on being human religiously

religiously

SELECTED ESSAYS
IN RELIGION AND SOCIETY

JAMES LUTHER ADAMS

edited and introduced by

Max L. Stackhouse

BEACON PRESS   BOSTON

Library of Congress Cataloging in Publication Data

Adams, James Luther, 1901–
  On being human religiously.
  Includes bibliographical references and index.
  1. Theology—Addresses, essays, lectures.
2. Social ethics—Addresses, essays, lectures.
3. Liberty—Addresses, essays, lectures.   I. Stackhouse,
Max L.   II. Title.
BR50.A28   230   75–36037
ISBN 0–8070–1122–3

"A sioun mai not bere fruyt
but if it stonde stable in the vyne."
John Wycliffe, 1380

To
Ruth Whitney Lyman
and
Herbert Lyman

Scions of a venerable tradition
in liberal religion and the arts

CONTENTS

ACKNOWLEDGMENTS

Grateful acknowledgment is made to the following for use of material in this book:

"Why Liberal," "The Liberalism That Is Dead," "The Changing Reputation of Human Nature," and "Unitarian Philosophies of History," reprinted by permission of the *Journal of Liberal Religion.*

"Man in the Light of the War," reprinted by permission of the Christian Century Foundation from the March 3, 1943, issue of *The Christian Century*; copyright 1943 Christian Century Foundation.

"On Being Human—The Liberal Way," an American Unitarian Association Pamphlet, reprinted by permission of the Unitarian Universalist Association.

"The Prophethood of All Believers" and "The Impact of Modern Thought on Unitarianism," from the *Christian Register*, reprinted by permission of the Unitarian Universalist Association.

"The Purpose of a Liberal Arts Education," reprinted by permission of the *Journal of Liberal Ministry.*

"The Voluntary Principle in the Forming of American Religion," from *The Religion of the Republic*, edited by E. Smith, reprinted by permission of Fortress Press.

"The Political Responsibility of the Man of Culture," reprinted by permission of *Comprendre.*

"The Love of God," from *The Meaning of Love*, edited by Ashley Montagu, reprinted by permission of Julian Press.

"Theological Bases of Social Action," reprinted by permission of the *Journal of Religious Thought.*

"From Psyche to Society," reprinted by permission of the *Perkins Journal.*

"Music as a Means of Grace," reprinted by permission of the *Crane Review.*

"Is Marx's Thought Relevant to the Christian?" from *Marx and the Western World*, edited by Nicholas Lobkowicz, reprinted by permission of the University of Notre Dame Press, Notre Dame, Indiana 46556.

" 'The Protestant Ethic' with Fewer Tears," from *In the Name of Life,*

EDITOR'S INTRODUCTION

It is presumptuous to "introduce" Professor James Luther Adams of Boston University, the University of Chicago, Meadville Theological School, Harvard University, and Andover Newton Theological School—a major American social ethicist of the two middle quarters of the twentieth century. Professor Adams is well known in a wide variety of religious, political, and intellectual communities, not only in North America but also in Europe and, more recently, in Asia. For at least half a century, Adams has been known as a serious scholar and teacher who is consistently involved in prophetic social reconstruction and deeply concerned about the welfare of his many friends. Surely no major theologian has preached in more local churches, attended more meetings where strategies for personal growth or social change were worked out, been president of so many academic societies, nor carried out a wider correspondence with leaders in many fields around the world. In fact, it is likely that no twentieth century theologian has been mentioned in the "acknowledgments" of other people's books more frequently than this man.

Yet it is characteristic of Adams that he has directed attention away from himself toward the thought of others. It is already well-known how much his scholarly effort has drawn attention to neglected themes in the work of Dean Fenn, the first important American Unitarian theologian of the twentieth century, and Harry Nelson Weiman. More than any other single person, Adams was responsible for introducing Paul Tillich to the English-speaking world before he was widely recognized; and Adams is currently at the center of the revival of scholarly interest in Ernst Troeltsch.

From his Fundamentalist childhood when he handed out tracts on the street, through his intense rebellion against all religious thought and organization and his later search for a satisfying religious humanism, to his position as "professor of Christian morals"—from which he led several generations of students into an abiding appreciation of the relationship of Christian thought to personal, social, and cultural perspectives—James Luther Adams has had an ever-expanding circle of acquaintance and apprecia- tion, one that overlaps and interacts with the circles around the other great teachers of Social Ethics of this same period— H. Richard Niebuhr of Yale, John Bennett of Union, and Walter Muelder of Boston University. His personal pilgrimage and in- fluence on others have indeed already been recounted in several ways among various groups.[1] Any "introduction" of this sort, therefore, is clearly redundant.

But there are good reasons to introduce this collection of essays by James Luther Adams. First, a book such as this makes some of Adams' contributions conveniently accessible to those already familiar with his scattered writings. Second, it allows still wider circles and the next generation to become acquainted with and to be taught by Adams. And lastly, it makes it possible to place certain key motifs in these essays—written for different audiences in different times—in the context of current debates and trends in his field and to show their continuing pertinence for contemporary clergy, church members, and students of ethics. Thus, it is especially to these, who have not known him over the years and who may never have the chance to meet Adams personally, that we present this view of some of Adams' important concerns.

In discussing the inefficacy of American policy in Southeast Asia, it became fashionable in the late 1960s to account for the resistance in Vietnam and among dissident groups in the United States by citing the "infrastructure." Ineffectiveness abroad and lack of support at home were attributed to unofficial, nongovern- mental patterns of trust and mistrust, expectation and suspicion, authority and freedom that governed the loyalties and lifestyles of everyday living. Whatever the official doctrines of official régimes, leading scholars, dominant religious groups, or family heritage, the "infrastructure" of a specific society seemed to have its own logic, ethic, and power. It is described as a variety of institutional life, one that relates very closely to the deepest values and life commitments of people in social groups.

The importance of the infrastructure has been acknowledged in a variety of ways. Some have turned to books such as *Fanshen*,[2] the documentary study of Maoist revolutionary processes, to find a model of how to grasp and alter the infrastructure of society. Others have formed caucuses or engaged in community organization of several descriptions. Some have formed communes or liberation groups. Still others have participated in T-groups, consciousness-raising, or encounter processes. Many more remain in church organizations and established labor, professional, or political organizations. (And secret intelligence organizations have evidently infiltrated a whole range of such groups.) All sought mastery or transformation of the infrastructure and, through that, the alteration of both personal meanings and patterns of the common life. In some cases, they have sought to establish or dismantle one or another worldview. Most efforts were shallow-rooted and, predictably, have been only partially successful.

The term "infrastructure," however, is not one Adams uses. It is of quite recent vintage and refers to those patterns of organized life not determined by an official régime or by genetic or inherited family patterns. And, while the above "assaults" on the infrastructures were newsworthy for a while—perhaps because they were thought to be bizarre—the concerns that surfaced in these often-superficial forms in the last decade are in fact rooted deep in history and involve a profound understanding of human nature. When the infrastructure becomes a matter of conscious intention, moral action, and group formation, the grounds for an associational theory are laid. Some religious, political, and cultural traditions have allowed and encouraged the development of an associational infrastructure, exercising a minimum of coercion and interference. In these traditions, the genuinely human is found in the twin reality that we are both social creatures—requiring relatedness to be whole—and creative agents—capable of making significant choices about that relatedness. We are, in short, associational beings with wills. For half a century, Adams has focused his attention on the history, philosophy, nature, power, character, and transformation of the associational infrastructure. It is here that persons are decisively formed and brought to decisions about their lives; it is here that wider human sensibilities about justice, beauty, hope, or meaning are nurtured, or stunted; it is here that the deepest religious loyalties become concrete, or dissipate; it is here that personal and social freedom lives, or dies.

There is something in contemporary thought, especially modern religious thought, that resists attention to the associational infrastructure. Humanity, in the more influential theories of the twentieth century, is understood as either intensely personal or radically collectivistic. Much psychology, literature, and existential philosophy suffer from what Jacoby calls "social amnesia" [3] while fascism, communism, and sundry nationalisms ride roughshod over persons. People experience an alienation of their personal feelings from their objective social situation; and many social workers, reformers, pastors, and psychiatrists feel an artificial division between the analysis of personal problems on one hand and the analysis of the social-political situation on the other. Perhaps such views merely reflect the fact that individuals are often cut off from significant social relationships in modern society. But it is also possible that there are ideological reasons for separating the personal from the social, thereby blocking out that range of experiences that could enable us to live our lives with greater integrity and solidarity. In any case, in nearly every essay Adams has written, we find a consistent concern for the intermediary structures of human life that stand between the isolation of individualism and the flood tides of collective authoritarianism. These associations are the locus, in Adams' thought, for being genuinely human.

One could, at this point, inquire into the reasons for this focus in the thought of James Luther Adams. The answer may lie partly in Adams' early sectarian background as a Plymouth Brother, when the mystery and power of an intense, disciplined community dominated his experience. In contrast to many who have repudiated such forms of religion, Adams continues to see several elements of value in it and can understand how and why this mode of religious life exercises such influence. His encounter with the Gestapo and with mass fanaticism in Hitler's Germany, while visiting some of Europe's leading philosophers and theologians in the 1930s, also led him to continuously examine the elements of loyalty and solidarity that allowed some groups and thinkers to engage in disciplined resistance to fascist nihilism while others acquiesced to or even celebrated such cultural-political influence.

Adams' present affinity for the Unitarian Universalist Association's freewheeling style, with its sense of minority solidarity against pretentious and mystifying forms of piety, and its religiously profound drive toward social involvement, is also important.

But three other influences are probably more significant and remove this emphasis from the sphere of the merely biographical and confessional: the prophetic–New Testament traditions, the history of sectarian movements in the West, and the philosophical-social impact of the Enlightenment. In the prophetic and New Testament writings, Adams sees the roots for a firm conception of the meaning of life that touches the theological grounds of existence and calls us into significant community. In the sectarian traditions, he finds evidence of the protest against the attempted routinization of that ground and against the domination of some by others that has frequently accompanied such domestication. And, since the Enlightenment, which split human subjectivity from the objective world, the problem of the basis for being and knowing and acting in common has beset us. Thus, not only biographical accident but, more importantly, theological conviction and objective social and philosophical conditions make this focus a decisive one for Adams.[4]

In mentioning the theological tradition of the Judeo-Christian heritage, I have already touched on the second reason for introducing Adams. Whenever he speaks of the issues involved in being human in a significant infrastructure, he speaks religiously. As there has been a tendency to separate individual meanings from social meanings, so there has also been an attempt to separate the religious from the humanistic dimensions of life. Theologians, in an attempt to protect notions of divine transcendence from secularization and reductionism, and humanists, in an attempt to protest the imposition of unwarranted claims, have often separated the realm of religious experience and reflection from basic human knowledge and concern. They have, to use Paul Tillich's term, made theology into a "heteronomous" element of life and thought. It is Adams' continual contention that such a separation destroys the integrity and depth of both theology and human life. To be sure, there are different levels of discourse; but all profound theology is directly pertinent to the genuinely human, and all that is genuinely human is pertinent to theology. In this regard, Adams is a "liberal" theologian, although as we can see, especially in Part I of this volume, Adams includes numerous critiques of liberalism in his own liberal affirmations.[5]

In his teaching and in innumerable conversations, Adams has shown himself to be an anecdotalist; that is, he tells a story to make his point. To illustrate the way in which theology and humanistic concerns interact in Adams' thought, I shall adopt his technique and recount a debate that occurred between Adams and several students. The debate centered around the ancient problem of "the one and the many." In one seminar it surfaced in the form of several questions: is it better for people to be highly integrated as individuals at the risk of losing diversity in their lives, or is it better to develop many sides of one's personality and risk losing intensity or excellence in any one area? Should society strive for an efficient coherence in order to solve social problems, or should it resist efforts at coordinated integration and centralized planning to preserve multiple subcommunities? Are we in a state of relativism for which we need an integrating principle, or are we in a state of oppressive conformity for which we need affirmations of variety to break up the monolith? What is our basic situation: chaos needing order, or uniformity needing diversity?

One student argued that Unitarianism/Universalism led logically to the weakest solution to such problems; for, on the one hand, it held to an undifferentiated, monolithic singularity and, on the other, to an affirmation that everything was of equal importance. Hence nothing could be distinguished from anything else. Another student pressed for a Trinitarian view as a pluralistic one that nevertheless held to an ultimate coherence through the concrete relations of persons. Adams, in responding, described a brilliant young black pastor who was leading the struggle for racial integration but losing a personal battle against drugs. He was one who could integrate the insights of several cultures in fresh ways and galvanize the black community into common action. Yet at the same time something beyond his control was driving him to disintegration.

"The pagans," said Adams, "knew something about the fates. There is a diversity of realities and of powers. But the biblical authors knew that the Lord God speaks in a council. There is a center, but it is heard in the midst of diversity, and most clearly only in community." "Could it be," someone asked, "that you really think that the meaning of life is ultimately an infinity of distinct centers of power and value?" Adams then embarked on a brief discussion of "henotheism," the view of the great scholar of Indian religions, Max Mueller, which holds that although there are many aspects of divine reality, only one is truly worthy of our highest attention and loyalty. Yet the one does not destroy the many.

The term "henotheism" has subsequently been abandoned by Adams and most scholars. But the double-edged point of this anecdote remains. First, Adams often points out that any mono-lithic definition of reality is wrong, for it cannot take account of genuine diversity. A pluralistic definition is necessary, but it is suspect if offered dogmatically or if it provides no coherent center. Second, the deeper we press into human dilemmas, the nearer we approach theological issues; and the more we understand theologi-cal debates, the better equipped we are to see the basic human options. In these areas, we see the kind of liberalism that pervades the essays of this volume, for Adams is a liberal theologian who is in responsive conversation with both traditional Western theology and the world's religions. He is one for whom basic psychological and socio-political problems require theological pondering; one who resists fixed dogmatic formulations, but who draws constantly on biblical and doctrinal resources; one who refuses to relinquish either side of the modern human dilemma of the need for inte-grated meaning and of the awareness of actual relativity. It is surely recognition of these concerns that led James D. Hunt, one of the leading students of Adams' thought, to write, "James Luther Adams is the only Unitarian actively engaged in significant conver-sation with the major figures of American theology, at the same time playing a decisive role in the Unitarian denomination . . . [and one of the few] religious liberals acknowledging the criticisms of liberalism . . . and making a defense of liberal theology." [6]

One of the distinguishing features of liberal theology as it has worked itself out on the American scene is the constant concern for social justice as a religious and not merely a secular matter. Nothing makes a theological liberal more angry than the sugges-tion that religion is a matter of the privacy of the heart only, that genuine religion, understood as deep personal experience, has no direct bearing on questions of justice, equality, and freedom in society. That is, nothing makes a theological liberal more angry except possibly the view that belief in official dogma is more important than sensitivity to what God is doing in the world in struggles for righteousness and compassion. To be sure, some liberals have become as individualistic as the pietists; some have fought orthodoxy while ignoring social and infrastructural questions; and some have subverted the theological dimensions of liberalism by holding that we humans finally save ourselves from emptiness, meaninglessness, and death by our own efforts. Nevertheless, American liberal theology has for the most part tended to be socially radical in the tradition of the Old Testament prophets and to assert that genuine faith is found in trusting participation in the dynamic source and end of life as it forms, sustains, and transforms human relationships and human community. Most call that dynamic source and end of life "God." As Adams shows, others find the word "God" too laden with mythic meanings that, in their experience, have distorted human knowledge, repressed valid feelings, corroded human relations, or subverted justice. But by whatever names, the dynamic source and end of life is, among liberal theologians such as Adams, seen as present and active in human interactions and in movements for liberation.

This focus has not led, in Adams, to a reduction of concern for personal life.[7] It does mean that the genuinely personal is understood in a nonindividualistic fashion. He believes that an individual is most adequately understood in the context of a wide variety of concrete relationships, loyalties, and networks of obligation—in contrast to atomistic or laissez-faire views of the self. The unique individual is the point of intersection of a wide variety of physical, social-cultural, and religious forces and cannot gain self-understanding without attention to these interdependencies. To be sure, the individual has a will that cannot be reduced to genetic, social, or cultural causations, a will that allows us to open or close ourselves to various influences or claims made upon us. It is the exercise of this capacity that makes us, as H. Richard Niebuhr wrote, capable of becoming "responsible selves"—selves "able and enabled to respond."[8] But, while freedom is a decisive human quality, it can only be exercised within a context of relations to other people and according to the range of real options in the social environment. Thus we only know the meaning of "responsible selfhood" and "freedom" when we see what social patterns they support or oppose, what forces they enhance or inhibit, and what structures they sustain or destroy.

Similarly, the concern for discerning the tracks of the divine as present and active in human interactions and in movements for liberation has not led, in Adams' case, to a reduction of concern for the integrity of ideas or symbols. Ideas and symbols are among the decisive social forces; they are not mere epiphenomena. They are, indeed, especially powerful social forces, for they both express and shape profound human choices and social relationships. They are rallying points for action and group behaviors. They legitimate or challenge the very existence of persons and collectivities. In this, Adams is not only a liberal, but he is something else often cursed in contemporary thought: he is an idealist. He thinks ideas are important and powerful, but he is not, and cannot be accused of being merely a liberal idealist; there is another dimension of his life and thought that is in constant dialectic with this appreciation of ideas. Namely, he constantly insists that those who deal in ideas must "lower the level of discourse" to say what they mean in terms of human life. That is, he insists that philosophers and theologians, psychologists and social theorists, metaphysicians and ontologists recognize that their ideas—perhaps especially the more "sublime" ones—are freighted with assumptions about and implications for the concrete shape of human life. Academics, consciously or not, often make descriptive and prescriptive statements about the character and direction of human life when they present presumably logical or abstract arguments. For Adams, it is necessary to recognize a genuinely dialogical perspective, not merely an idealistic or a reductionistic one. This concern can be seen especially well in Part II of this collection.

It is fascinating to note that in Adams' attempt to relate person to community and idea to experience he has certain "ritual enemies," as Herbert Richardson once called them. Everyone who struggles for a point of view has certain contrary views that are seen as the most dangerous threats to life's meaning. For Adams, the threats arise on two fronts, each the dark side of the other. On one side is "pietism," a view occurring when nonsocial personalism is wedded to a disincarnate idealism. He sees the roots of this in Gnosticism, the ancient heresy of Christianity, and present in much evangelical, existential, and psychiatric thought. All give succor to the pathological aspects of commercial, bourgeois society as can be seen in Adams' aphorism "Nothing is so marketable as egoism wrapped in idealism." On the other side is patriarchal collectivism, the view that there is a primordial, natural, and hierarchical order that is present in the pregiven social-political arrangement, so that neither personal wills nor human ideas can alter the organization of life or the logic of history. Adams has called the attempt to embrace the whole of racial, sexual, political, intellectual, and religious life under an autocratic rulership the "Theodosian heresy," after Theodosius the Great, who attempted to establish an "Orthodoxy" and persecuted all deviations. Adams sees its correlate in aspects of traditional Orthodoxy and Catholicism, in Protestant notions of the Orders of Creation, in communist and fascist tendencies of the twentieth century, and in contemporary sexism and racism.

A phenomenon that Adams consistently identifies and points out is the frequency with which the two tendencies go hand-in-glove. Half of life is thought to deal with personal spirituality, or the transcendence of the individual, while the other half is left—as a matter of exterior, "merely secular," or natural and rational concern—to whatever powers are believed to be in command of them. In Part III of this volume, we can see Adams working through the major ideas from Europe, where such divisions are struggled with—and against—in an effort to mediate key questions and perspectives on these issues to an American audience.

The relationships of person to collectivity, of idea to experience, of piety to politics are among the critical problems of religion and society. And it is such concerns that led Adams to make a distinctive mark on his field of ethics. Ethics, in his view, is best approached through the resources of theology and social analysis. Hence he aided the development of the sub-discipline of Christian Social Ethics, or, more broadly, Religious Social Ethics or Religion and Society. It is in relation to his place in the field that I offer a final set of observations by way of introducing these essays.

Religious Social Ethics, as an academic discipline, is an American contribution to intellectual life. To be sure, most religious traditions of Asia and Africa bear implications for the organization of the common life, and European ecclesiastical and academic traditions have various indirect ways of dealing with the questions of religious social ethics. Still, it is in North America, and most specifically in those Protestant seminaries where concern for the social implications of theology, and a fresh willingness to use the new social science tools of this last century appeared, that this discipline began to develop. Its boundaries and center are still in dispute, but it continues to grow.[9] Two writers in this field are perhaps most influential. One dominated thought from the 1930s through the 1950s. He is still highly respected. The other has only recently become widely known, but his work has been much discussed in the 1960s and 1970s. Indeed, I would suggest that Reinhold Niebuhr's *Nature and Destiny of Man* and John Rawls' *A Theory of Justice* are the two most important works in Social Ethics written in twentieth-century America. Further, each represents a stream of thought that is important for Adams. Thus, it may be useful to compare and contrast them on certain crucial issues.

Adams, Niebuhr, and Rawls would all agree on a number of issues central to Social Ethics: all hold constitutional democracy to be the best form of political governance devised. All see a dramatic need for increased socialization of certain economic institutions and are sharply critical of present capitalistic arrangements. All insist on a radical principle of equality in society, yet each demands an accent on freedom and excellence. Each has had an impact on social thought beyond their initial intentions. As it can be said that Adams is the most profound theologian of voluntary associational life, it can properly be said that Niebuhr was a "prophet to politicians." [10] And Rawls is being discussed not only by philosophers, but also by theologians and social scientists.[11] But perhaps their most important common feature is their focus on the social and theoretical (theological and philosophical) preconditions for meaningful existence in community. In this emphasis they differ from a number of contemporary ethicists who focus on the making of decisions in a pregiven context. The primary job of Social Ethics, in the views of these three figures, is less the guidance of specific decisionmaking in a casuistic fashion—as one might find in such otherwise-divergent figures as Paul Ramsey and Joseph Fletcher— than the clarification of the social, ideational, and dispositional circumstances under which human life can become most significant and least destructive, most just and least corrupt, most open and least repressive. But the finding of a vantage point from which the present context of life may be assessed requires a critical principle beyond the present context. On this principle, the three differ.

Reinhold Niebuhr, a liberal pastor in Detroit who became engaged in the city's social and religious life, felt the poverty of his own liberalism and subsequently experienced a "theological shift to the right and a political shift to the left." Only the former, he held, could provide an adequate basis for the latter. He turned to the study of biblical, Augustinian, and Reformation views of the nature of human nature as well as to contemporary social theory. He was deeply influenced by Christian existential thought and political realism. He developed a polemic style and, in the work mentioned above, set out to expose the frailties, indeed the pathologies, that ensued from dominant Western philosophies. He turned to traditional theological symbols and showed how they, rightly understood and taken seriously but not literally, were more accurate in estimating the depth of human sin and the height of the human self-transcendence, in preventing utopian or cynical views of life that led most modern thought to irrelevance or destruction, and in grasping the subtle interactions of vitality and form that are real in human historical experience. His use of biblical and traditional materials is not easy to grasp, but it is a very distinctive and complex view of Christian thought. He recognized that many previous syntheses—for examples, classical forms of Judaism, Catholicism, and Protestantism, as well as modern liberal Protestantism—have been as dangerous or irrelevant as many secular philosophies. Yet, he holds that it was possible to bring about a new synthesis, involving aspects of Pauline, Augustinian, and Reformation thought as well as the Renaissance protest against pretentious religion. This synthesis, he felt, could give modern humanity and society a rooted sense of direction without illusion.

At the center of Niebuhr's argument stands his view of Jesus Christ. Niebuhr is what the theologians would call a Christological or Christocentric thinker. In the life, death, and resurrection of Jesus Christ, Niebuhr finds the clue, the critical principle, by which human nature and the historical context of life is to be evaluated. For here the power of grace, the undeserved divine gift, is made manifest. It empowers us to live amidst the judgment and mercy of historical life in faith—with its attendant demand to quest for

truth—in love—with its attendant demand to quest for justice—
and in hope—with its attendant demand for realistic expectation.

James Luther Adams' thought is not unlike Niebuhr's in several
respects. He would applaud Niebuhr's social engagement, his
willingness to draw on traditional materials in a reconstructive
fashion, his recognition of the power and importance of symbols,
his quest for a new synthesis pertinent to human existence in
history, and his appreciation of grace—that sense of divine gift and
empowerment that transcends rational discourse. All this, he
would agree, is directly pertinent to Social Ethics at its most
profound levels. But Adams, in the final analysis, is not a Christological thinker. He is what Christian theologians sometimes call a
Pneumatological theorist; that is, his emphasis is on the Holy
Spirit. Indeed, the Holy Spirit is present in Christ as one in
continuity with the Old Testament prophets, as the one who broke
the limitation of Hebraic religious insight making it pertinent to all,
as the center of Christian liturgical life, and as the paradigmatic
"Son of God" and "foretaste of the Kingdom of God." The dynamic
Holy Spirit, understood as the power of life that moves where it
will in human experience—bringing new meaning and wholeness
—is the theological core and decisive critical principle of Adams'
thought.[12] It appears among peoples and in groups not consciously
Christian. It inspires and transforms, it invites and guides, it
propels and grasps, and it calls all under its influence into new
associational communities of liberation, righteousness, and inner
depth.

It is on this last point that Adams might well disagree with
Niebuhr most sharply. In Niebuhr's thought the antinomy of
personal existence and social-political reality are held in creative
tension and are shown to be important for the interpretation of
historical experience. But the actual tissues of relational and
associational life are seldom dealt with. In brief, the infrastructure
of community formation is neglected by Niebuhr and many of his
disciples.

One could make this point in more traditional theological terms
by saying that there is very little ecclesiology in Niebuhr. Tradi-
tionally, the doctrine of the Holy Spirit has been connected to the
understanding of the "true church" as a community of faith
signified by the organized, visible church, frail as it is, and called to
a life of worship, discipline, social engagement, and compassion.

For Adams, the church is the prototype of the networks of meaningful life that stand between the privacy of the individual and large social-political structures, influencing both. It has its own internal integrity, and it carries out its mission by caring for the least and the lost and by prophetically discerning the signs of the times (all the while celebrating the meaning of life together). Niebuhr was surely reacting against the triumphalism or triviality of much churchiness. Adams too protests these, but he reacts by extending—not constricting or ignoring—the significance of "church" so that it includes other, even explicitly "anti-religious" groups that manifest the marks of the church spoken of by theologians more than many churches do. This broader interpretation is surely the theological reason for his involvement in a variety of voluntary associational activities besides those in his denomination. Thereby he maintains the connection between his basic perspective and the actual matrices of life in communities where people live. Thereby he gives institutional embodiment to the Spirit and to the pluralism he affirms. Thereby he maintains a social-theological basis for combating the twin perils of pietistic and Theodosian tendencies in much Christian thought. And thereby he has a ground for resisting the subtle combination of these perils that has appeared again and again in world history. Niebuhr, too, opposes these perils, but the question can be raised as to whether or not he has provided enough accent on the connective tissues of community that stand between the contrite self confronting the reality of God and the *Realpolitik* analysis of national interests and balances of power as they stand under divine majesty.

One further implication of the differences that Adams might well have with Niebuhr, and with most Christocentric theologians, involves the relationship to the nonbiblical religions. Adams has often been involved in cross-cultural, interreligious exchanges, although space prevents inclusion of essays in this area of his thought. The chief element for which he strives in these encounters is the formation of a global community of mutual trust that can form a common basis for discerning the activity of the Spirit that calls all peoples into the struggles for truth, liberation, and justice. In his view, the proclamation of any particular theological doctrine is to be evaluated in part according to its practical capacity to evoke prophetic commitment in community. Thus, any who claim to know and proclaim the true faith are well advised to test it in genuine dialogue: does it, when exposed to other people in other contexts, open common horizons of meaning, righteousness, and compassion? At the same time, he holds that it is foolish for those influenced by the Judeo-Christian tradition to go chasing after esoteric religions without first coming to terms with the tradition we have some chance of knowing in its depth from the inside.

Quite different issues are at stake when we compare Adams to John Rawls. A philosopher, and self-consciously not a theologian, Rawls draws on Continental resources as diverse as Kant and Rousseau, but he works essentially within the Anglo-American, liberal, philosophical tradition of ethics. Some see his work as the best contemporary restatement of John Locke as modified by post-capitalist social theory. Rawls' specific purpose is to provide a rational ground for choosing a social system regulated by principles of equality or fairness that also maintains a maximum range of liberty. He also attempts to sketch the outlines of such a society and to show that it is not incompatible with basic aspects of human nature. In this effort, he contradicts a number of contemporary views, which hold that it is impossible to derive a genuine and rational social ethic by taking individual preferences as a point of departure. It can be done, Rawls argues, if we make only a few simple and rather obvious assumptions: first, that while people's tastes, life goals, and abilities will differ, we are all interdependent; that there will be conflict in society as well as cooperation and both will involve some inequalities of wealth, authority, and influence; that all normal adults will know some things about the social world in which we live, but no one will know everything; and, finally, that if we want to choose basic rules to govern the common life—for surely all would recognize that there must be some rules—we have to fashion them so that they could be agreed upon by, for example, a Chinese nuclear physicist, an American labor leader, and an Egyptian peasant. With these assumptions in mind, could people arrive at a set of basic, rational principles to govern the common life? Rawls thinks that we can indeed and suggests that such principles would, in fact, involve the most extensive latitude for liberty compatible with liberty for all, plus an attempt to arrange necessary inequalities so that the least advantaged have the maximum chance to become advantaged. Such a chance must be commensurate with opportunities to make greater contributions to the common life and to have a basis for self-respect.

In his argument, Rawls can be said to have provided a liberal, rational basis for a pluralistic, constitutional, democratic society that presses toward socialization of wealth and opportunity. In this he breaks what Robert Bellah has called the "American Taboo" [13] by discussing a kind of nonideological socialism pertinent to a society properly interested in maintaining democratic principles in legal and political life. From another perspective, Rawls can be said to have provided a new, peculiarly modern, "natural rights" argument that is highly significant for interreligious, cross-cultural, and transideological contact. Furthermore, he sets forth a view that takes the choices and potential choices of persons seriously, even though he has a clear sense of the priority of social ethics over individual ethics, as Roy Branson, one of Adams' former students, has pointed out.[14] And, finally, Rawls accomplishes something Bredemier accents in his treatment of Rawls: we have, "a persuasive rationale for distinguishing social science from other sciences by . . . insisting on the necessity for social science to be concerned with 'justice' as a distinct feature of the objects of social science inquiry. Justice is not relevant to membranes, atoms or need dispositions: but it is 'the first virtue' of social institutions. For social scientists to ignore the variable of justice, Rawls is implying, is as derelict as to ignore the variable of truth. *Both* virtues infect the proper pursuit of social science, even if only the latter constrains the other sciences." [15] One of Adams' best-known students, Donald Shriver, President of Union Theological Seminary, has recently shown how such concerns can be worked out in his book, *Spindles and Spires.*[16]

Adams would applaud much in Rawls,[17] but he would surely pose several questions to Rawls that would distinguish their views. At the core would be questions of history in several senses: first, whence derived the notions of deciding individuals and constitutionally governed collectivities? Are these not, at least in part, secularized and universalized versions of a "covenantal" theological tradition that could have developed only in localities where Puritanism and the Independency of the "Radical Reformation" once held sway? Second, is it not possible that Rawls' work is a product of and a rationale for a progressive welfare state, an idealized picture of the best features as they exist at the present time? And third, can such notions be sustained by rational argument in the future, when the ultimate commitments and beliefs informing Western history in the past may not obtain? In brief, Adams would suggest that a moral philosophy is limited if it does not have an explicit philosophy or theology of history present at its core.

The kinds of questions that are here put to Rawls out of Adams' perspective suggest that Adams and Rawls have very different senses of what it is that is likely to be the most reliable basis for social ethical thought and action, what it is that can serve as a foundational critical principle for Social Ethics. In short, it is the ground, less than the content, of Rawls' arguments that Adams would question, although it is both that Rawls wants to defend. For Adams, as a key representative of *religious* Social Ethics in comparison to a most articulate representative of *philosophical* Social Ethics, there is a serious question whether reason can, does, and ought to rule so absolutely. There is no sense in which Adams can be called anti- or non-rational; rationality is necessary to every attempt to understand or express anything. But for Adams, it is a serious question whether human reason is not—and by its nature and its relation to prerational dimensions of the human apprehension of life and meaning in history *must* be—always in the service of the historically rooted spirit and the commitments and sensibilities that govern it. He insists that no community can survive that does not have a high estimate of rationality and a hard-nosed capacity to use it in the sciences, in policy formation, and in serious analysis of personal and social commitments. But while reason, basically, can correct and critique, it is an open question whether it can construct or sustain a context for its own life out of its own powers. In this, Adams would surely agree with his former student Wayne Proudfoot who, in offering a critique of Rawls, points out that knowledge, rationality, and a sense of right depend in part on prior participation in many and varied social tissues and rituals, actions and conventions, and affiliative and religious ties. He points to other philosophical traditions that accent the need to understand ethics by considering the social and cultural contexts, the shared concepts, and the historic senses of the sacred that are available to people.[18] In brief, imaginative, emotive, relational, mythic, and symbolic patterns are as powerful and significant as rational elements of human experience and are also proper bases for moral decision in community. By setting these aside, Rawls distorts the understanding of root forces that are pertinent to a constructive statement in Social Ethics.[19] In certain respects on this point, Adams is closer to a variety of divergent contemporary efforts ranging from Michael Novak to Paul Lehmann to Gibson Winter to Franklin Sherman than he is to Rawls. These and many others want to include an "interpretive" element in social ethics in addition to the rational accents on right and wrong, good and evil (or, more technically, deontological and teleological modes of moral discourse). That is, Adams contends, there are basic background beliefs and historical conditions that are directly pertinent to and necessary for a viable social ethic. Humanity is not saved nor made most ethical by intelligence alone. For Adams, this is manifestly clear and it characterizes much of his writing. But the question is not settled in contemporary ethics and is the topic of continued debate, as can be seen in recent work by Charles Reynolds, Frederick Carney, and James Gustafson, all, again, former students of Adams.[20]

In any case, it should be clear that the issues posed by the essays in this volume, written over several decades, have a pertinence to current redefinitions of "liberalism" and "liberal religion," to contemporary human self-understanding, and to the scholarly debates that are carried on today about the relation of person to community, God to humanity, and history to Social Ethics. In selecting and editing these essays, I have been much aided by several people—especially by Herbert F. Vetter and Paul Vogel, who made the initial proposals for this volume; George H. Williams and Wilson Yates, who made valuable suggestions about emphases and inclusions; and by MaryAnn Lash, whose editorial expertise taught me much over several months. I am also indebted to Meadville-Lombard Theological School and Beacon Press for making the volume possible. Kay Caughlin was a competent and cheerful typist throughout.

A final word about the editing of these essays. I have deleted all footnotes to make them more accessible to a general audience. For scholars, however, I have cited original sources where Adams' documentation can be investigated. I have edited several essays considerably, as is noted in the prefaces to those chapters, but most of them have been only moderately altered so as to best fit the design of this volume. In each preface, I have attempted to show how the essay fits into Adams' biography or represents a major motif in his thought. As Professor Adams has given me considerable latitude to reshape his essays for this volume, I must also take full responsibility for all failures of an editorial nature. I am grateful for the confidence he has shown and his openness to suggestion, but especially for the chance to work on the material of one to whom I am deeply indebted in many ways. Thereby I have been forced to a critical distance in the midst of a deepening and continuing sense of appreciation.

—Max L. Stackhouse

NOTES

1. See James Luther Adams, *Taking Time Seriously* (Glencoe, Ill.: Free Press, 1957), especially Chapter 1; and D. B. Robertson, ed., *Voluntary Associations* (Richmond, Va.: John Knox Press, 1966), especially Chapters 17 and 18.

2. William Hinton (New York: Vintage Books, 1966).

3. Russell Jacoby, *Social Amnesia. A Critique of Conformist Psychology from Adler to Laing* (Boston: Beacon Press, 1975).

4. It would be a fascinating study in the history of American Social Ethics to compare and contrast Adams with those other influential teachers of Social Ethics who have been deeply engaged in church affairs and political problems and who have been influenced by many of the same currents of theological and social thought—H. Richard Niebuhr, John Bennett and Walter Muelder. Major students of Adams, such as David Little, Douglas Sturm, Ralph Potter, and Theodore Steeman, to mention a representative variety, tend to focus quite differently than the students of the other two. Cf. Paul Deats, ed., *Toward a Discipline of Social Ethics* (Boston: Boston University Press, 1973).

5. In this regard, Adams shows throughout his work an affinity to other contemporary directions now that the wave of neo-Protestant positivism is subsiding. I would cite several contemporary authors who exemplify these directions: Georg Iggers, *The German Conception of History* (Middletown, Conn.: Wesleyan University Press, 1968); Karl H. Hertz, *Politics Is a Way of Helping People* (Minneapolis: Augsburg Publishing House, 1974); and especially George Rupp, *Christologies and Cultures* (The Hague: Mouton, 1974).

6. James D. Hunt, "James Luther Adams and His Demand for an Effective Religious Liberalism," unpublished Ph.D. dissertation (Syracuse University, 1965), p. 10.

7. In particular, I call attention to James L. Adams and Seward Hiltner, eds., *Pastoral Care in the Liberal Churches* (Nashville: Abingdon Press, 1970), especially the "Foreword" and pp. 174–220.

8. It is in this area that Adams most clearly approximates the work of H. Richard Niebuhr, especially his *The Responsible Self* (New York: Harper

& Row, 1963), and of those deeply influenced by him, such as James Gustafson, James Fowler, and James Nelson.

9. Cf. Deats, *op. cit.*, and G. Stassen, ed. *What Is Social Ethics?* (forthcoming).

10. See especially Ronald Stone, *Reinhold Niebuhr: Prophet to Politician* (Nashville: Abingdon Press, 1972); Gabriel Fackre, *The Promise of Reinhold Niebuhr* (Philadelphia: J. B. Lippincott Company, 1970); and M. L. Stackhouse, "Eschatology and Ethical Method," unpublished Ph.D. dissertation (Harvard University, 1965), written under the direction of J. L. Adams.

11. I am especially indebted to two critical review articles on Rawls, by a theologian and a social scientist respectively: Wayne Proudfoot, "Rawls on the Individual and the Social," *Journal of Religious Ethics*, vol. 2 (Fall 1974), pp. 107–28; Harry C. Bredemeier, "Justice, Virtue and Social Science," *Society* (Sept.–Oct. 1974), pp. 76–83.

12. On this point, the biblical scholar Pheme Perkins has suggested that Adams is actually closer to classical theological traditions in which the Holy Spirit is seen as the principle of continuity between the Old and New Testaments and the foundation for their interpretation.

13. In *The Broken Covenant* (New York: Seabury Press, 1974).

14. "Bioethics as Individual and Social," *Journal of Religious Ethics*, vol. 3 (Spring 1975), p. 132.

15. *Op. cit.*, p. 77.

16. Donald Shriver et al., *Spindles and Spires* (Richmond: John Knox Press, 1975).

17. For a fascinating comparison, read Rawls, on Civil Disobedience, *op. cit.*, pp. 363–91, and Adams, "Civil Disobedience: Its Occasions and Limits," in *Political and Legal Obligation: Nomos XII*, J. Pennock and J. Chapman, eds. (New York: Atherton Press, 1970).

18. *Op. cit.*, especially pp. 114 ff.

19. In fact, it can be suggested that in order to make his argument viable, Rawls must appeal to these kinds of concerns, especially in his concepts of "original position" and "veil of ignorance," ideas that are not unlike classical theological notions of "Covenant" and "Sin" or stoic notions of the Golden Age and the broken natural law, at least as they function in efforts to construct a basic and compelling social ethic. In this regard, compare Adams, "The Law of Nature in Greco-Roman Thought," *Journal of Religion*, 25, no. 2 (April 1945), pp. 97–118; "The Law of Nature: Some General Considerations," *ibid.*, pp. 88–96; and "Natural Religion and the Myth of the Eighteenth Century," *Harvard Divinity School Bulletin*, 16 (1951), pp. 17–32, for representative treatments of these continuing concerns.

20. Charles Reynolds, "Editorial Notes," *Journal of Religious Ethics*, vol. 3 (Spring 1975); Frederick S. Carney, "On Frankena and Religious Ethics," *ibid.;* and James Gustafson, *Can Ethics Be Christian?* (Chicago: University of Chicago Press, 1975).

Part I

THE SPIRIT AND FORMS OF FREEDOM

BETWEEN 1939 and the present, the fascists, the communists, orthodox and neo-orthodox Christians, university intellectuals, and Populist conservatives have joined in a many-sided attack on liberalism. It is said that as World War I and the Depression destroyed Continental liberalism, so World War II and subsequent involvements in Asia demonstrated the poverty of liberalism as it developed in the Anglo-American tradition. As an editor of the *Journal of Liberal Religion*, an activist in several liberal political organizations, and professor at liberal schools of theology, Adams recognized the ambiguous roots and character of liberalism, acknowledged the accuracy of some of the criticism, and proceeded to sort the gold from the dross. Liberalism is sometimes at its best when under pressure, for then it must decide what must be fought for, preserved, and renewed, and what must be jettisoned. The following chapter is a composite of eight editorials and speeches he wrote on different occasions between 1939 and 1955.* While the basic outline of the presentations remained fairly constant, Adams expanded here on one point, there on another. The lengthier arguments have here been edited into a single statement representing a major dimension of his thought.—M.L.S.

CHAPTER 1 · GUIDING PRINCIPLES FOR

A FREE FAITH

URING THE RISE of Hitler in Germany, I visited a philosopher whom we Americans consider to be one of the most distinguished representatives of what was left there of the liberal tradition—the tradition that claims such men as Harnack, Troeltsch, and Otto. During our conversation I casually referred to my host as a liberal. He immediately demurred, saying, "Please do not call me a liberal. That word is taboo here. And besides, I am not a liberal." Certain allowances must, of course, be made for the fact that the word "liberal" has had a

---

* "Why Liberal," *Journal of Liberal Religion*, vol. 1, no. 2 (Autumn 1939), pp. 3–8; "The Liberalism That Is Dead," *Journal of Liberal Religion*, vol. 2, no. 1 (Winter 1940), pp. 38–42; "On Being Human—The Liberal Way," American Unitarian Association pamphlet, no. 359 (n.d.); "A Faith for Free Men," in *Together We Advance*, S. H. Fritchman, ed. (Boston: Beacon Press, 1946), chap. 4; "Unitarian Philosophies of History," *Journal of Liberal Religion*, vol. 7, no. 1 (Summer 1945), pp. 91–107; "Impact of Modern Thought on Unitarianism," with Thaddeus B. Clark, *Christian Register*, vol. 127, no. 5 (May 1948), pp. 21–23; "Man in the Light of the War," *Christian Century* (March 3, 1943), pp. 257–59; "The Liberal Christian Looks at Himself," mimeographed speech dated March 6, 1955.

different meaning among the Germans then from that among us now. Still, even now, it is difficult to find a writer "in the vanguard" who does not make some assertion—in a tone of finality—concerning the demise of liberalism.

Presumably what is meant by those who say liberalism is dead is that liberals today are attempting to maintain life in a corpse by means of artificial respiration, while the critics are pleading for prompt burial. Their "description" of the situation is in fact a value-laden prescription.

For, if liberalism is dead, then we say, "Long live liberalism." As will be seen, we would not venture to continue the paraphrase by asserting that liberalism can do no wrong. But we do affirm that the royal lineage is not dead and will not die. Having once got into the world, the liberal spirit will blow where it listeth. It may, along with the scientific spirit, be driven underground but only in appearance. We remember that Christianity has from time to time been reported dead; and those who have wished to be a little more cautious have assured us that its days are numbered. In the nineteenth century, when the idea of progress was glorified as the faith once for all delivered, we were told that "the religion of the future" would leave Christianity behind. Yet even today many people persist in avowing critical allegiance to Christianity; indeed, there is evidence that the Christian religion is now waxing rather than waning. Simultaneously, many of the faithful admit the validity of certain of the charges that have been brought against Christianity. How is this apparent ambivalence to be explained? Clearly, by observing that the loyal Christian of this sort believes he is retaining the essence of Christianity and relinquishing only its accidental elements.

The question of the essence of Christianity is, in the technical sense, a modern one. In the form with which we are familiar, the question is little more than a century old and is one of the fruits of the scientific spirit. But it has been posed in an acute and importunate fashion many times throughout history. One need mention only the names of Paul, Marcion, Augustine, Abelard, Luther, Kant, Schleiermacher, Hegel, and Ritschl to indicate the wide variety of approaches and answers to the question, "What is the essence of Christianity?" Each of these names symbolizes a period when Christianity was at a crisis and a turning point. The question has repeatedly been asked in determining whether a given element in Christianity was a foundation stone or merely a vestigial organ. But all along, those who have served to keep alive the one holy catholic church have acted on the principle, Christianity is dead, long live Christianity.

Now, we will confuse the situation by bringing in metaphysical swim-bladders in the form of essences or by arguing from analogy that liberalism's course will precisely resemble that of Christianity. The point is rather that liberalism may, like Christianity, also have its apostolic age and acute secularization, its reformation and renaissance, its loss and (we should hope also) its recovery of proletarian interest. And, as it passes through these or other phases, the question will continue to be posed, "What is the essence of liberalism?" And so it is today.

THE AMBIGUITY OF LIBERALISM

In order to answer this question, we must have the courage not to oversimplify. Liberalism is in part divided against itself. While some might celebrate the dialectic in liberalism and others decry its contradictions, it is clear that there is tension in liberalism. This tension in both liberal Christianity and within liberalism in general is an aspect of the morphology of ideas and of social movements.

Alfred North Whitehead pointed out that when we examine the intellectual agencies that function in "the adventure of ideas" we find a rough division into two types, "one of general ideas, the other of highly specialized notions." As an example of a general idea he cites the ancient ideal of the intellectual and moral grandeur of the human soul; as an example of a highly specialized notion he cites the ideals of early Christianity. The distinction is pertinent for an understanding of the tensions and ambiguities within liberalism and within liberal Christianity.

Liberalism's "general idea" has been to promote liberation from tyranny, provincialism, and arbitrariness and thus to contribute to the meaningful fulfillment of human existence. This aspect of liberalism we may call its progressive element: it is always critical of the status quo and seeks new paths of fulfillment. A "specialized notion" of liberalism has developed during the last two centuries, namely a doctrine of pre-established harmony coupled with the laissez faire theory of society. Under the conditions of early capitalism, this doctrine was vindicated in economic progress. But beginning a century ago progressive liberalism became critical of this "specialized notion." From the point of view of progressive liberalism, the laissez faire society was producing new structures of arbitrary domination that frustrated both equality and justice. Accordingly, the more general idea of liberalism has come into conflict with a specialized version of it. Progressive liberalism has criticized laissez-faire liberalism as being closely bound up with the narrow interests of the middle class, and also with its dogma of political nonintervention in the economic sphere. Progressive liberals have also protested against the status quo that was defended by laissez faire liberals. In support of the labor movement, and, subsequently, of the minorities ignored by labor, they demanded a more responsible society—a political intervention on behalf of the disinherited. Here the specific aims took the form of attack on monopolistic use of power and also on the form of attempts to control inflation and depression. So great has been the tension between the general and the specialized forms of liberalism that some people have rightly asserted that the strategies of progressive liberalism are in fact the opposite of laissez faire liberalism. We see, then, that there is an ambiguity in the meaning of the word "liberalism" and that it is the consequence of a tension between two related versions of liberalism. Indeed, the ambiguities are far more complex than we have indicated.

Liberal Christianity is not by definition identical with liberalism considered either as a generalized or a specialized notion. Liberal Christianity is explicitly oriented to the ultimate resources of human existence and meaning discerned in the Old and the New Testaments and in Christian experience, and in Anglo-American society, it finds its modern roots primarily in the "Left Wing of the Reformation." At the same time, liberal Christianity has been associated with several kinds of liberalism, both generalized and specialized. Indeed, because of its intentional entanglement in the secular order—in contrast to the orthodoxies that claim to remain aloof—liberal Christianity is never in its actuality easy to distinguish from one or another of these associated forms of liberalism, except perhaps in terms of its ultimate orientation. At the same time liberal Christianity has aimed to be critical of these forms of liberalism. The relationships of creative involvement and critical tension are roughly analogous to those that Paul Tillich takes into account in his conception of the "Protestant principle," a principle that is creative but that also brings into question every actualization of Protestantism. Thus liberal Christianity must protest the confusions in liberalism itself.

THE ROOTS OF AMBIGUITY

The roots of ambiguity can be traced to the contrast between the liberalism of John Locke and Thomas Jefferson on the one hand, which is constantly invoked by both laissez faire and progressive liberals, and the liberalism of the Left Wing of the Reformation on the other. These two types of liberalism differ fundamentally in ultimate orientation. Locke's picture of the individual (with his property) required both a government and a religion that let him alone. Thomas Jefferson too had a great faith in the individual. A man was a law unto himself, and the purpose of government was to protect him—him and his property. In him resides the final appeal. Nothing can overrule him: he is sovereign. This view of man fitted with the prevailing theory of knowledge. Locke had found the world divided into material and mental substances. The mental substance was "the soul of man and the political person," a unified, isolated entity having a body that was its most immediate "property," being acted on by the material substances and projecting impressions on them in turn.

Such a view of man cannot be set aside as a mere chapter in the history of philosophy. It accords too closely with pervasive modern feelings. Indeed, it is embedded so deeply in us that it is almost below the level of consciousness. Many other influences have come into liberalism, but every influence has had to cope with this original inclination and each successive one has been accepted or rejected to the degree that it has or has not fitted this initial view. The individual is to us still inviolate, and it is Locke's and Jefferson's theories we have in mind. Try as we will to introduce other conceptions that might limit the individual's primacy, the notion of personal sovereignty continues to rule. Progressive liberals turned this notion into the positive obligation of the political order to promote individual fulfillment through economic intervention.

In religious circles, major liberal theologians, such as the eminent Unitarian, Channing, have been permitted to contribute little more than the clearing away of elements in Protestantism that did not harmonize with this view. The devil and hell were dispatched, although sin was still recognized. In due time, however, the idea of sin was also in large measure liquidated. The individual now possessed an innate purity that harmonized with innate sovereignty; the individual was, then, a being worthy of the unalienable rights of life, liberty, and the pursuit of happiness. Jesus was important because of his human qualities; it was not derogatory in this view to find him so human, because the human had been deified.

The science of the nineteenth century was readily acceptable to this view since it derived by a somewhat different route from the same origin. Empirical science concerned so exclusively with observation was congenial, for the sovereign mental substance of the individual and the scientific observer were one and the same person—that had been Locke's initial idea. Thus, among liberals, the clash between science and liberal religion was interpreted as a mistaken view of both. Progress and evolution were acceptable ideas since they gave an explanation of the achievement of mankind as the result of a long and arduous struggle, and they opened endless vistas into the future—"the progress of mankind onward and upward forever." The foundation of scientific humanism is obviously here, as are the bases for a middle-class philosophy of history and the defense of private property as the individual transcends himself to gain control over all that is around him.

This form of liberalism has been in conflict with, yet often in uncomfortable alliance with, the form of liberalism deriving from the "Radical Reformation," or, as it is sometimes called, the "Left Wing of the Reformation." It originated less as a philosophy than as a protest against the authoritarian organization of the churches, both Protestant and Catholic, which were ruled from the top down. Like the philosophical liberals in the traditions from Locke, the Radical Reformers, especially in England, rejected the notion that the cosmos was a hierarchy and that society must be organized on the pattern of hierarchy controlled by priest and monarch. But they focused their protest against the use of state force in matters of religious belief. Accordingly, proponents of the left wing demanded the separation of church and state. And rather than finding their defense in the rational individual, they typically appealed to the belief in the freedom of the spirit—"The spirit bloweth where it

listeth"—to create new community. The Left Wing of the Reformation, therefore, also insisted that the church is a lay church; it is not
to be controlled by "officials." Every child of God has the guidance
of conscience, for the Holy Spirit is available to every child of God.
But this conscience and the living presence of the Holy Spirit is
found in the mutuality of community. The individual transcends
himself not, in the first instance, through rational control of
property, privately or governmentally, but through life with others.
In this "fellowship" the so-called minority position was to be
protected in the very name of the Holy Spirit. According to this
view, God works in history where free consensus appears under
the great Taskmaster's eye. Thus the sanction for the maintenance
of Freedom was held to be a covenant between people in community and under God. Here we see the "gathered" church, a pattern
promoting the religious pluralism characteristic in modern society.
Variety was seen as the law of creation, truth to emerge in the
battle of ideas among free persons in free communities.

Contrary to the ideological interpretation of history by the
philosophical liberals, many scholars today recognize that it was
out of these ideas that political democracy was born. Basic to this
whole development was the demand for coarchy in place of
hierarchy on one side and a distrust of individualist notions of
humanity on the other. These ideas were first applied to the church
and then next to the state. Thus some proponents of the Left Wing
considered their free church to be a model for a democratic state.

The political conceptions were drawn by *analogy* from the
conception of the free church. What were originally elements of a
doctrine of the church appeared now as ingredients of a political
theory; the consent of the governed, the demand for the extension
of universal suffrage, the rule of law over the executive, and the
principle of the loyal opposition. The conception of the democratic
society is, then, a descendant of the conception of the free church.

From these sources modern liberal Christianity gained its major
thrust. In face of the traditional pecking orders, liberalism of this
sort developed its characteristic feature, namely, the conviction
that people should be liberated, indeed should liberate themselves,
from the shackles that impede religious, political, and economic
freedom, that impede the appearance of a community characterized by a rational and voluntary piety, and that impede the reality

of equality and justice for all. Here we can discern vigorous reformist (and even utopian) elements that have biblical roots and press liberalism always toward the future.

This type of liberalism has had to struggle not only against the old idolatries of authoritarianism but also against an idolatry latent within liberalism, that is, within a specialized form of it. Idolatry occurs when a social movement adopts as the center for loyalty an idol, a segment of reality torn away from the context of universality, an inflated, misplaced abstraction made into an absolute. Liberalism in its generalized form has been the chief critic of the idolatries of creedalism, of church or political authoritarianism, of nationalistic, racial, or sexual chauvinism; but in its specialized form it has generated a new idolatry, the idolatry of "possessive individualism." This possessive individualism has served as a smokescreen, an ideology, concealing or protecting a new authoritarianism of corporate economic power. This idolatry in the name of individualism and the "free market" eschews responsibility for the social consequences of economic power—it has become virtually unaccountable to the general public. Accordingly, it rejects responsibility for the character of a society that requires, or at least comfortably tolerates, the built-in poverty of almost one-third of the populace (not to speak of the poverty of the underdeveloped countries). What began as a liberating individualism has become a pervasive conglomeration of power, an oppressive idolatry, a new absolute.

THE LOSS OF DIMENSION

In face of this devotion to a new absolute, some liberals have experienced a "loss of nerve," allowing liberalism to lose its inner amplitude of form or shape. In these quarters liberalism has sometimes retreated into a superficial and provincial backwash of "progress" ideology, sometimes into the mere privatization of religion, and sometimes into up-to-date but provincial zeal for the spirit of the times. This kind of liberalism is impotent to deal intellectually and responsibly with the ultimate issues of life. No philosophy of life, no religion, can remain viable unless it possesses a sense of depth, a sense of breadth, and a sense of length (or continuity) in history.

The liberal has properly been concerned with ethics, but under the influence of utilitarianism, and also of some forms of Kantianism, liberal religion in wide sectors has tended to identify religion with the good life. Here we have the thinning out of liberalism into moralism and the reduction of religion to the observance of ethical precepts. Little attention is given to the tragedy or the pathos of life, or to the ultimate sources and resources of life. The depth dimension is lost.

Liberals have also been concerned with the natural and cultural sciences. For the liberal, these methods and findings must take their place within the integrity of knowledge. Moreover, literature, the fine arts, and philosophy offer interpretations and criticisms of life that contribute to self-understanding and must be evaluated. In these respects, liberalism is properly broadminded. But breadth has its hazards. It may be misinterpreted to mean the acceptance of a little bit of this and the rejection of a little bit of that and with little sense to the whole. Breadth of this sort may be tantamount to irresponsibility; it may systematically prevent the achievement of integrity. To many people the attraction of liberalism has been its openness, its tolerance, its freedom. But, unchecked, precisely these qualities can produce the mind that is simply open at both ends; they can spell the loss of character and serve as an invitation to confusion, sheer variety and fissiparous freedom—diffused identity.

A more adequate conception of breadth than mere openmindedness is the breadth that relates the personal to the social-institutional dimensions of existence. Authentic liberalism protests equally against the mere privatization of religion and against its mere externalization in "social action." In terms of basic orientation, we may say that Kierkegaard and Marx need each other. What one lacks the other demands.

Liberalism in its several major forms has been conscious of time. Indeed, the modern world is indebted in part to liberalism for the profound historical consciousness that is in us all, a consciousness that had made modern humanity aware of the inevitability of change, of the necessity to be critical of the past and the present, and of the possibilities of the future, motifs also present in biblical sources. Things are not all what they were or what they will be. But in some liberal circles this critical stance has issued in an uncritical antitraditionalism. It tempts liberalism into a provincialism in time, an historical illiteracy, and finally a debilitating rootlessness. But nothing significant in human history is achieved except through long-standing continuities. A sense of "length" is required for any genuine liberalism.

In the face of the loss of depth, width, and length in liberalism, we must engage in the criticism of liberalism from the inside. As liberals, we assume that liberalism, like any other movement, can remain alive only through "coming to itself," through repentance and return. Only where there is a sincere recognition of incompleteness and failure, only where there is the recovery of depth, breadth, and length, only there is the authentic spirit of religious liberalism to be found. Hence, the liberal expects to hear over and over again: liberalism is dead; long live liberalism. Indeed, the spirit of liberalism can live only where "the liberalism that is dead" is identified and where the life that makes all things new is appropriated. This life may be found, of course, within the traditions of liberalism itself; but liberalism has no monopoly upon the fount of life. The transcendent belongs to no party and it perennially eludes domestication. But we are not helpless, nor may we remain silent. The prophetic religious insights which have been catalytic for vibrant and enduring elements of liberalism in the past demand new articulation today. With a self-denying ordinance that disclaims finality or authoritativeness, we venture the following characterization of the essential elements of a genuine and vital religious liberalism.

THE FIVE SMOOTH STONES OF LIBERALISM

I.   Religious liberalism depends first on the principle that "revelation" is continuous. Meaning has not been finally captured. Nothing is complete, and thus nothing is exempt from criticism. Liberalism itself, as an actuality, is patient of this limitation. At best, our symbols of communication are only referents and do not capsule reality. Events of word, deed, and nature are not sealed. They point always beyond themselves. Not only is significant novelty both possible and manifest, but also significance is itself inchoate and subject to inner tensions of peril and opportunity.

The ground for this first tenet is the human dependence for being and freedom upon a creative power and upon processes not ultimately of our own making. The liberal's ultimate faith is not in himself. We find ourselves to be historical beings, living in nature and history, and having freedom in nature and history. The forms that nature and history take possess a certain given, fateful character, and yet they are also fraught with meaningful possibilities. Within this framework, humanity finds something dependable and also many things that are not dependable. One thing that is dependable is the order of nature and of history that the sciences are able to describe with varying degrees of precision.

How long the order of nature will continue to support human life is beyond the ken of our science. Possibly our earth and our sun will one day cool off and freeze, or they may dissipate or explode. Moreover, everyone is condemned to what we call death. Whether beyond this death there is a new life is a matter of faith, of a faith that trusts reality as we have known it. Like one of old we may say to this universe and its ruling power, "Into thy hands I commend my spirit."

Whatever the destiny of the planet or of the individual life, a sustaining meaning is discernible and commanding in the here and now. Anyone who denies this denies that there is anything worth taking seriously or even worth talking about. Every blade of grass, every work of art, every scientific endeavor, every striving for righteousness bears witness to this meaning. Indeed, every frustration or perversion of truth, beauty, or goodness also bears this witness, as the shadow points round to the sun.

One way of characterizing this meaning is to say that through it God is active or is in the process of self-fulfillment in nature and history. To be sure, the word "God" is so heavily laden with unacceptable connotations that it is for many people scarcely usable without confusion. It is therefore well for us to indicate briefly what the word signifies here. In considering this definition, however, the reader should remember that among liberals, no formulation is definitive and mandatory. Indeed, the word "God" may in the present context be replaced by the phrase "that which ultimately concerns humanity" or "that in which we should place our confidence."

God (or that in which we may have faith) is the inescapable, commanding reality that sustains and transforms all meaningful existence. It is inescapable, for no one can live without somehow coming to terms with it. It is commanding, for it provides the structure or the process through which existence is maintained and by which any meaningful achievement is realized. Indeed, every meaning in life is related to this commanding meaning, which no one can manipulate and which stands beyond every merely personal preference or whim. It is transforming, for it breaks through any given achievement, it invades any mind or heart open to it, luring it on to richer or more relevant achievement; it is a self-surpassing reality. God is the reality that works upon us and through us and in accord with which we can discern truth, beauty or goodness. It is that reality which works in nature, history, and thought and under certain conditions creates human good in human community. Where these conditions are not met, human good, as sure as the night follows the day, will be frustrated or perverted. True freedom and individual or social health will be impaired.

This reality that is dependable and in which we may place our confidence is, then, not humanity. Nor is it a mere projection of human wishes. It is a working reality that every person is destined to live with. In this sense, we are not free; we are not free to work without the sustaining, commanding reality. We are free only to obstruct it or to conform to the conditions it demands for growth. This reality is, then, no human contrivance; it is a reality without which no human good can be realized and without which growth of meaning is impossible. Theists and religious humanists find common ground here. They differ in defining the context in which human existence and human good are to be understood. The liberal's faith, therefore, is a faith in the giver of being and freedom. Dignity derives from the fact that we participate in the being and freedom of this reality.

But we not only participate in divinely given being and freedom; through the abuse of freedom we also pervert and frustrate them. We distort or petrify the forms of creation and freedom. Hence we cannot properly place our confidence in our own creations; we must depend upon a transforming reality that breaks through encrusted forms of life and thought to create new forms. We put our faith in a creative reality that is re-creative. Revelation is continuous.

II. The second major principle of religious liberalism is that all relations between persons ought ideally to rest on mutual, free consent and not on coercion. Obviously, this principle cannot be advocated in any strict or absolute sense. Education, for example, may be compulsory within the liberal state, if not in the liberal church. All responsible liberals recognize the necessity for certain restrictions on individual freedom. They also recognize that "persuasion" can be perverted into a camouflage for duress. Nevertheless, free choice is a principle without which religion, or society, or politics, cannot be liberal.

Some time ago there was a good bit of excitement about the study of social organizations among birds. Scientists studying how long it takes a group of fowl to form a social organization reported that within eighteen to twenty-four hours, a group of chickens hitherto unacquainted with each other formed a tightly structured social organization—a rigid hierarchy of pecking rights. Liberalism, in its social articulation, might be defined as a protest against "pecking orders."

This second principle, like the others, can be stated in religious terms in various ways. Historically, the more profound forms of liberalism began in the modern world as a protest against ecclesiastical pecking orders. Protest against political and economic pecking orders soon followed. This protest often found its sanction in the basic theological assertion that all are children of one Father, by which is meant that all persons by nature potentially share in the deepest meanings of existence, all have the capacity for discovering or responding to "saving truth," and all are responsible for selecting and putting into action the right means and ends of cooperation for the fulfillment of human destiny. These religious affirmations are thus the basis of the liberal's belief that the method of free inquiry is the necessary condition for the fullest apprehension of either truth or justice, and also for the preservation of human dignity. This method of free inquiry and persuasion is the only one consistent with both the dignity and the limitations of human nature, and it is the method that yields the maximum of discovery and criticism.

Now it should be clear that if some people wish infallible guidance in religion, they are not going to find it in liberal religion. Of course, orthodox mentors will claim that this is the reason we need a divine guide, in a book or a church doctrine. Further, they sometimes tell us that the mortal sin of the liberal is the unwillingness to submit to divine authority and that this unwillingness grows out of intellectual pride. What the orthodox overlooks, however, is this: the most pretentious pride of all is that of the man who thinks himself capable of recognizing infallibility, for he must himself claim to be infallible in order to identify the infallible.

In contrast, the liberal seeks in the words of prophets, in the deeds of saintly men and women, and in the growing knowledge of nature and human nature provided by science meanings that evoke the free loyalty and conviction of people exposed to them in open discourse.

III. Third, religious liberalism affirms the moral obligation to direct one's efforts toward the establishment of a just and loving community. It is this which makes the role of the prophet central and indispensable in liberalism.

A faith that is not the sister of justice is bound to bring men to grief. It thwarts creation, a divinely given possibility; it robs man of his birthright of freedom in an open universe; it robs the community of the spiritual riches latent in its members; it reduces man to a beast of burden in slavish subservience to a state, a church or a party—to a manmade God. That way lies the grinding rut and tyranny of the superpatriot line, the Nuremberg line, and the Moscow line, different though these lines are from each other in their fear and obstruction of freedom. To try to manipulate or domesticate the integrity of freedom is to rely upon the unreliable —an attempt that ends in reliance upon unjust arbitrary power and upon unjust arbitrary counsels. Sooner or later the arbitrary confronts either stagnation from within or eruption from both without and within. The stars in their courses fight against it.

This faith in the freedom that creates the just community is the faith of the Old Testament prophets. They repudiated the idea that the meaning of life is to be achieved either by exclusive devotion to ritual or by devotion to blood and soil, or by self-serving piety. The "holy" thing in life is the participation in those processes that give body and form to universal justice. Injustice brings judgment and suffering in its train; it is tolerated only at the peril of stability and meaning.

Again and again in the history of our civilization this prophetic idea of the purpose of God in history comes to new birth. Jesus deepened and extended the idea when he proclaimed that the kingdom of God is at hand. The reign of God, the reign of the sustaining, commanding, transforming reality is the reign of love, a love that fulfills and goes beyond justice, a love that cares for the fullest personal good of all. This love is not something that is ultimately created by man or that is even at our disposal. It seizes and transforms life, bringing us into a new kind of community that provides new channels for love and new structures of justice.

Jesus uses the figure of the seed to describe this power. The power of God is like a seed that grows of itself if man will use his freedom to meet the conditions for its growth. It is not only a principle by which life may be guided; it is also a power that transforms life. It is a power we may trust to heal the wounds of life and to create the job of sharing and of community. This is the power the Christian calls the forgiving, redemptive power of God, a power everyone may know and experience whether or not these words are used to describe it. It is the power that leads to integrity of personal life, to the struggle for justice in social-institutional life, and to a creative tension between them.

Not that it demands no wounds. It drew Jesus up Golgotha to a cross. Thus Jesus was not only a martyr dying for his convictions, but also the incarnation of the affirmative power of love transforming life, even in death, and creating a transforming community, a fellowship yielding to the tides of the spirit.

This commanding, sustaining, transforming power can, at least for a time, be bottled up in dead words or in frozen institutions. The sustaining, transforming reality can be perverted by willful men, abusing their freedom, into a power that up to a point supports evil—yet, if we could not so abuse our freedom, we would not be free.

In history and in the human heart there are, then, destructive as well as creative powers. These destructive powers are manifest in the social as well as in the individual life, although they are most subtly destructive in the social life where the individual's egotism fights under the camouflage of the good of the nation, the race, the church, or the class. These destructive impulses (thoroughly familiar to the psychologist if not to their victims) seem veritably to possess people, blinding them, inciting them to greed, damaging the holy gifts God provides. This is precisely the reason for the need of the redemptive, transforming power. Indeed, the "pious" are often most in need of the transformation.

The community of justice and love is not an ethereal fellowship that is above the conflicts and turmoils of the world. It is one that takes shape in nature and history, one that requires the achievement of freedom with respect to material resources as well as with respect to spiritual resources. Indeed, the one kind of freedom is not fully authentic without the other. Freedom, justice, and love require a body as well as a spirit. We do not live by spirit alone. A purely spiritual religion is a purely spurious religion; it is one that exempts its believer from surrender to the sustaining, transforming reality that demands the community of justice and love. This sham spirituality, far more than materialism, is the great enemy of religion.

IV.   Now, anything that exists effectively in history must have form. And the creation of a form requires power. It requires not only the power of thought but also the power of organization and the organization of power. Thus we are led to the fourth element of liberalism: we deny the immaculate conception of virtue and affirm the necessity of social incarnation. There is no such thing as goodness as such; except in a limited sense, there is no such thing as a good person as such. There is the good husband, the good wife, the good worker, the good employer, the good churchman, the good citizen. The decisive forms of goodness in society are institutional forms. No one can properly put faith in merely individual virtue, even though that is a prerequisite for societal virtues. The faith of the liberal must express itself in societal forms, in the forms of education, in economic and social organization, in political organization. Without these, freedom and justice in community are impossible.

The faith of a church or of a nation is an adequate faith only when it inspires and enables people to give of their time and energy to shape the various institutions—social, economic and political—of the common life. A faith in the commanding, sustaining, transforming reality is one that tries to shape history. Any other faith is thoroughly undependable; it is also, in the end, impotent. It is not a faith that molds history. It is a faith that enables history to crush humanity. Its ministry prepares people to adjust to the crushing by focusing on, and salving, the personal experiences of hurt.

The creation of justice in community requires the organization of power. Through the organization of power, liberated persons tie into history; otherwise they cannot achieve freedom in history. Injustice in community is a form of power, an abuse of power, and justice is an exercise of just and lawful institutional power.

The kind of freedom that expresses itself only within the family and within the narrow confines of one's daily work is not the faith of liberals. It is as lopsided as the other kind of freedom that tries to express itself only in larger public affairs and forgets that the health of the body politic depends upon the health and faith of its individual members. At best it creates and expresses cloistered virtues of loyalty, honesty and diligence. This kind of faith can be oblivious of the injustices of the domestic, economic, and political orders; it can be a form of assistance to the powers of evil in public life and consequently also in the private life.

V.   Finally, liberalism holds that the resources (divine and human) that are available for the achievement of meaningful change justify an attitude of ultimate optimism. This view does not necessarily involve immediate optimism. In our century we have seen the rebarbarization of the mass man, we have witnessed a widespread dissolution of values, and we have viewed the appearance of great collective demonries. Progress is now seen not to take place through inheritance; each generation must anew win insight into the ambiguous nature of human existence and must give new relevance to moral and spiritual values. A realistic appraisal of our foibles and a life of continuing humility and repentance is all that will do, for there are ever-present forces in us working for perversion and destruction.

Perhaps nothing exemplifies this better than the twentieth-century experience of war. To be sure, there are many liberals who deny that war reveals anything fundamental about human nature and possibility. There are those for whom war is only an anachronism, a temporary aberration not to be taken seriously as a comment on human possibility. Still others would ignore war as a revealer of the human because they consider it one of those calamities, one of those accidents that comes from without, like earthquakes and storms, or from exterior political and economic machinations; as such it neither confirms nor challenges their view of the human condition. But war is a relentless revealer. It presents the human powers and aspirations as dramatically as does peace. Indeed, it reveals that the humanity of conflict is essentially the same as the humanity of "peace"; but in war the humanity that is almost hidden in times of peace, the *homo absconditus*, comes into fuller view.

Still, there is something in the genuine liberal perspective that, while recognizing this tragic nature of the human condition, continues to live with a dynamic hope, with the optative mood as one of its voices. It is a mood that derives ultimately from the ancient prophets and from the white-hot heart of the New Testament. No reputable scholar today would deny that Christianity was in its origin an eschatological religion. The recognition of this fact has become a source of embarrassment to many liberals. Yet liberalism denies to its peril that it was brought into being by people who, like the prophets and the eschatologist of Nazareth, turned from retrospect to prospect.

The optative mood alone offers only a truncated and, in the end, frustrated conjugation; the full paradigm demands the penitential and imperative moods as well. It demands also the declarative mood that speaks of the resources of fulfillment. This fuller paradigm, governed by the optative mood, has taken many forms in the thought of the West. Paul with his joyous faith in redemption, Augustine with his vision of the City of God, Joachim of Fiore with his hope of a new era—the reign of the Spirit—Lessing with his expectation of a third era, Channing with his prophecy of a new spiritual freedom, Marx with his battling for a new humanity, all speak in the optative mood without neglecting the realistic and the tragic. They utter their faiths in differing accents, although each has something to learn from the others, and all are severely critical of much around them. But all sense that at the depths of human nature and at the boundaries of what we are, there are potential resources that can prevent a retreat to nihilism.

Thus, each of these thinkers passes the litmus test of all prophetic religion. In response to the primary question of whether history has a meaning and a demanded direction or not, they all answer, finally, Yea. This is the issue that cuts through all others. It cuts through the ranks of those who believe in God as well as through the ranks of the unbelievers. The affirmative answer of prophetic religion, which may be heard in the very midst of the doom that threatens like thunder, is that history is a struggle in dead earnest between justice and injustice, looking towards the ultimate victory in the promise and the fulfillment of grace. Anyone who does not enter into that struggle with the affirmation of love and beauty misses the mark and thwarts creation as well as self-creation.

Thus, with all the realism and toughmindedness that can be mustered, the genuine liberal finally can hear and join the Hallelujah Chorus—intellectual integrity, social relevance, amplitude of perspective, and the spirit of true liberation offer no less.

THROUGHOUT HIS LIFE, Adams stood on the boundary between the community of faith and the academic community. He thus exemplifies both the liberal religious tradition of the "learned pastor" and the academic demand that religious commitments be held with intellectual integrity. However, he does not believe that human salvation is, in the end, derived from intelligence, that rational excellence is the key to human fulfillment, nor that the disciplined mind is an end in itself. On the contrary, he argues in the following essay that in a proper understanding of the arts and sciences as taught in the universities can be found basic questions of the purposes and ends of life, questions that involve profound religious sensibilities and demand profound human commitments.* Modern society denigrates the liberal arts college at its peril; religion sacrifices its concern for education at a dear price; yet neither the religious liberal nor the liberal intellectual can ignore the qualities of identity, choice, and community that shatter narrow concepts of rationality and rational utility.—M.L.S.

CHAPTER 2 · THE PURPOSES
OF "LIBERAL" EDUCATION

IN HIS autobiography *The Education of Henry Adams* the eminent American historian relates that one day, now more than a century ago, he asked an undergraduate at Harvard why he wanted a college degree. The student promptly replied, "The degree of Harvard College is worth money to me in Chicago." The student possessed at least the virtue of candor, but his answer was the perfect answer of the "interchangeable man," what Emerson called "the pea in the pod." Education of this kind seeks improved means for unimproved ends. One can readily see the fallacy of this concern for means to the exclusion of reflective concern for ends. According to the traditional definition, a liberal education is oriented primarily to terminal values and only secondarily to instrumental values. This has been the meaning of the word liberal since the time of Aristotle.

"Improved means for unimproved ends." The words from Henry David Thoreau are worth our pondering, and they bring into question much more than the cash-register view expressed in the

---

* First published as "The Purpose of a Liberal Arts Education," *Journal of the Liberal Ministry*, vol. 9, no. 2 (Spring 1969), pp. 3–8.

Henry Adams' story. For example, they bring into question the recently issued statement of a National Education Commission that the central purpose of American education is the development of the ability to think. The document says a good many other things as well; it recognizes that people are more than merely rational creatures, and it speaks of the interdependence between rationality and freedom, and of the necessity of developing the rational powers with respect to values in specific situations. But it stresses the point that the student's ability to think "enables him to apply logic and the available evidence to his ideas, attitudes and actions, and to pursue whatever goals he may have."

But is the major purpose of education adequately stated if one says that it is to develop the student's rational powers to the end of pursuing whatever goals he or she may have? I think not. So far as it goes, this statement of purpose is not essentially different from that offered by Henry Adams' student. It is, to be sure, extremely important that one be able to recognize fact, to distinguish, to classify, to relate, and thus to achieve the clarity appropriate to the subject matter. Abraham Lincoln was once asked why the president of the United States should receive seventy-five dollars a day, while a ditchdigger received only a dollar a day. In reply Lincoln said that if the president is able to dig abstractions aright, his worth is incalculable. One must insist that the capacity to dig abstractions aright, to define fundamental terms cogently, is a skill indispensable for civilized living. It belongs to the purpose of higher education. But this purpose *can* issue in only improved means for unimproved ends. It does not encompass the larger purpose of the study of the arts and the sciences in the liberal arts college.

With respect to the study of the sciences, we are often told that the principal purpose is to acquire the scientific method. But here again one is concerned with means and not with ends. The scientific method enables us to determine more efficient means for achieving a given end, but this is not the principal role of the study of the sciences. The primary purpose is a terminal value, an intrinsic end—the desire to know, to satisfy significant human curiosity. Dante, speaking of Aristotle, underlined this dimension of human existence when he said of him that he is the master of all who would *know*. Science grows out of wonder, Aristotle tells us.

The primordial father of science, let us say, was the first tadpole that raised its head above the surface of the water and asked the question, "What is going on here anyway?" The pure scientist is not a utilitarian; he is not primarily concerned with *use*. He wants to know what is going on in the course of nature and of human affairs. He rejects the demand, "Of what use is this knowledge?" The desire of science simply to satisfy curiosity, as Whitehead used to say, is the aspect of science that has been characteristically overlooked by the Dewey pragmatist.

The contrast between the intrinsic, terminal value of science, in contrast to the utilitarian value, is well illustrated by a conversation that took place one day when Prime Minister William Gladstone visited the scientist Michael Faraday, to see his laboratory. After Faraday had spent an hour showing Gladstone his scientific apparatus, his drums and batteries, and his instruments for the measuring of electromagnetism, the prime minister drew himself up and in pontifical condescension asked, "But what good is it all?" Faraday was in despair, for he had not been able to communicate to Gladstone a sense of the desire to know the nature of electric power for the sake of the knowing. In a fashion calculated to be intelligible to the utilitarian politician, Faraday replied, "Well, Sir, perhaps some day you will be able to tax it." Of course, Faraday was not indifferent to the use of electricity for human welfare; but in this reply to Gladstone he gave the answer that presupposes and prefers the liberal conception of the motive for scientific study, whether it be in the natural or the social sciences. Here the rational powers are developed, the scientific method is refined, in order to satisfy the desire to know.

As in the sciences so also in the arts—literature, philosophy, history, and the plastic arts—the ability to think clearly and to come to terms with evidence is indispensable; and it is also an arduous discipline. But to what end?

You will forgive me if I seek a shortcut through the discussion of this complex subject. Let us say with Emerson that to be human is to be a belief-bearing animal. We live on meaning, we demand purpose. We want to locate ourselves in time and space. We want to know who we are, we want to become. We want to achieve self-identity. We can do this only through relating ourselves to past and present, with some sense of direction for the future. How do we do this? Matthew Arnold's word here is familiar. He says that the educated person wants to know the best that has been thought and said. The discriminating student of literature seeks touch-stones by which he or she may judge the new literature it confronts. A more dynamic and historical conception than this is possible. John Galsworthy explained that the novelist understands that all the great novels comprise a long spinal column, and the several styles and forms of the novel serve as vertebrae in this spinal column.

A somewhat similar recognition is involved in the development of the human person. The psychologist Erik Erikson, concerned to understand the process of human maturation, has asserted that every person experiences a series of crises in the process of achieving self-identity. The youth finds in culture a great variety of models; development takes place as he or she tries on these models, not only for size but also for achieving a direction and purpose. One becomes a person when a personal style is achieved. This process, however, involves making decisions, and the decision provides a centerstance in the midst of circumstance.

An apt story is told about the Harvard geologist Nathanial Shaler of several generations ago. To the great annoyance of a number of his colleagues on the faculty, Shaler persisted in objecting to the award of a top scholarship to a certain student. Repeatedly Shaler was reminded that this student possessed an all-A record. But Shaler would not approve the award. Finally, Barrett Wendell of the English Department put the question squarely to Shaler at a faculty meeting, "Why are you set against this man who has such a superb record?" In reply, the tall, red-bearded Scotsman stood up and said, "I am voting against this student because of his cantankerous whatlessness."

A liberal arts education is a failure if it develops the ability to think but issues in "whatlessness"—a Laodicean lack of commit-ment. Does this mean that liberal education should attempt indoctrination? By no means. At least, not if indoctrination entails the transmission of a neat package of dogma that is exempt from criticism. Students, as well as teachers, if they are to be liberated from whatlessness, must avoid two equally enervating attitudes— a diffused identity, an unintegrated congeries of self-identifications on the one hand, and a foreclosed self-identity on the other hand. The formed self requires structure; and if a structure is to grow and to become relevant to changing situations, it must be a dynamic structure.

In the liberal arts college the student encounters the opportunity and responsibility of achieving through choice and decision, a self-identity—a self in relation to the past and present of the reigning culture—and an awareness of other styles of self-identity. This process involves the definition and integration of sensitivity and the criticism of sensitivity. Often it requires the achievement of the ability to suspend judgment. But the mind of a developed person cannot remain open at both ends; it makes decision and commitment. Unhappy and irresponsible and "whatless" are those who acquire no enduring enthusiasm, no identification with an idea that informs purposes. Human persons, in short, are not one whit greater than the ends with which they identify themselves.

These ends seldom function as mere abstractions of the sort to be found in a textbook. They function through incarnations in other persons; here the great teacher again and again turns out to be pivotal in the life-development of the student. They also function through incarnations in the treasures of culture. I recall a student who, with a group of others, had been preparing for weeks to hear the Bach Mass in B Minor, by listening to the phonograph recordings and by discussing with other students and the teacher everything that came to mind about the music, the text, and the composer. Finally, we all attended together the performance of the Mass in B Minor at Symphony Hall in Boston. Afterwards, as we were walking together down Huntington Avenue, the student stopped abruptly and brimming over with conviction and feeling, he said to me, "I want you to know that this is the greatest day of my life." The student felt this way because he had found in a work of art an object for self-identification. Later this man became a major figure in the effort to rescue German intellectuals from Fascist persecution and slaughter. I recall another fellow student who would come to my room in the dormitory from time to time to play phonograph records. I observed that when he was particularly discouraged with himself and his studies, he would play a recording of Mozart's aria, *Voi che sapete*. One day I asked him why he chose that particular music in his moments of discouragement. He answered, "When I play that aria I say to myself, 'Well, at least I belong to a race of man that can create that supreme beauty'."

This is the process of achieving self-identity and commitment. In a long conversation lasting well into the early hours of the morning, I once asked Erich Fromm if he would be willing to answer a personal, Boswellian question. I put it very bluntly, "Erich, what makes you tick?" "I know the answer to that question," he replied. "It is the Messianism of the Old Testament prophets." In this moment, Fromm defined himself in part by reference to an object of identification in the past, an object that gave dynamic for the venture into the future.

The liberal arts college exists in order to elicit the sort of identification that can become the nucleus for the achievement of what I have called centerstance in the midst of circumstance. In order to characterize this sort of self-identification, we could say of the student, of the teacher, of the human being, "By their roots shall ye know them." The liberal arts college aims to provide the possibility of one's finding roots from which one may grow into integrity. In large degree the liberal arts college aims to cultivate, transmit, criticize, and transform significant tradition. It does so with the presupposition, so well stated by Goethe, that a tradition cannot be inherited, it must be earned.

Now for one final consideration. The definition of a special kind of sensitivity and of self-identity is fundamental for responsible existence in the democratic society. The liberal arts college, like the democratic society, is pluralistic; it encourages and protects a variety of perspectives, so that these perspectives may (so to speak) water each other. Now just as this process requires the association and discipline of the liberal arts college for its cultivation, so also in later life, in post-college life, disciplined association is required. The growth and improvement of sensitivity and self-identity require sharing, and sharing is possible only in community, in a fellowship that provides the opportunity for participative enjoyment, mutual correction, and implementation in the life of the society at large.

ADAMS' TEACHING as well as his writing often takes a concrete, personal experience as a point of departure. In the following chapter, he begins by recalling his Fundamentalist past. In the course of his intellectual and personal pilgrimage, Adams had left most of his earlier religious training behind; but he continued to treasure two elements from that past that show up again and again in his work. Fundamentalists often hold that history consists of periods, epochs that have identifiable characteristics prophetically anticipated in the Scriptures. However obscurantist this concept became at the hands of some Fundamentalists, Adams saw a quality of thought in these esoteric efforts that is neglected at a considerable sacrifice by those concerned with human liberty. Moreover, Fundamentalists often emphasized the notion of radical laicism—the participation of all community members in decisionmaking and in discerning the signs of the times. Recently, non-Fundamentalist theologians of liberation and hope have moved to the recovery of these motifs. Their efforts are both anticipated and, in part, corrected by this 1947 article by Adams.*—M.L.S.

CHAPTER 3 · LIBERATION AND
EPOCHAL THINKING

O NE OF THE more vivid recollections of my youth in a Fundamentalist group is of their eager interest in the prophecies of the Bible. The prophecies were believed to encompass almost the entire range of human history. One all-embracing "prophetic" image that looms in my mind is that of an immense chart that adorned the wall of the church auditorium. The chart depicted the pivotal events of creation and redemption, beginning with the original chaos and proceeding through the six days of creation, the first day of rest, the fall, the various dispensations of Old Testament history on down to the annunciation, the incarnation, the crucifixion, and the resurrection, and thence to the second coming of Christ, the Battle of Armageddon, the seven years· of tribulation, the thousand-year reign of Christ, the chaining of Satan in hell, the last judgment before the great white throne, and the eternal peace or torment of the re-

* First published under the title "The Prophethood of All Believers," *Christian Register*, vol. 26, no. 3 (March 1947), pp. 95–96. It also appeared in Adams' *Taking Time Seriously* (Glencoe, Ill.: The Free Press, 1957).

spective final destinations of all human souls. In short, the epochs of "salvation history" were set forth as "by prophet bards fore-told."

Modern religious thinkers are accustomed to emphasize the prophetic task of the church too, but they long ago abandoned the whole idea of predicting the future by means of interpreting biblical prophecies. In conformity with the findings of modern historical research, we have held that prediction is a secondary and even an unimportant aspect of Old Testament prophecy. Accordingly, we say that the prophets were primarily *forthtellers* and not *foretellers*; they proclaimed the action of God in history, thus they disclosed the meaning of history. We see the prophet as one who stands at the edge of a community's experience and tradition, under the Great Taskmaster's eye, viewing man's life from a piercing perspective and bringing an imperative sense of the perennial and inescapable struggle of good against evil, of justice against injustice. In the name of the Holy One the prophet shakes us out of our pride and calls for a change of heart and mind and action; with fear and trembling he announces crisis and demands ethical decision here and now.

This function of prophecy is well symbolized by a visual metaphor that appears in a church in Toronto. On the altar in this church there stands a large crucifix on which the figure at first seems to be an importunate question mark, the prophetic question mark that stands over human ways that are not the ways of truth and right. It is the question mark we all would often like to liquidate, for it reminds us of the death-dealing effect of our egotism and our pretentious "virtue."

But we fall far short of understanding the full nature of prophecy (and of the prophetic task of the church) if we think of the prophets merely as critics dealing with religious and ethical generalities. In the great ages of prophecy the prophets (whether inside or outside the churches) have been *foretellers* as well as *forthtellers*. They have been predictors—proclaimers of doom and judgment, heralds of new fulfillment. They have attempted to interpret the signs of the times and to see into the future. They have stood not only at the edge of their own culture but also before the imminent shape of new and better things to come. At times of impending change and decision, they have seen the crisis as the crisis of an age; they have felt called to foresee the coming of a new epoch; that is, they have been what Karl Jaspers called "epochal thinkers." Wherever you find a prophet of world-historical significance you find a foreteller, and you find epochal thinking. By this kind of prophecy the signs of the times are interpreted as parts of a pattern, an old pattern in the structure of society that is passing away or of a new pattern of life that is coming into being. Jeremiah and Isaiah, Jesus and Paul, Augustine and Joachim di Fiore were all epochal thinkers in this sense; they saw themselves as standing between the times, between the epochs.

Prophetic prediction and epochal thinking have played an equally significant role in modern times. But not all prophets have appeared within the churches. Indeed, some of the most influential epochal thinkers of the nineteenth century prophesied against "religion," teaching that it was inextricably bound up with the passing epoch and as such marked for elimination. Karl Marx, for example, in his attempt to interpret the signs of the times, predicted the end of the age of the bourgeoisie and the advent of a new epoch, the real beginning of history in the age of the classless society. He tried to support this prophecy by means of a "science" of society. The influence of Marx upon even non-Marxist thinking has been profound, for he has given to masses of men a new concern for the "trend" of history and for epochal thinking. Even the proponents of "free enterprise" (the defenders of an earlier progressivist epochal thinking) have been constrained to defend their outlook in terms of prediction and of a theory of the inexhaustibility and viability of the present age. Friedrich Nietzsche, the great critic of Christian "slave morality" and of Prussianism, demanded, like Marx, that the scientist become a philosopher of culture and of history, a demand that many a scientist in the atomic age is now beginning to recognize; and he predicted (with shrewd accuracy) the nihilism of Western culture and conventional religion as the consequence of the loss of spiritual vitality. He also heralded the coming of a new man. "Man is something that shall be surpassed." Auguste Comte, an even more influential epochal thinker, took up the theme of the coming "third era" (proclaimed in varying ways before him by Joachim and Lessing and Hegel and Marx) and heralded the "third era" of science—the era that was to replace the ages of theology and metaphysics. Under his influence and under similar influences, many social scientists have come to hold that their work should include prediction. Indeed, many would say that the ideal of science is to acquire the sort of knowledge that will provide a basis for prediction. So the social scientists (or at least some of them) have become interpreters of the signs of the times, attempting to discriminate among the trends of the time and to describe our present position in the changing epoch. Edward Alsworth Ross of the University of Wisconsin, in considering the prophetic elements in contemporary sociology, has recently asserted: "Insight into the future is, in fact, the 'acid test' of our understanding. . . . From the days of Comte our slogan has been *Voir pour prevoir*, i.e., see in order to foresee."

It is not an exaggeration to say that the anti-Christian critics of our culture (such as the above) have done more than the church-men to revive prophetism as prediction and as epochal thinking. As *forthtellers* (that is, as interpreters of the ultimate meaning of life) they could learn much about the religious character of true prophetism; but as foretellers and as epochal thinkers they cannot be ignored. We live in a world of change, and we have the obligation to confront the problems posed by the present phase of our social economy. Only those who have a priestly attachment to the *status quo* (which changes whether we like it or not) will try to persuade us that we are living in a former stage of our epoch or that new occasions do not teach new duties. This sort of attach-ment produces the false prophets who say, "Ye shall have peace at this time." They say "unto everyone that walketh after the imagination of his own heart, no evil shall come upon you."

When we speak of prophecy, of prediction, of epochal thinking, a host of questions comes immediately to mind. Can one predict with accuracy what will happen to the entire economy? Do we know enough to make our predictions more than wild guesses? Should we not confine ourselves to piecemeal predictions? Is it not fanciful and even dangerous to talk about new epochs? Does this talk not lead to utopianism and irresponsible, tinkering experimen-tation? How does one choose from among the predictors? How big is an epoch, and how do we know one when we see one—or are we in a period of rapidation where the epochs come in such waves that we have a new agenda every generation, every decade, or every year? And how can religious belief contribute to prophetic criticism anyway? These questions demand and deserve answers.

But whatever the answers may be, this much we can say. A

group that does not concern itself with the struggle in history for human decency and justice, an expert who does not show concern for the shape of things to come, a church that does not attempt to interpret the signs of the times, is not prophetic. They are but representations of the past. We have long held to the idea of the *priesthood* of all believers, the idea that all believers have direct access to the ultimate resources of the religious life, that every believer has the responsibility of achieving an explicit faith, and that there are resources from the past that need to be mediated to the present. As an element of this radical laicism and sense of history, we need also a firm belief in the *prophethood* of all believers. The prophetic forces in society will appear where people think and work together to interpret the signs of the times in the light of their faith, to make explicit through discussion the epochal thinking that the times demand. They will arise wherever it becomes a responsibility to attempt to foresee and foretell the consequences of human behavior (both individual and institutional) and whenever there is the intention of participating in the creative dimensions of the future in place of merely being dragged into it. Only through the prophetism of all believers can we together foresee doom and mend our common ways.

Hope is a virtue, but only when it is accompanied by prediction and by the daring venture of new decisions, only when the prophethood of all believers creates epochal thinking. If this foresight and this epochal thinking do not emerge from the churches, they will have to come from outside the churches. Humanity can surpass itself only by being grasped by that which surpasses it and calls it to a new future. Do we have access to the religious resources for this surpassing of the present? If not, the time will come when others will have to say to us what Henry IV said to the tardy Crillon after victory had been won, "Hang yourself, brave Crillon! We fought at Arques, and you were not there."

ADAMS' CONCERN for an authentic religious liberalism, which was shaped by a deep appreciation of the arts and sciences and a sense of continuity with the prophetic tradition of the Bible, forced him to press the question of the relationship of human rationality to human freedom. In this chapter he combs the philosophical tradition to see how basic concepts of rational order are, or have been, related to concepts of choice and liberty, as aspects of human nature. This material was first presented by Adams at the annual "May Meeting" of the American Unitarian Association in 1941. Subsequently it was revised and published in the *Journal of Liberal Religion.** It appears here in still a third, moderately abridged, form. It finds renewed pertinence today, for although many current philosophies speak of the quest for the "genuinely human" or protest "dehumanization," they give few clues as to what basically constitutes "the human."—M.L.S.

CHAPTER 4 · ROOT IDEAS OF HUMAN FREEDOM

THE CHANGING REPUTATION OF HUMAN NATURE

EW THINGS in human history are fixed, least of all reputations. As Santayana remarks of Hamlet, the reputations both of the great figures of fiction and of their creators have usually had an evolution and a history. One age extols Shakespeare as abiding our every question; another devotes itself to "improving" him. One age wishes Milton could be living at this hour; another regards him as the blight of English poesy. One school honors Plato as the "father of all orthodoxy"; another excommunicates him as the "source of all heresy." Hence, the admonition "Let us now praise famous men" raises again and again the questions "Which men?" and "How praise them?"

But not only individual reputations change. The reputation of the whole species also changes. Indeed, it has been changing a good deal of late. The reasons for this are legion. One reason is, of course, that among men above the primitive level some change of outlook is always taking place. It may be slow or devious, but it is inevitable. There is a sort of dialectic in the history of ideas, which over and over again manifests itself in a dissatisfaction with "established" views and a demand for novelty. Moreover, every

* Originally titled "The Changing Reputation of Human Nature," *Journal of Liberal Religion*, vol. 4, no. 2 (Autumn 1942), pp. 59–72, and no. 3 (Winter 1943), pp. 137–60.

idea that persists in history has what Hegel calls its own "cunning." No idea can remain static, not even the conception of man. The values and insights of a given orientation or emphasis seem to exhaust themselves, and the moving finger of time points in a new direction—and sometimes in the opposite direction. Another reason for the change in the reputation of man is the fact that many of the generalizations applied to human nature in one period of the world history have only a restricted validity in another period. The structure of society at a given time in large measure determines which aspects of human nature shall receive fuller expression and which shall be suppressed or called very little into play. But there are also reasons for changes in the reputation of human nature that are peculiar to our age. For one thing, both the natural and the social sciences have in the recent past brought forth new knowledge about human nature that is affecting its reputation. Equally significant as a cause for the changes taking place today in this area is the profound change in the historical situation. History has its "cunning" too, and this affects man's estimate of the human condition.

But there are two additional things that should strike the attention of any one interested in the changing reputation of human nature. The first is that the reputation of human nature in any epoch or movement is closely associated with a general worldview, and it cannot be understood apart from this worldview. The second is the fact that in modern times the major changes in this reputation represent to a large extent variations on a few very old themes. A novel fundamental idea does not appear often in human thought, whether the thought is concerned with man, nature, or God. Only a few basic rival conceptions are available in any one of these areas of thought, and most of these we have inherited from ancient times.

When the reputation of human nature changes, then, it is almost inevitable that either some variation of the prevalent attitude toward human nature and existence or a new version of a neglected earlier conception should emerge. This latter trend has been taking place in our day. In the very process of assimilating the new knowledge of man that has resulted from the application of modern scientific methods and that has accrued from viewing man in a changed historical situation, many people have been led to a new appreciation of certain earlier estimates of human nature and the human situation.

We now turn our attention to a consideration of three of these basic rival conceptions. Our purpose in presenting them is not merely to provide an orientation for the consideration of the current changes in the reputation of human nature, but also to indicate the relative merits of these conceptions and to draw from such a study an indication of the changes needful in the older liberal doctrine of man.

EARLY ALTERNATIVE VIEWS

Nietzsche pointed out to us, some time ago, that in the ancient Greek tradition we find two of these typical estimates of human nature and the human situation. One view is associated with the classical philosophers, and is usually called the intellectualistic or rationalistic view, the Apollonian view. According to this view, reason is the masterful principal of creation, and the cosmos is a moving shadow of a world of eternal ideas, essences, or forms. Correspondingly, man's primary, distinguishing faculty is his reason, and through it he can release a vitality that will enable him to achieve control of himself and of the human situation by subjecting them to clearly envisaged forms. What is to be especially noted here is the tendency of this intellectualistic view, first, to interpret existence in terms of a rational, unified, harmonious structure, and, second, to exalt the cognitive, nonaffective aspects of the human psyche. The conjunction of these two elements leads to a preoccupation with the forms and structures of being and to a "theoretical attitude of distance" that aims at the development of the form and harmony of the Olympian calm. Thus the vitality of nature, man, and history is presumed, but creativity is identified with the operations of reason.

The other view of human nature in the Hellenic tradition to which Nietzsche drew our attention interprets existence more in terms of vitality than of form, a vitality that is both creative and destructive, that imbues every form but that also eludes and bursts the bounds of every structure. It is associated with one of the major traditions in popular Greek religion, with certain pre-Socratic philosophers very close to this religious tradition, and in certain respects, with the great tragedians. It has usually been characterized as the Dionysian view. In recent decades this view and certain modern variations of it have been spoken of as "voluntarism."

In general, this view exalts the dynamic aspects of existence; therefore it conceives of man's proper goal as the fulfillment of the life-giving powers inherent in existence. But here the elements of struggle, contradiction, and tragedy, rather than the element of harmony, are emphasized. Thus in popular Greek thought and even among certain of the élite, a large place is assigned to Fate. Man is believed to be confronted by divine and demonic forces that either support and inspire or thwart and pervert him in his attempt to fulfill his destiny. Although there is here a keen sense of tragedy, man does not in this view necessarily lose his dignity and worth. Quite the contrary. In the great Greek tragedies, for example, the tragic element is discovered at the very point at which human greatness and the divine sphere come into conflict. It is precisely human greatness that makes possible tragic guilt and self-destruction. Indeed, according to this view, not only man is plagued by a Fate that drives him to tragic grandeur and self-destruction; but even the gods are subject to it, since no one of them can be identified with the highest principle. Fate is considered to be sovereign over both man and the gods just because it is viewed as a causal manifestation of a primordial creative principle. The point to be stressed, however, is that man is here understood in terms of the dignity and fate of a human agent confronted by a will or power that cannot be created or controlled by any merely rational technique. The tragic process is master of all forms, causing them to undergo change and transformation and even destruction.

This tragic view of the human condition, as it was held among the Greeks, was largely ignored in eighteenth- and nineteenth-century "Hellenism," as was also the fact of its affinity with ancient Hebrew conceptions. The Hellenism that has been influential since the Renaissance has taken its nourishment chiefly from the intellectualistic tendency in Greek life and thought. Nietzsche and Jacob Burckhardt were among the first influential modern historians to become aware of the great significance of the tragic, Dionysian tendency in Greek thought. The work of later scholars such as Butcher and Diels has contributed much to the achievement of a new appreciation of what Butcher has characterized as "the melancholy of the Greeks." Nevertheless, the Apollonian interpretation of Hellenism as set forth by Matthew Arnold has continued to exercise a wide influence, and it has veiled from the eyes of many the predominantly tragic attitude of the Greeks, an attitude much more similar to that of the Hebrews than Arnold recognized. The Hellenism described by Arnold deserves the praise he bestows upon it. But we should bear in mind that it was shared by only a small élite in ancient Greece and also that it was only for a short time able to maintain the optimistic attitude that we associate with the glory that was Greece.

In modern usage, the Dionysian motif shows up in a variety of ways. Ferdinand Tönnies coined the term "voluntarism" in 1883, and it has subsequently been employed by several sociologists to denote an emphasis upon the decisive significance of "the social will" in the development of society. As an epistemological method, voluntarism may be said to depend upon the view that the substantial character of reality cannot be understood merely by achieving clear and distinct ideas. For reality not only *does*, but *should* determine the ideas and not the ideas the reality. Hence, knowledge is an active understanding and a participation in creativity. In psychology, the older conceptions of the "will" as a faculty have disappeared. Terms such as "conation," "striving," "impulse," "desire," and "action" have replaced it. In religion, the term "voluntarism" denotes any theory that stresses the primacy of divine will or of human decision in religious knowledge, faith, or experience.

In the light of what has been said, it should be clear that we cannot properly understand the third influential attitude toward humanity and existence—the Judeo-Christian view—if we interpret it as constituting a complete contrast with the Greek views of life. It is true that there is little in common between the Jewish-and-early-Christian view and the Apollonian attitude. Insofar as Matthew Arnold confines his attention to these two points of view he is a reliable guide when he characterizes the differences between Hellenism and Hebraism. In addition to the differences Arnold describes, we should note that another difference between the Judeo-Christian and the sophisticated Greek outlook is to be discerned in their contrasting views of time and history; the one looked on history as "forward-moving" toward a particular End (*eschaton*), while the other viewed it as cyclic.

On the other hand, the Greek Dionysian view and the Judeo-Christian attitude bear a resemblance to each other in their possession of a "tragic sense of life," as well as in their emphasis upon the dynamic elements in the world and in human life. According to the Judeo-Christian view, God is a righteous will fulfilling its purpose in history; humanity and nature are fallen; our natural will is at variance with the divine will; our sin, guilt, and conflict with the principalities and powers of this world are an inextricable part of human experience. Thus, in both the Greek tragic view and the Jewish prophetic and primitive Christian outlook, there is an awareness of an ontologically grounded tendency in humanity toward rebellion, perversion, and self-destruction. Moreover, in both views the attention is centered upon the dynamic, creative-destructive aspects of humanity and upon the affective aspects of the psyche.

Yet, there are also certain fundamental differences to be observed between the Judeo-Christian and the Greek "tragic" view. Two of these differences may be noted here. The first has to do with the ultimate valuation they place on existence. The Judeo-Christian doctrine of creation involves the idea that in substance the world is good because it is God's creation. Nothing in existence is absolutely antidivine, for in order to exist an object must contain something of the divine. *Esse est bonum qua esse.* The Christian confession: "I believe in God the Father Almighty, the Creator of heaven and earth," has this idea as its real import. Even suffering may be a means of grace. Indeed, the Cross itself is the highest revelation of the character of God, for through it divine providence overcomes sin and death. Likewise, the Pauline belief in original sin is outweighed by the emphasis on providence and the hope of redemption. Thus God is beyond tragedy; and, ultimately, existence and history are not tragic. On the other hand, the Greek popular view, from pre-Homeric times onward, was unable to find a principle of transcendence beyond the tragedy of existence. This view finds philosophical expression in the famous fragment of Anaximander: "Things perish into those things from which they have their birth, as it is ordained; for they pay to one another the penalty of their injustice according to the order of time." For Anaximander, "the separate existence of things is, so to speak, a wrong, a transgression which they must expiate by their destruction." The contrast between Judeo-Christian optimism and the melancholy of the Greeks cannot be discussed in further detail here.

The other major difference between the Judeo-Christian and the Dionysian view concerns their contrasting attitudes toward reason and morality. The Dionysian view was strongly characterized by "enthusiastic" irrationalism and amoralism, defects made familiar to most of us through the diatribes of Euripides against Dionysianism. The Judeo-Christian mentality in its formative period made no virtue of irrationalism, and it strongly opposed amoralism. Whether we think of the Old Testament prophets, the writers of the Wisdom literature, or of the great rabbis of normative Judaism, whether we think of Jesus, Paul, the author of the Fourth Gospel, or of the Greek fathers or Augustine—the main line of the Christian tradition—we find no exaltation of irrationalism, and we find a great emphasis placed on conformity to the righteous will of God. With respect to the attitude toward reason, it is no accident that the Christian outlook could be merged with Greek theology. It is largely because of this coming together of Judeo-Christian voluntarism and Greek intellectualism that Christianity became the transmitter of much of the best in both the ancient Semitic and the ancient Greek traditions.

Much of the history of thought in the West may in its broader perspectives be interpreted as a history of the combination of, and the tension and interplay between, the three attitudes toward existence that we have briefly described. In view of the fact, however, that the *pagan* tragic view was effectually overcome in the Middle Ages, modern thought about man and existence for the most part represents an interplay between only two of these attitudes, the Greek intellectualist and the Judeo-Christian voluntarist view. The views that prevailed in the Middle Ages, in the Renaissance and the Reformation, and even in the periods of the Enlightenment and of Romanticism are to be interpreted as modern developments, combinations or perversions of motifs already present in these ancient Greek and Hebrew traditions. The increasingly dominant force in modern Western culture, however, has been the rationalistic tradition. Although intellectualism reached its high points in Thomism, in the Cartesian tradition, and in early eighteenth-century rationalism, and although it met with strong opposition in Romanticism—a form of Dionysianism—it has in many quarters continued to hold its own. To be sure, it has in this process undergone certain transformations. Indeed, its "success" is perhaps due to this very fact. Thus the earlier static rationalism was replaced, in the eighteenth century, by a dynamic, progressive rationalism that has exercised a considerable variety of influence. This dynamic rationalism is to be seen, for example, in the revolutionary rationalism of the late-eighteenth century; it has served as the core of modern bourgeois democracy; and, alongside the influence of empiricism, it has also decisively affected eighteenth- and nineteenth-century science and technology. This change to a dynamic rationalism took place at the time when bourgeois man was freeing himself from the feudal system and bringing about the modern industrialist society. This has no small bearing on the character that modern rationalism has assumed in its various stages.

Meanwhile, the voluntaristic view also has undergone many changes. Its peregrinations may be roughly identified through its many variations, as in Bonaventura, Duns Scotus, and Luther, and through essential changes, as in Schelling and Nietzsche. A list of the significant figures who in the modern period have in one way or another stressed the role of creative will and conflict rather than of unitary reason and harmony would be long and imposing. Yet it would for the most part include philosophical outlooks that have been subdominant in modern thought until recent decades. Some of these thinkers have set forth a basically irrational philosophy; others have stressed the role of the nonrational or the alogical; and still others have attempted to combine rational or metalogical analysis with a recognition of the decisive role of the will.

In general, however, we may say that whereas intellectualism as a consequence of its having centered attention on the cognitive aspects of human nature has emphasized rational poise, harmony, and "a theoretical attitude of distance," voluntarism, although for the most part insisting upon the basic significance of the intellectual disciplines, has tended to stress the dynamic and contradictory elements in existence and the affective aspects of human nature. Hence, the latter point of view has emphasized what is today called the existential attitude, that is, "an ultimate concern about the meaning of being for us, demanding an attitude of decision." In the light of these contrasts in typology we must interpret the age-old conflict between those who assert the primacy of the intellect and those who assert the primacy of the will. And it must be noted again that the voluntaristic tradition, especially in Christian theology, has stressed the fateful, tragic aspects of human existence. Indeed, in its most extreme forms voluntarism has asserted the arbitrary sovereignty of God and the helpless corruption of human nature; and in secular thought it has asserted the arbitrary sovereignty of some particularist loyalty to tradition, blood, class, or nation, or the existential sovereignty of the self that chooses only its own authenticity and arbitrarily creates its own moral world.

MODERN DEVELOPMENTS: RATIONALIST

The modern development of intellectualism must be understood as a reaction against these extreme forms of voluntarism. In large degree the Renaissance was a revolt against the obscurantism and authoritarianism of the Middle Ages and also against certain forms of earlier voluntarism (though it must be added that the Renaissance was also voluntaristic in some respects). Likewise, intellectualism in later centuries represents a revolt against the extreme forms of voluntarism found in orthodox Calvinism and Lutheranism.

Indeed, religious liberalism itself can be understood in its proper perspective only when interpreted as an aspect of this opposition. In religious liberalism the rationalistic view of human nature and of the human situation appeared as a revolt against the older forms of authoritarianism, a revolt in the name of the principles of freedom of mind and freedom of conscience. But concomitantly the liberal movement represented also a revolt against the Protestant dogma of the total depravity of human nature, that is, against a depraved, lopsided, rationalized form of the Christian doctrine of original sin. In short, it was a revolt against a voluntarism that had gone to seed.

The fruits of this struggle and of the great humanitarian impulse of the nineteenth century represent no mean cultural accomplishment. This fact can scarcely be overemphasized. Moreover, contemporary Protestantism owes to religious liberalism the social emphasis that in the past century has been reintroduced into Protestant thought and action.

But, unfortunately, not all the fruits issuing from the new movement were actually intended or expected by its proponents.

Nor was the movement able to maintain in the main body of its adherents the prophetic power of its early days. The new intellectualism, which in its early stages was powerfully dynamic, more and more moved in the direction of emphasizing again the cognitive aspects of human nature—"the theoretical attitude of distance"—and thus neglected the affective side of human nature and "the attitude of decision." The influence of the scientific method, despite its value in other respects, played no small role in accelerating this tendency.

As a consequence, the emphasis on the quality of the will, on the disposition of the *entire* personality, was replaced by a onesided emphasis on "reason." The attitude of Greek rationalism, as mediated through Stoicism and scholasticism and transformed by modern rationalism, was taking the place of the older Augustinian emphasis on the will and the affections. Here we find, then, the element that has given liberal religion its reputation for being intellectual. The appeal to affective experience, the belief in the necessity for conversion, and the use of the emotive symbols of the religious tradition were more and more deprecated. Thus religious liberalism, in the name of *intellectual* integrity, tended to neglect the deeper levels both of the human consciousness and of reality itself. As a consequence, it gradually became associated with an ascetic attitude toward the imagination as well as toward enthusiasm and gripping loyalties. Instead of confronting people with the demand of inner commitment to the ideals of prophetic religion, it more and more provided a cosmic or religious sanction for the interests of a "respectable" group. Conversion was relegated to the underprivileged classes or taken as a sign of ignorance. In the end "the attitude of distance" won the day, and liberalism achieved poise by living at the low temperature of "detached, middle-class common sense," as Whitehead called it.

These tendencies were not the consequence of a loss of faith. They were merely the negative aspects of a new faith. Nor was this a faith merely in human reason or in man alone. It was a faith that found its support in a new idea of the character of the universe and of humanity as a part of that universe.

This faith and its supporting conception of the universe is what is generally referred to when the modern historian of culture speaks of Liberalism (with a capital L). It is against this type of Liberalism and its contemporary residues that much of the current criticism of religious liberalism is directed. Insofar as it is valid, this criticism does not involve a repudiation of the liberal idea of liberating the human spirit from the bondage of economic, social, and ecclesiastical tyrannies. Instead, it is directed against the view of human nature and of the nature of reality that is explicit in eighteenth- and nineteenth-century Liberalism and which is still implicit in much liberal thought of today. Hence, it is directed also against the tendency of this type of Liberalism to become associated too closely with the interests of one class in society. Let us now examine these conceptions.

Dean Fenn once pointed out that the favorite concept of modern rationalistic Liberalism is its belief in the unified structure of the world. This belief is the modern counterpart of the Greek rationalistic view of ultimate reality as a unified pattern behind phenomena, a pattern that is viewed as the source of vitality and with which the rational soul feels itself akin. It has found a great variety of expression, as in Descartes' faith in the existence of a divine power that harmonizes both mind and nature, or in Spinoza's view that thought and extension are different attributes of the same substance and that God is the substance, or in Leibniz' theory of a pre-established harmony that preserves unity despite apparent diversity, or in his view that the individual is a unified whole within the macrocosm. Jung's psychology is one of the more influential current forms of this basic view.

We are all familiar with the result of this tendency. Because of the pre-established harmony, separative individualism was given a divine sanction, and the modern Liberal's overoptimism about human nature, its possibilities for growth, and its progressive and ultimate perfectibility was born. Mandeville does, to be sure, recognize the contrast between the selfish desire of the bourgeois man and his desire for order and education. But he resolves the conflict by appealing to the pre-established harmony: hence, he says, private vices are public virtues. Shaftesbury and Hutcheson discover a moral sense in everybody. This moral sense, they say, is an invariant norm, the violation of which would alone introduce discord. Helvetius even goes so far as to assert that self-love leads ultimately to the love of others. Condillac says that the brain is a *tabula rasa,* but the laws of matter operative in brain vibrations will bring forth truth. How? Through the pre-established harmony. And many of the scientists of the eighteenth and nineteenth centuries, following the lead of Francis Bacon, believed that if only the scientists would individually specialize and then pool their findings the kingdom of man would be ushered in. Finally, Liberal economics proclaimed the faith that if markets were made free and state interference were reduced to a minimum, the rationality of economic forces would do the rest and harmonious well-being for everybody would ensue. This view was supported by the doctrine of the harmony of interests, according to which the individual could be relied on, without external control, to promote the interests of the community for the reason that those interests were identical with his own. The harmony was believed to be none the less real if those concerned were unconscious of it. The pre-established harmony would operate willy-nilly. According to Adam Smith, the popularizer of the doctrine of the harmony of interests, the individual "neither intends to promote the public interest, nor knows how much he is promoting it. . . . He intends only his own gain, and he is in this, as in many other cases, led by an invisible hand to promote an end which was no part of his intention."

Out of roots such as these grew the ideas of growth, progress, and perfectibility characteristic of the secular as well as of the religious Liberalism of the eighteenth and nineteenth centuries. In some quarters, these ideas were related to a new faith in humanity; in others they were related to a thoroughly worked-out philosophy of history; and in still others they were rooted in a belief in "cosmic progress." Within these variations, there were still others. Some liberals, for example, emphasized the natural power of Reason, while others, under the influence of Romanticism, emphasized the natural power of Sympathy. In 1885 belief in "the progress of mankind onward and upward forever" became one of the main articles of the Unitarian faith. And, as an eminent Unitarian historian says, Dr. James Freeman Clark "leaves us in no doubt concerning the importance" he ascribed to the famous Point Five: "He did not intend 'the Progress of Mankind' to be an *omnium gatherum,* or an anti-climax; on the contrary, he regarded the belief in human progress as an essential and a summary of a true Liberal's religion." Dr. Clark's sermon in which the "Five Points of the New Theology" were first set forth concludes with this affirmation: "The one fact which is written on nature and human life, which accords with all we see and know, is the fact of progress; and this must be accepted as *the purpose* of the creation." The historian already quoted comments as follows on Dr. Clark's general position: "There is ground for believing, indeed, that Dr. Clark was influenced by the doctrines of Herbert Spencer and August Comte regarding the inevitability of progress—a process and a consummation implicit in the course of evolution and assured by the trend of natural forces."

Since the turn of the century some religious liberals have greatly altered their attitude toward the older ideas of growth, progress, and perfectibility. Indeed, some of them no longer even mention the ideas, except when singing hymns written a generation or so ago. Moreover, liberalism has sometimes taken on new forms as a consequence of the influence of scientific positivism, of ethical relativism, and even of Marxian dialectical materialism—not to mention the influence of Marxian Utopianism. Nevertheless, it would be wrong to suppose that the outlook on the world entertained by the majority of religious liberals has undergone radical modification in respect to belief in the unified structure of the world or in the continuous progress of the race. As operative presupposition, if not as explicit doctrine, the old beliefs in harmony and perfectibility still serve as a groundwork for faith. This is especially true among the laity of all the denominations in the left wing of Protestantism, not to mention millions of people outside the churches. In short, the general outlook on life of many people continues to have its roots in the rationalistic, non-tragic tradition, especially as it took form in the eighteenth century. It is therefore necessary for us to examine critically the basic presuppositions of this tradition in order to understand the present "changing reputation of human nature."

MODERN DEVELOPMENTS: VOLUNTARIST

From the point of view of the modern voluntarist, the seventeenth- and eighteenth-century view of nature as a beautifully working mechanism or as a manifestation of reason was subjective—it did not sufficiently take into account stubborn external reality. The voluntarist, agreeing with the empiricist, holds that although nature lends itself to rational methods of inquiry, existence as fact comes first and man's rational interpretation only later. The conditions under which existence is maintained or modified are "given." The world might have been any one of an infinite number of possible worlds, but actually it is the kind of world it is. This actual existence is a primary datum; or, as the British empiricist F. R. Tennant said, it is an alogical datum. It is not legislated by reason or by necessary being. Indeed, humanity's reason itself has roots in a being and in a history that might have been different. Nor is the alogical datum of existence identical with an idea that is "clear and distinct." Actuality is richer than thought. There is always a tension between *logos* and being. Hence, natural laws must be viewed as only tentative generalizations formulated on the basis of certain observed data.

But the older Liberalism was not just subjective in its view of nature. It also interpreted nature in terms of form rather than of vitality, in terms of reason rather than of "the divine fecundity of nature." Moreover, structural centripetal forces, rather than individual centrifugal tensions, were stressed. Insofar as a man bases his religious convictions upon this rational conception of nature he tends to develop an overharmonious view of it, and thus also to develop a "simple" belief in the immanence of God. For this reason, I take it, Dean Fenn recommends to those who adopt a monistic view that they "seriously consider what sort of God it is that nature reveals." As he says, "We cannot be so enamoured of the loveliness of nature as to be blind to its terrible aspects." The heavens may declare the glory of God, and nature may exhibit the operation of a principle of mutual aid, yet the struggle for existence in nature amply justifies Tennyson's description of it as "red in tooth and claw." No doubt it was because of this internecine struggle in nature that St. Paul, as well as the ancient Hebrews, looked upon even the world of nature as a fallen world, a world to be restored to love by the New Age or by the atonement of Christ. At all events, nature exhibits both creative and destructive tendencies, both a will to harmony and a will to power. Neither of these tendencies appears without the other. Moreover, the power to exist and the power of love (or mutuality) do not possess perfect correlation; disharmony as well as harmony, devolution as well as evolution are to be found in nature.

Analogous objections may be directed against the older Liberalism's view of the human level of existence—history. Again, the rationalistic conception is criticized because it is subjective and also because it overlooks the element of vitality or creativity as it appears on the level of human freedom. That is, it ignores the alogical character of history, and it rationalistically formalizes history by interpreting it as a progressive movement toward harmony. Thus it fails to take fully into account the elements of conflict and perversion; it fails to recognize that vitality in history does not issue from logic (which is a regulative and not a constitutive principle); and it fails to recognize that this vitality brings forth both harmony and disharmony, both creation and destruction.

The great liberal Ernst Troeltsch, who anticipated much of contemporary voluntarism, has decisively set forth these criticisms in his famous work, *Historismus und seine Probleme.* History, Troeltsch says, is something "given," and the forces that operate there share the alogical character inherent in existence itself. This alogical character of history is manifest both in necessity and in freedom. Neither the necessity nor the freedom can be understood merely in terms of reason and its self-evident premises. In the first place, knowledge of the character of that necessity can be acquired only by observing it inductively and not by deduction from *a priori* principles. In the second place, the very fact of human freedom gives to history a singularity peculiar to all human creations. "In history," as Troeltsch says, "a qualitative unity and originality is assumed to be originally given . . . which may be called fate, destiny, creation, or something else." He speaks of this aspect of history as metalogical and not logical. For whereas organic nature is practically enclosed within the biological circle of birth, growth, procreation, and death, history does not repeat itself—it generates novelty. And because of this also, it cannot be interpreted in strictly rationalistic terms. As Bergson and Whitehead (as well as Troeltsch) have pointed out, strict rationalism precludes the possibility of novelty.

Now, there are certain implications for the nature of humanity that must be seen to follow from the fact that history is the realm of both necessity and freedom. Humanity is fated as well as free. As Wilhelm von Humboldt puts it, "humanity always ties on to what lies at hand" *(Der Mensch Knüpft immer an Vorhandenes an).* Certain fateful conditioning factors always operate in the individual as well as in society. Humanity must act in terms of the historical process and of psycho-physical organism. Our actions must be of a certain kind in order to be relevant and also in order that we may avoid destruction. We cannot act merely in accordance with logical canons of an *a priori* order. Even our ethical ideals emerge through our experience of being and of history. In this sense, it may be said that "being is older than value." Yet, despite these conditioning factors, humanity is fated also to be free; we are compelled to make decisions. For we can transcend our situation and in some measure we can freely change it; we can even change ourselves. As creative beings we can act to preserve or increase, destroy or pervert, mutuality—though it must be remembered also that conditions over which we have little control may affect the results of our action. Thus, humanity lives both in and above history. We are fatefully caught in history, both as individuals and as members of a group, and we are also able to be creative in history.

Through the use of this creative freedom, humanity expresses the highest form of vitality that existence permits. Indeed, since this creativity is a manifestation of a divinely given and a divinely renewing power, we say that humanity is created in the image of God, that is we participate in the divine creativity. This and not reason alone is the basis for the liberal's faith in humanity, and no change in the reputation of human nature could involve a denial of this fact without also repudiating the very essence of the liberal understanding of humanity.

Because of this freedom, human history not only exhibits a singularity that transcends all *a priori* conceptions of the intellect; it also provides a more complex and spiritual form of conflict than to be found on the level of nature. For history is a theater of conflicts in which the tensions between the will to mutuality and the will to power appear in their most subtle and perverse forms. In short, history is tragic. Let it be said immediately that this does not mean merely that people violate the moral code or disobey the law. That they do these things is obvious and universally recognized. The changing reputation of human nature does not depend upon any such "discovery."

It is at this point that we come to the consideration of the major deficiencies in the older Liberal doctrines of man and progress. These deficiencies can be brought into bold relief by showing concretely what is meant by the assertion that history is tragic. We shall use the Liberal epoch as an illustration of this view of history, not because that epoch is different from other epochs as a revelation of the nature of history, but rather because the tragic outcome of Liberalism in the present crisis presents the major problem confronting contemporary society and also because Liberalism provides certain of the principles that are of decisive positive significance for the continued development of a democratic society and of liberal religion. In dealing with these problems we shall have to go over some very familiar ground. But it would seem worthwhile to do this, not only in order to show how the monistic, Liberal doctrines of humanity and progress actually contributed to the tragic outcome of the Liberal epoch but also in order later to indicate how a voluntaristic interpretation of man and history purports to correct the deficiencies of the "harmonistic" conception.

When we say that history is tragic, we mean that the perversions and failures in history are associated precisely with the highest creative powers of humanity and thus with our greatest achievements. One might call this the Oedipus motif in the sphere of history: nemesis is very often encountered almost simultaneously with the seemingly highest achievement. The very means and evidences of progress turn out again and again to be also the instruments of perversion or destruction. The national culture, for example, is the soil from which issue cherished treasures of a people, their language, their poetry, their music, their common social heritage. Yet nationalism is also one of the most destructive forces in the whole of human history. Progress in transportation has assisted tremendously in the raising of the standard of living: yet it has produced also a mobility in our cultural life which has brought in its train a new rootlessness and instability. Improved means of printing have made the treasures of the printed page available even to those who run as they read. But it has also made possible the appearance of the irresponsible manipulators of the idea industries, with the consequence that literacy is now also a powerful instrument for demagogy and the corruption of taste. The growth of a machine civilization has made available to the peasant objects that kings used to pine for; yet the machine doth man unking, and it has necessitated so rapid an urbanization of the population that a sense of community has been destroyed for millions of people, and intimate, colorful family life has become largely a rural phenomenon.

Or, consider another aspect of progress. There is no such thing as a unilinear development in the area of *moral* achievement. We see this in the fact that each generation has to acquire wisdom over again, and within this process "the war of the generations" arises. The son of the Philistine becomes a Bohemian, and his son becomes a communist. The mystical Body of Christ becomes an autocratic ecclesiastical hierarchy, and this in turn gives place to a spiritual anarchy or a militant secularism. There is progress here, regress and a new attempt or perversion there; one year a Revolution for the Rights of Man, but four years later a Reign of Terror and then a Napoleonic era; an American Revolution then, Daughters of the American Revolution now; emancipation of the slaves then, suburbanized senators now; the extension of suffrage then, the "right-to-life" movement now. Certainly, if there is progress, it is no simple configuration of upward trends. At times, it looks more like a thing of shreds and patches. The general tendency of Liberalism has been to neglect this tragic factor of history. It is true that most of the theorists of Liberalism were definitely pessimistic concerning man's worthiness of being entrusted with concentrated political power, but the general and prevailing trend of their thinking was nevertheless lopsidedly optimistic.

It is true also that in the heyday of the idea of progress a few expressed skepticism concerning the progress "assured by the trend of natural forces," but they were given little heed. A poet here and there, an orthodox Calvinist or a cranky social prophet spoke out, but the idea that some people when released from bondage to superstition or to political and ecclesiastical domination, might use their newly acquired freedom and reason to build a new Bastille does not seem to have occurred to many.

Now, what should be noticed here is that this contradiction in human nature derives from the fact that human will is a decisive element in human structure. And it is a will that is ambiguous in character. We can use our freedom by expressing a will to mutuality, but we can also abuse it by exercising a will to power. Freedom and liberation is therefore both the basis of meaning and the occasion for the destruction of meaning. Here we see again the tragic nature of the human condition. The tragedy does not derive merely from the fact that humanity carries an inheritance from the jungle within. It derives also (and primarily) from the fact that we have a freedom that we did not have in the jungle, a freedom to exercise the infinitely higher powers of human nature in terms of creative love, and a freedom to waste them in mere lassitude and triviality, or to pervert them for the sake of a will to power.

It is this coexistence in humanity of the possibility of using our freedom *ad majorem gloriam dei* and the possibility of perverting it to our own destructive ends that constitutes the deepest contradiction of our nature. And this contradiction is no merely human, subjective phenomenon. As Martin Luther suggests, humanity is the *Schauplatz* of opposing cosmic forces, the forces of love and of power. The contradiction penetrates our innermost spiritual life. It goes to the very center of our being; and it reaches out through the individual and permeates all our social relations. It is not, as the Marxists contend, merely a precipitant of the structure of society.

MODERN DEVELOPMENTS: THEOLOGICAL

It was in connection with the sort of interpretation here set forth that the historic Judeo-Christian doctrine of sin was developed. The "orthodox" theory of "original sin," because of its association with the notion of Adam's Fall "in whom we sinned all" as well as with an ascetic conception of sex, has been rightly abandoned by religious liberals. It is doubtful, however, if there is any word available that has more profound metaphysical implications than the word "sin," for the word has the theonomous reference necessary for any truly theological category. But, whether the liberal uses the word "sin" or not, he cannot correct his "too jocund" view of life until he recognizes that there is in human nature a deep-seated and universal tendency for both individuals and groups to ignore the demands of mutuality and thus to waste freedom or abuse it by devotion to the idols of the tribe, the theater, the cave, and the marketplace. The old triumvirate of tyrants in the human soul, the *libido sciendi,* the *libido sentiendi,* and the *libido dominandi,* is just as powerful today as it ever was, and no man can ignore its tyranny with impunity. It cannot be denied that religious liberalism has neglected these aspects of human nature in its zeal to proclaim the spark of divinity in man. We may call these tendencies by any name we wish, but we do not escape their destructive influence by a conspiracy of silence concerning them. Certainly, the practice of shunning the word "sin" because "it makes one feel gloomy and pious," has little more justification than the use of the ostrich method in other areas of life.

Obviously, a correction here does not involve any lending of support to the old view of "total depravity," at least not among liberals. We ought to have enough faith in humanity and God to believe that even a "realistic and credible doctrine of humanity" will not separate us from the love of God. Certainly, we ought to be willing to take the risk that we would incur by giving more serious consideration than we have in recent years to the sinful side of human nature, and even to the biblical myth of the Fall as a description of the contradictions in human nature.

But extreme pessimism is not the only danger of the tragic view of life that is now emerging. Just as rationalism had its characteristic besetting sin, namely, "feeling terribly at ease in Zion" and "cuddling up to the Almighty," so voluntarism has its own peculiar danger. Certain types of voluntarism, it must be remembered, have often been infected with irrationalism. Indeed, they have even exalted irrationalism into a virtue. Duns Scotus illustrates this tendency when he urged acceptance of the Catholic faith without question and without reference to reason. National Socialism took the same attitude of authoritarian subjection to blood and soil. Observers from the Orient have long noted this tendency to irrationalism in the Christian Occident. Charles Chauncy valiantly opposed it in the New Lights, and many oppose it today as it appears in new nationalisms and new spiritual fanaticisms of various stripes. But such irrationalism is not the only alternative to rationalism. We find keen rational analysis in great historic exemplars of voluntarism—for example, most of all in the Buddha, and to a marked degree in St. Paul and St. Augustine, or—to cite three modern examples—in Jonathan Edwards, Ernst Troeltsch, and Rudolph Otto. What is needed, of course, is that combination of *logos* and *dynamis* that can effect a vitalizing tension between the attitude of distance and the attitude of decision. One of the best characterizations of this sort of relation between the reason and the will is suggested in the metaphor repeated by most of the voluntarists of the Middle Ages and especially by the anti-Thomists; they compared reason to a torch lighting the paths ahead; and the will under God's grace, the whole self, they said, both guides the reason and chooses the path to be taken. We see, then, that a recognition of the large role of the will, a recognition of the fundamental significance of the basic orientation and predisposition of humanity, does not necessarily involve a deprecation of reason. Indeed, the voluntaristic theory of human nature is itself the result of an intellectual and rational analysis of the human condition.

The older Liberalism underestimated the destructive possibilities of the contradictions in human nature and was thus unrealistic. It offered salvation through the "restraints of reason." But the "restraints of reason" are inadequate for entering the "war within the cave." Merely intellectual education is not enough. The world has many educated people who know how to reason, and they reason very well; but, curiously enough, many of them fail to examine the pre-established premises from which they reason, premises that turn out on examination to be antisocial, protective camouflages of power. Where our treasure is, there will our heart be also. And where our heart is, there will be our reason and our premises. The "theoretical attitude of distance" needs for its completion the existential "attitude of decision." St. Paul underlines this fact when he speaks of the foolishness of the wise. The element of conflict inherent in us and in human relations with our neighbors can, as St. Paul knew, be dealt with only by a regenerated will, a will committed to the principles of liberty and justice and love, a will prepared by a faith, a decision, a commitment sufficient to cope with the principalities and powers of the world.

Kant, who in this respect stands in the Pauline tradition, suggests that the *root* of evil must be touched. What is needed, he says, is not piecemeal reformation with minor adjustments of character and conduct, but an alteration of the basis of character and of the habitual way in which the mind works. Nor is this reformation a "conversion" of the evangelistic order, a conversion that takes place at one moment and is then complete: Martin Luther came much nearer to describing it when he said that our whole life should be a repentance *(metanoia)* that brings forth fruits meet for repentance. Nor is this conversion merely what we do with our solitariness. It is a conversion that affects our social relations and brings about some conversion in society.

These principles can be stated in nontheological terms also. The way in which the reason operates depends upon the aims and interests around which the personality is organized. Morality has as its basis an underived commitment to certain guiding principles and purposes. Thus the basis of choice is not irrational in that the direction taken by choice is determined by the evidence or principles that can be applied. Accordingly, the decisive quality of a personality is its commitment, for the basic commitment determines the self and its interests, instead of being determined by them.

The way in which a personality will interpret its freedom and use its reason depends, then, upon the character of the self and upon its relation to and attitude toward the rest of reality. A readiness even to enter into discussion for the sake of reaching agreement (or of reaching at least a common understanding) depends upon our total character and not upon our intellectual capacities alone. It depends, in short, upon a proper relation to the creative ground of meaning and existence. Moreover, science as well as religion, politics as well as art, properly flourish only when the primary quality of human character or integrity is the foundation and when that integrity has a positive and critical relation to larger integrities, both social and metaphysical.

We have now seen the ways in which the rationalistic tradition has optimistically taken for granted the idea of unity in the world, in society, and in the structure of the individual psyche. We have also seen how it stresses the role of reason in such a way as to offer a truncated view of the functions operative in both society and the individual and also in such a way as to encourage both separative individualism and "the attitude of distance." The voluntaristic outlook, we have seen, aims to correct and supplement this view by stressing the significance of the alogical factors in existence, in human nature and history, by emphasizing also "the tragic sense of life" arising from human entanglement within its deep-going conflicts, and by stressing the significance of the creative depths of the entire personality (and of the group to which it belongs) for the dynamic achievement of relevant and vigorous action. But often it focuses so narrowly on touching the roots of feeling and will that it provides no guide to relevant or vigorous action or careful learning.

Theology is, in the language of Bonaventura, "an affective science," the science of the love of God, and the function of the church is to bring people into communion with a group wherein the divine power of transformation and the ethical standards rooted in it are operative. When we say operative, we mean that this power is capable of changing people, of eliciting commitment to a way of life that makes a difference in their attitude toward themselves, others, and God; in short, it aids them in the achieving of voluntary community. Only by some such commitment can we, in Channing's words, be always young for liberty. And without such a commitment, we become content with "philosophic" objectivity and "distance" that insulate us from the source of true vitality, from openness to the power of the Spirit. We become attached to the forms that have given us our cherished securities; or, as Augustine puts it, we give our devotion to creatures rather than to the creative power from which issue all forms and all true vitality. We substitute our aspirations and "virtues," our reason and our moralism, for God's power and goodness. Thus our rationalism and our moralism "miss and distort reality and the real possibilities for improvement of the human situation." They give us a "poise" that freezes the knees and keeps us erect and "harmonious" in face of the divine demand for repentance, for change of heart and mind. The early Christians (and also the Dionysians) saw that the creative and redemptive power is not subject to domestication by means of these techniques. It breaks into a human situation destroying, transforming old forms and creating new ones, manifesting the expulsive and creative power of a new affection—the *amor dei.*

It is not reason alone, but reason inspired by "raised affections" that is necessary for salvation. We become what we love. Not that information and technique are dispensable. Even a St. Francis with commitment to the highest would be impotent when confronted with a case of appendicitis if he did not recognize the malady and did not know what to do. One sector of the problems of society is its intellectual problems—problems of statecraft, economics, pedagogy, and the like. Here no amount of good will alone can suffice. But something of the spirit of St. Francis is indispensable if the benefits of science and of society are to be in widest commonalty spread, and, for that matter, if even the intellectual problems are to be dealt with adequately. The desire to diagnose injustice as an intellectual problem as well as the power of action to achieve a new form of justice requires "raised affections," a vitality that can break through old forms of behavior and create new patterns of community. But the raising of the affections is a much harder thing to accomplish than even the education of the mind; it is especially difficult among those who think they have found security.

This element of commitment, of change of heart, of decision, so much emphasized in the Gospels, has been neglected by religious liberalism, and that is the prime source of its enfeeblement. We liberals are largely an uncommitted and therefore a self-frustrating people. Our first task, then, is to restore to liberalism its own dynamic and its own prophetic genius. We need conversion within ourselves. Only by some such revolution can we be seized by a prophetic power that will enable us to proclaim both the judgment and the love of God. Only by some such conversion can we be possessed by a love that will not let us go. And when that has taken place, we shall know that it is not our wills alone that have acted; we shall know that the ever-living Creator and Re-creator has again been brooding over the face of the deep and out of the depths bringing forth new life.

THE BASIC CONCERN for freedom and human liberation not only has roots in thought, it must also have roots in society. It is one of Adams' teaching aphorisms that, no matter how good an idea, "if it does not incarnate, it will dissipate." The means by which ideas of liberty and liberation have incarnated in Western social history is through the "voluntary association," of which the free church is a paradigm. Adams has been the chief American theorist of the voluntary association for nearly four decades. In the following essay, compiled from three major essays on this topic,* Adams traces the religious roots of the voluntary principle, its impact on American religion, some of the pathologies and creative possibilities that attend such organizations, and the reasons why voluntary associations are indispensable to genuine freedom.—M.L.S.

CHAPTER 5 · FREEDOM AND ASSOCIATION

$\mathcal{S}$EVERAL YEARS AGO at the annual meeting in Boston of the American Philosophical Association three philosophers from Russia were guest lecturers on the program. One afternoon during the conference I joined several other Americans for a closeted discussion with these Russian philosophers. Inevitably, questions regarding freedom of speech in Soviet Russia and the United States were introduced into the discussion. The great philosophers were quick to assert that in Russia today the citizen is allowed this freedom. They claimed that Soviet Russia is fundamentally democratic. At this juncture one of the Americans responded that freedom of speech is scarcely sufficient to meet the criteria of democracy, and that the crucial question is whether there is freedom of association, freedom of citizens to organize a group to promote an idea or a cause and particularly to promote a cause that may be in conflict with the policies of the establishment, in short, the freedom to organize dissent. Is there social space for liberating activity? The interpreters, however, were unable successfully to communicate this question to the guests, even though they made a persistent attempt. The

* "The Geography and Organization of Social Responsibility," *Union Seminary Quarterly Review*, vol. 29, nos. 3 and 4 (Spring and Summer 1974), pp. 215–60; "The Voluntary Principle in the Forming of American Religion," in *The Religion of the Republic*, E. Smith, ed. (Philadelphia: Fortress Press, 1970), pp. 217–46; and "The Political Responsibility of the Man of Culture," *Comprendre* 16 (1956), pp. 1–15.

Russians insisted that they could not see the significance of this question about freedom of association.

After the discussion came to an end and when we Americans were out in the corridor, a British Marxist philosopher who had served as one of the interpreters assured us that the guests from Russia simply could not afford to understand the question. Actually the Russians might well have pointed to certain limited forms of freedom of association that obtain today in Russia. On the other hand, they could have pointed to the infringements upon freedom of association in the United States that were characteristic of the Joseph McCarthy period, and they could point to the more recent report that about three-fourths of the 1,136 people interviewed under the auspices of the Columbia Broadcasting System said that "extremist" groups should not be permitted to organize demonstrations against government policy, even if there appeared to be no clear danger of violence.

Why do we in entering upon a discussion of freedom introduce this issue of association? Precisely because it impinges in a crucial way upon the definition of "the voluntary principle" as simply the freedom of the individual—for example, freedom of belief or of speech or of self-determination. At other times voluntaryism is defined as the rule of persuasion instead of coercion. These features, to be sure, belong to freedom, but definitions of this sort fall short of grasping its essential social meaning, for they center attention too much upon the individual as an isolated entity; thus they fail to take explicitly into account the institutional ingredient, namely, the freedom to form, or to belong to, voluntary associations that can bring about innovation or criticism in the society. Freedom in this *institutional* sense distinguishes the democratic society from any other. Yet, as we have observed, it is by no means exempt from attack in our society. The reason is that freedom of association, viewed as a social function in the open society, represents a dynamic institutional force for social change or for resistance to it. As such, the voluntary association brings about differentiation in the community, a separation of powers.

Freedom, then, involves more than freedom of choice. Many people entertain *attitudes* in favor of freedom, but socially effective freedom requires participation in associations that define or redefine freedom and that attempt to articulate or implement that freedom in a specific social milieu. Voluntaryism is an associational institutional concept. It refers to a principal way in which the individual through association with others "gets a piece of the action." In its actual articulation it involves an exercise of power through organization. It is the means whereby the individual participates in the process of making social decisions. This process, particularly when it affects public policy, requires struggle, for in some fashion it generally entails a reshaping, and perhaps even a redistribution, of power. This means that it demands a special commitment and expenditure of directed energy in the institutional context of the society; it also means that there must be the social "space" to do so.

SPACES IN AND FOR ASSOCIATIONS

In a modern pluralistic civilization, society is constituted by a variety of associations and organized structures. The constituent organizations cannot function if they do not have turf. Even in order to hold meetings an organization must have a *place* of meeting and also office space. Anyone who has had experience in these matters knows that the recurrent and acute problem for many a voluntary association is the payment of the rent and the telephone bill. A "warrior" friend of mine used to say that any organization worth its salt will have to face this crisis repeatedly, the crisis of being obliged to pay the rent or "vacate."

If we expand the term *space* metaphorically, we can say that a pluralist society is one that is made up of a variety of relatively independent and interdependent "spaces." An effective organization must be able to elicit the loyalty that maintains the organization. More than that, it must be able, standing on its turf, to get a hearing if effective social criticism, or innovation and new consensus with respect to social policy, are to ensue. A concrete example of a struggle over a relatively simple goal of social policy will quickly identify some of the spaces within which and through which social participation and responsibility are articulated. An example may be drawn from the sphere of what is today called "environmental action," specifically the struggle of over half a century to "save" the Indiana Dunes (at the southern end of Lake Michigan) from industrialization and for a national park. In this enterprise we can identify different spaces in cooperation and conflict; the spaces and boundaries are characteristic of a pluralistic society composed of relatively independent associations: citizens' groups, political parties, industrial corporations, newspapers, labor organizations, national associations for environmental action, and the official engines of public government—the government ostensibly representing the common good and consensus. In short, both public and private governments have been involved. The people in these associations are never exclusively affiliated with any one of them: indeed, they may belong to several of them.

Here, then, we see a kind of separation of powers analogous to the separation of powers obtaining within the constitutional state. Some of the associations possess the limited powers of segmental groups in the society, and they function in face of the power of the state (albeit limited), which possesses a monopoly of legitimate force and the power to make a final decision. In this congeries of associations we see the dispersion of power and group creativity characteristic in principle of a pluralistic, democratic society. The agents of the struggle described in the case of the Dunes Council represent a variety of social spaces in the commonwealth, each organization having its own locus and its limited jurisdiction, and each having its own conception of responsibility. The price of consensus is a heavy one, requiring the skills of organization, of fact-gathering, of analysis and propaganda, of confrontation, of bargaining, of compromise, of vigilant persistence—with thousands of people participating in hundreds of meetings in assigned or acquired spaces, sharing in conflict and cooperation.

If we multiply these efforts and organizations to take into account the 40,000 registered, voluntary associations in this country today, we grasp readily what is meant when our people are called "a nation of joiners" and when the society is spoken of as a "multi-group society." Max Weber has called the United States "the association-land *par excellence.*" The most frequently cited statement on this matter comes from another foreign observer, Alexis de Tocqueville who, in *Democracy in America* (1835), said: "In no country in the world has the principle of association been more successfully used, or applied to a greater multitude of objects, than in America. . . . Wherever at the head of some new undertaking you see the government in France, or a man of rank in England, in the United States you will be sure to find an association." Tocqueville goes on to describe the multitude of associations in the United States at that time, association for libraries, hospitals, fire prevention, and for political and philanthropic purposes. One could summarize Tocqueville's account by saying that where two or three Americans are gathered together it is likely that a committee is being formed. To be sure, not all associations of this sort work for the general welfare. One is reminded of the aphorism of Henry Mencken that where two or three Americans are together and speaking of "service," you may be sure that someone is going to get "gypped."

TYPES OF ASSOCIATIONS

We must turn now to sort out the different types of voluntary organization. As voluntary associations they depend upon volunteers who do not look for monetary rewards: the financial support comes from voluntary "contributions." These features distinguish voluntary associations from other private institutions, such as business and most labor organizations. Moreover, the member may in principle freely join an association, and he is free to withdraw from membership. As voluntary organizations concerned with public policy, they require high and sustained motivation on the part of the members for the performance of tasks.

Broadly considered, voluntary associations have a wide variety of purposes and methods. Some associations are spoken of as instrumental: they aim to influence nonmembers and thus to affect public policy at many levels—from the neighborhood through the municipality to the region and the country at large. Some associations reach beyond the national boundaries, aiming to affect international or transnational policies. Some of these associations promote charitable and philanthropic causes and do not attempt to influence the public government. They may even prefer remedies that are purely voluntary.

Another type of voluntary association is called expressive. This type exists mainly to promote the interests of the members in their association with each other, such as in hobby groups, recreational groups, social clubs, self-help, educational or cultural groups. Max Weber points out that monarchs always love these associations, for they make "good (that is, passive) citizens" by "draining off their energies in warbling." This is not to deny the values of these associations, which in certain instances define, redefine, or protect significant privacy. Professional associations, on the other hand, combine instrumental and expressive purposes, aiming to define the occupational interests of the members (for example, in maintaining professional standards) but intending also to influence public opinion or public agencies. We may say that both instrumental and expressive purposes are components of most ostensibly instrumental associations. In both types of association, latent as well as manifest functions obtain. For example, highly significant friendships may develop in an instrumental association concerned with promoting the general welfare without expectation of any but psychic rewards. Or again, voluntary associations may engender leaders who later transfer their efforts to serve government.

Voluntary associations are generally contrasted with nonvoluntary organizations, that is, with associations to which everyone in the territory belongs without choice. In principle, one has no choice as to whether one will or will not be under the political jurisdiction of the territory and no choice as to whether one will be a member of a family. In certain instances perhaps little choice obtains as to whether a worker will belong to a trade union. Although the state and the family are referred to as nonvoluntary associations, they may permit or encourage certain forms of intramural voluntary action, particularly in the democratic state and in the "consensual family."

In addition to these voluntary and nonvoluntary associations there is another type, in which membership is more or less voluntary but which have the purpose of making a profit—as in business or industry or finance. Large associations of this type, beside providing goods or services, sometimes form pressure groups to affect public government policy. Labor unions in the main belong to this class, although (like business corporations) they may promote enterprises of general cultural benefit quite separate from the benefits they achieve for members of the corporation or the union. Union members constitute such a large segment of the population that what benefits them, for example as consumers, will be to the interest of all consumers. If the unions achieve the upgrading of women and blacks, these groups in general begin to enjoy new status and privilege. Women's liberation and black liberation were encouraged by the unions long before the civil rights movement and the current movement for women's liberation. Taken together, these economic associations in a technological society increasingly represent the most powerful sector of the territory. Although they are private governments, these associations are not usually classed as purely voluntary.

And then there are the churches. Since the time of separation of church and state they have been classified as voluntary associations: they depend in principle upon voluntary membership and voluntary contributions. The collection plate in the Sunday Service is sometimes objected to for aesthetic reasons, but it is an earnest, indeed a symbol, of the voluntary character of the association, and it should be interpreted in this fashion. It is a way of saying to the community, "This is our voluntary, independent enterprise, and under God's mercy we who believe in it will support it. We do not for its support appeal to the coercive power of the state."

By reason of adapting a usage initiated by Montesquieu, voluntary associations are spoken of as intermediary associations standing between the individual and the family and between the individual and the state. If we contrast these intermediary associations with the corporations of the Middle Ages, we observe that these associations have served to break the kinship pattern that dominates in a traditionalist society. We see an anticipation of this break with kinship patterns in the early Christian churches. More than this, however, occurred in the early Christian period. The authoritarian civil religion of Rome was also broken by the primitive church. Whitehead has put the matter pithily. Commenting on the maxim, "Render unto Caesar the things that are Caesar's and unto God the things that are God's," he says that "very quickly God was conceived as a principle of social organization in complete disjunction from Caesar."

THE HISTORICAL ORIGINS OF VOLUNTARYISM

Voluntary associations did not come into history, ancient, medieval, or modern, without dust and heat. We cannot here trace these forces backward into the abyss of time. But we should observe that in the history of Christianity the first expression of voluntaryism appears in the primitive church, a voluntary association. In referring to the voluntaryism of the primitive church, however, we should not overlook the fact that the concept of voluntary association is not wholly adequate, for the Christian viewed the church in its origin and development as the work of divine grace, and thus its ultimate orientation was transcendent. Yet on the human side the church was a voluntary association. The church appealed to the individual for a voluntary decision to join the movement. It rejected civic religion, the rule of Caesar and of territoriality in the sphere of religious commitment and faith; it transcended the ethnic bonds of traditional Judaism; it gave to the individual certain responsibilities in the new organization; it was open to people of all classes and races; it gave new status to the common man, to the slave, and to women; and it soon developed forms of responsibility with respect to charity and philanthropy; it even formed credit unions. But the institutional aspects of the early church included also other features. In order to become viable this primitive church had to develop new skills of communication and of organization. Primitive Christianity, then, did not only promote new attitudes; nor is it to be understood merely in terms of its message, its *kerygma*. It gave institutional incarnation to a new covenant, a new commitment, a new community. Indeed, in order to continue to exist it formed an institution that could bear its message to the world—an institution that in important respects adumbrated or illustrated the meaning of the message in its social consequences. Here we see one of the great innovations in the history of the West. More than that, the ethos and organization of the early church again and again served as a stimulus or model for new forms of voluntaryism.

In modern history the first crucial affirmation of voluntaryism as an institutional phenomenon appeared in the demand of the sects for the separation of church and state, though these sects were of course anticipated by certain heresies. (The word "heresy" means "*I* choose," rather than the choice being made by the church or state.) In England, for example, and then later in America, the intention was to do away with direct state control of the church and also to remove official ecclesiastical influence from the political realm—toward the end of creating a voluntary church. In the voluntary church, religious faith as well as membership was to be a matter of individual choice. The individual was no longer automatically to become a member of the church simply by reason of his being born in the territory. Moreover, he could choose not to be a member of a church. Nor was rejection of the established confession any longer to be considered a political offense or a reason to deprive the unbeliever of the civil franchise. In rejecting state control, the church (and the theological seminary) were no longer to be supported by taxation. The objection to taxation in support of the church was twofold: tax support, it was held, not only gave the state some right of control; it also represented a way of coercing the nonmember or the unbeliever to give financial support to the church. Freedom of choice for the individual brought with it another freedom, namely, the freedom to participate in the shaping of the policies of the church group of his choice. The rationale for this voluntaryism was worked out theologically by the sectarians of the sixteenth and seventeenth centuries and in terms of social and political theory by John Locke in the next century.

From the point of view of a theory of associations, the demand for the separation of church and state and the emergence of the voluntary church represent the end of an old era and the beginning of a new one. The earlier era had been dominated by the ideal of "Christendom," a unified structure of society in a church-state. In the new era the voluntary church, the free church, no longer supported by taxation, was to be self-sustaining; and it was to manage its own affairs. In the earlier era, kinship, caste, and restricted community groups had determined most of the interests and the forms of participation. In the new era these interests became segregated. In this respect the freedom of choice was increased. The divorce of church and state and the advent of freedom of religious association illustrate this type of increase in freedom of choice.

In accord with this new conception of religious freedom and responsibility in the voluntary, self-governing congregation, the voluntary principle amounts to the principle of consent. One must add, however, that although the struggle for voluntaryism on a large scale in the church began over 250 years ago, it was not achieved generally and officially in the United States until the nineteenth century—except in those colonies that from the beginning had had no establishment.

The thrust toward the separation of church and state could succeed only by carrying through a severe struggle for freedom of association. Initially, the authorities who opposed it asserted that the health of society was threatened by the voluntary principle. They held that uniformity of belief was a prerequisite of a viable social order. As a separation of powers, voluntaryism was viewed as a wedge for chaos. In order to defend the unrestricted sovereignty of the commonwealth, Thomas Hobbes published in 1651 *Leviathan*, the most cogent attack of the times upon the voluntary principle. In his view the church should be only an arm of the sovereign; indeed, no association of any sort was to exist apart from state control. Therefore he spoke of voluntary associations, religious or secular, as "worms in the entrails of Leviathan" (the integrated social whole). Analogous attacks upon the voluntary church came also from conservatives in the American colonies where establishment prevailed.

Hobbes recognized that freedom of religious association would bring in its train the demand for other freedoms of association. His fears were fully justified. Indeed, with the emergence of this multiple conception of freedom of association, a new conception of society came to birth—that of the pluralistic, the multigroup society.

THE THEORY OF ASSOCIATIONS

The pluralistic conception of society entails a modern view of the relations among the community and the state and other associations. According to this view, the institutional system is made up of a complex of nonvoluntary and voluntary associations. The state and the family are involuntary in the sense that one cannot choose whether or not he will belong to a state or to a family; nor can he ordinarily choose his particular state or his family. Other associations are voluntary in the sense that one may choose to belong or not to belong. Of central significance for voluntaryism within the context of these associations is the claim that the community at large is the embracing association within which the other associations live. The state is one of these associations. It is the creature and the servant of the community, not its creator. The state therefore is not omnipotent or omnicompetent. Between the individual and the nonvoluntary associations of state and family stand the voluntary associations that provide forms of freedom that transcend both the family and the state and that may also exercise some influence upon both of these institutions. The pluralist society, then, is not a mere aggregate of individuals. It is a group of groups that in turn are made up of individuals.

The individual is not viewed here as wholly comprehended in the community or the state or the family or the other associations. He possesses an integrity and freedom of his own. Luther hints at this idea of privacy when he says that everyone must do his own believing. For him and for other Protestants the individual has direct access to the divine in and through and beyond all institutions and all human mediators. Yet in the developed theory and practice of pluralism the individual's freedom is articulated in the choices he confronts or contrives in the context of these associations. The dependence of the individual upon these intermediary associations for freedom is succinctly stated by the British historian J. N. Figgis: "More and more is it clear that the mere individual's freedom against an omnipotent state may be no better than slavery; more and more is it evident that the real question of freedom in our day is the freedom of smaller unions to live within the whole." In this view of humanity and society, we have the rudiments of an anthropology and also the framework for a philosophy of history. Humanity is essentially associational and human history is the history of associations. The history of any open society is the history of the changing character of the associations and of the changing relations between the individual and the associations, and of the changing relations among the various associations.

In the light of this conception of humanity and history we may see the historical significance of the advent of voluntaryism wherever it appears, and especially its significance for the formation and the expression of the religious mentality. These features became evident in the American colonies.

VOLUNTARYISM IN THE NEW WORLD

In its initial stages the development of voluntaryism in the New World varied considerably in the different colonies, though in the course of time essentially the same dominant tendencies appeared. These tendencies exhibited voluntaryism as the burgeoning characteristic feature of the religious mentality in this part of the world.

In New England and the South the old conception of establishment had been transported from England. The colonists in the middle region, on the other hand, were committed to disestablishment. Here, as well as in New England, variants on covenant theory played a large role. Given the absence of any establishment in the middle colonies, the churches there could affirm and implement their voluntaryism without any significant struggle with proponents of establishment, and therefore without the necessity for compromise with establishment. From the start, then, there were voluntary, "gathered" churches in the middle colonies; so it was unnecessary for them to carry on a struggle for freedom of association. That struggle had been ended by their leaving the Old World. So strong was the spirit of independence that for well over a century these churches held out against any strong centralized organization. This spirit of independence also appeared in the colonies where an establishment prevailed. Indeed, long before disestablishment was officially legitimated, the laity had asserted itself in the management of the congregation. Moreover, by reason of geographical factors, local autonomy was practically unavoidable. Here voluntaryism and localism worked hand in hand.

But in all of the colonies a deterioration of energy—we might call it the law of entropy—served to alter the development of voluntaryism. Whereas there was a great release of energy in religious circles in the early days, this energy became less readily available as the temperature of commitment diminished. Through adoption of the halfway covenant, for example, the New England churches recognized a changing identity in the succession of the generations. With the increasing number of the unchurched in all of the colonies, the problem of maintaining church commitment became all the more acute. This commitment could not be automatically transmitted from generation to generation. What initially had been a voluntary self-sustaining church gradually became a church seeking to elicit commitment and voluntary support. A new voluntaryism had to be promoted. Faced with this change, the churches in all regions found it necessary to employ the techniques of persuasion "in order to win support and gain recruits by voluntary means." The Great Awakening and the subsequent revivals are to be understood in part in these terms. The law of entropy could be countered only by the attempt to activate the voluntary principle in new ways.

This attempt involved the adoption of new means and forms of communication—the itinerant preacher, the psychic excitement of revivals, the dissemination of tracts, the distribution of Bibles, and even a new rhetoric. In this effort the churches, themselves voluntary associations, began at the end of the eighteenth century to form new, specialized voluntary organizations as instrumentalities to carry out the task of persuasion. Some of these new associations were supported by several denominations in cooperation. This sort of cooperation became even more widespread in the nineteenth century. A full roster of voluntary associations founded before the end of the first quarter of that century would be long. We name only a few of them: The Missionary Society of Connecticut (1798), the Massachusetts Missionary Society (1779), the New Hampshire Missionary Society (1801), the Massachusetts Baptist Domestic Missionary Society (1802), the American Board of Commissioners of Foreign Missions (1810), the American Bible Society (1816), the American Sunday School Union (1824), the American Tract Society (1825), the American Home Mission Society (1826), and so on. By the 1830s many of these "benevolent societies" met every May in New York so that the interlocking directorates could be in ready communication with each other.

The formation of some of these missionary associations brought about severe conflict when they were autonomous and sought to raise funds outside the denominations, thus avoiding accountability to these organizations. In this connection Elwyn Smith has shown that the willingness of the church groups to enter into cooperation in the formation of intergroup associations may be taken as a sign of the emergence of a new church form. The sect became a denomination, a type of association that combined "the separative and the unitive spirit of American Christianity" and that became "the fundamental church structure of the country."

It should be noted here that this proliferation of associations not only provided a means for concentration upon special purposes; it also offered new definitions of vocation and even of self-identity. Accordingly, it gave occasion for the release of new energies in new directions of voluntaryism.

A new stage of development is marked by the rise of nonecclesiastical associations concerned with specific problems, social and political. In the eighteenth century these associations began to appear with variety of purpose. In the developing frontier all sorts of land-development companies were formed. Later, mounting opposition to British colonial policies gave rise to a multitude of associations both local and interprovincial. In the 1740s the Masonic Order appeared on the stage—though, to be sure, it encountered continuous opposition. For a time Benjamin Franklin served as provincial grand master of the Masons. He also formed or belonged to several international societies concerned with learning and with politics. Not without knowledge of Cotton Mather's earlier proposals for the formation of associations "to do good," Franklin showed himself to be one of the major initiators of local and national voluntary organizations concerned with educational, philanthropic, and civic purposes. He also instituted the American Philosophical Society, America's oldest learned society.

After the Revolution, freewheeling political activities resulted in local associations concerned with opposing views on public policy. For example, associations disseminating pro-French propaganda produced anti-French associations. So vigorous were these associations and so intense were the disagreements that President Washington in his Farewell Address warned against "all combinations and associations, under whatever plausible character, with the real design to direct, control, counteract, or awe the regular deliberation and action of the constituted authorities." This formulation approximates the kind of statement that had become familiar in the opposition to freedom of religious association. It is perhaps significant that although the First Amendment to the Constitution protects freedom of speech and assembly and rules out the establishment of religion, it makes no explicit mention of freedom of association. Nevertheless, by the end of the first quarter of the nineteenth century the country was alive with associations —religious, quasi-religious, and secular. During the nineteenth century thousands of these associations were formed. As early as the 1830s religious periodicals were saying that the benevolent societies had grown beyond the most sanguine expectations of their founders; the revenues were "such as kings might envy; together they formed a benevolent empire," "a gigantic religious power . . . systematized, compact in its organization, with a polity and a government entirely its own, and independent of all control." Yet most of the societies referred to were less than ten years old.

THREE AMERICAN PROTESTANT THEORIES OF ASSOCIATION

Starting early in the nineteenth century, a Protestant literature on "the principle of association" began to appear. Testimony regarding the ways in which this voluntaryism was giving shape to American religion in its moral and social outreach is found in the writings of three of the principal theorists, Lyman Beecher, Francis Wayland, and William Ellery Channing—a Presbyterian, a Baptist, and a Unitarian—men who differed from each other as much in theology as they agreed with each other on the significance of associations.

Continuing an interest acquired in 1797 as a student under the influence of a religious revival at Yale, Beecher (1785–1863) preached in favor of the formation of societies for the suppression of vice and "the promotion of morality." He viewed these societies as watchdogs and aides in support of the magistrates' efforts to enforce the laws. The vices mentioned for correction were swearing, drinking, gambling, playing cards, and dueling. Moreover, the laws of several of the states prohibited blasphemy, atheism, Sabbath-breaking, and other gross violations of general Christian morality. The societies were to "constitute a sort of disciplined moral militia, prepared to act upon every emergency and repel every encroachment upon the liberties and morals of the state." They were also to promote the careful selection of law enforcers and to lend them "support requisite to the full discharge of their official trust." These efforts were calculated also to "prepare the way for the acceptance of such offices by men who will be faithful." The branch societies were to scrutinize the character of schoolteachers and tavern keepers; they could also encourage boycotts of businesses run by those who violated the moral law as set forth in the Bible. In these efforts the clergy and the laity were to cooperate.

Beecher coupled the rationale for the formation of voluntary societies with a defense of the establishment (in Connecticut). But soon after disestablishment in 1818, however, he came to approve the fact that it "cut the churches loose from dependence on state support. It threw them wholly on their own resources and on God." In 1826 he preached a sermon to praise the effectiveness of voluntary associations. "Now we are blessed," he says, "with societies to aid in the support of the Gospel at home, to extend it to the new settlements, and through the earth." In these societies, he pointed out, the evangelicals of different types could unite in opposing rationalism and "infidelity." In association he saw strength. During his six-year pastorate in Boston, Beecher extended the range of purposes for associations by organizing or sponsoring at least a dozen societies, ranging in character and purpose from the Boston Lyceum to the Franklin Debating Society to the Young Men's Temperance Society to the Young Men's Christian Association. He supported the antislavery societies, and at the same time belonged to the American Colonization Society.

Beecher went beyond the confines of the parish and also beyond the boundaries of the "denominations," toward the end of promoting societies concerned with public policies as well as with private morals. This was, in effect, an extension of the voluntary principle to the sphere of public affairs. One can see in Beecher, however, a strong element of elitism, or what Sidney Mead has called paternalism. A Federalist, he intended his voluntaryism mainly for the middle-class protectors of private and public morals rather than for underlings or "delinquents"—these were supposed to be under scrutiny and guidance. Indeed, he injected a vigorous spirit of intolerance into his crusading efforts. Beecher's attack on the Roman Catholics was probably a contributing cause for the burning of the Ursuline convent in Charlestown, Massachusetts. Moreover, he apparently did not conceive of a voluntary association that could legitimately promote a cause fundamentally incompatible with his conception of Christian private or public morals. In any case, he was the head and fount of associational theory in American church life, though he did not work out a systematic theory regarding the relations between the voluntary and the involuntary associations.

The Reverend Francis Wayland (1796–1865), at one time president of Brown University, wrote extensively on associations both voluntary and involuntary. He was the author of *The Elements of Political Economy* (1837), a popularization of Adam Smith's views and one of the most widely used textbooks of the period. As a Baptist, Wayland was a promoter of radically congregational polity. He opposed every kind of denominational centralization. He rejected also every attempt of the congregation to coerce the believer or the unbeliever, including any attempt of the congregation directly to regulate the behavior of members; the congregation was simply to "withdraw" from the recalcitrant deviant.

Unlike Beecher, Wayland attempted to work out a theory of associations that would relate the Christian to universal mental and moral "sensitivity" and also to natural religion. In the spirit of Bishop Joseph Butler he adopted an antiutilitarian system of conscience and duty. Natural religion and conscience, properly understood, together with Baptist voluntaryism, were viewed as conducive to the establishment of a coercion-free society. Mutual edification and education rather than compulsion, he surmised, would one day direct men's affairs. He viewed teaching as the counterpart of the church's preaching.

Wayland assigned to voluntary associations a crucial role, conceiving of them in contractual terms. The association was an instrumentality of conscience based upon contract. Just as commitment to Jesus Christ was the basis of the Christian voluntary church and just as the autonomy of the individual believer must be protected there, so the voluntary association was a contractual arrangement and the autonomous individual might not properly be coerced into any obligations he had not assumed freely upon entering the association. Since conscience was the basis of social order and also of authentic associations, the voluntary association was to serve to enhance individual conscience and responsibility. "Autonomy" was Wayland's watchword. Therefore voluntary associations of great size were to be viewed with skepticism and caution. They threatened always to pervert individual conscience and to dislocate responsibility.

In the guidelines Wayland set up for associations one can see the rudiments of a philosophy of voluntaryism that gives central place to the principle of consent. The purpose of an association and the manner of pursuing it should be clear, and they should be agreed to by all members. Moreover, they "should be perfectly and entirely innocent; that is, they must be such as are incapable of violating the rights of any human being." Accordingly, he opposed abolition societies that demanded forced emancipation. He held that in face of the slaveholders the conscience-bound citizen should set an example "of the most delicate regard to their rights." Anyone "whose first act is an act of injustice" violates the dominion of right.

In practice, however, the dominion of right would at times be egregiously violated not only by voluntary associations but also by "the civil society." In this situation neither passive obedience to the state nor resistance to it by force was ethically justifiable. Here the conscientious citizen might find the only recourse to be "suffering in the cause of right." Wayland's view of "righteous suffering" approximates what we today call civil disobedience; it presents, he said, "the best prospect of ultimate correction of abuse by appealing to the reason and conscience of men . . . , a more fit tribunal to which to refer moral questions than the tribunal of force."

It is worth noting that whereas Beecher's theory of associations was engendered initially in the milieu and spirit of an established church and a firm authoritarianism, Wayland's conception derived primarily from his Baptist ecclesiology and from a sectarian heritage that had suffered from persecution at the hands of the establishment. Another contrast with Beecher is to be observed in Wayland's search for a universal religious-ethical basis, a sort of doctrine of natural law in terms of which the Christian might cooperate with the unchurched. Most noticeable, however, is Wayland's intention to develop with complete consistency the ramifications of the voluntary principle, the principles of persuasion and consent, not only giving special emphasis to the methods appropriate in associations but also stressing the rights and sensitivities of others in face of voluntary associations bent on persuasion. Nothing of Beecher's paternalism is to be found here. Fearful of the dangers of the crusading mentality, Wayland would have sympathized with the aphorism that was current in England during the period of the Restoration: "Nothing is more dangerous than a Presbyterian just off his knees." On the other hand, with his ironic temper he would scarcely have understood Nietzsche's claim that some things must be loved for more than they are worth if they are to make an impact on history. Morever, with his stress on autonomy, he seems to have been little aware that autonomy is often the cloak for a hidden heteronomy. Such are the dilemmas of voluntaryism in an imperfect world.

In the midst of the Great Awakening, Jonathan Edwards wrote his *Treatise on the Religious Affections.* In an age when voluntary associations have become "a mighty engine," William Ellery Channing (1780–1842) presents in his "Remarks on Associations" (1830) a treatise on associations. Whereas Edwards deals only with individual behavior, Channing, with a moral, social concern, deals also with institutional behavior. In his treatise he aims to suggest "a principle by which the claims of different associations may be estimated." In doing so, however, he gives primary status to the individual. In his explication of a criterion for the voluntary principle one finds a formulation of the essential intention of voluntaryism, which Wayland could readily have approved. He states his major premise succinctly:

> The value of associations is to be measured by the energy, the freedom, the activity, the moral power, which they encourage and diffuse. In truth, the great object of all benevolence is to give power, activity, and freedom to others. We cannot, in the strict sense of the word, *make* any being happy. We can give others the *means* of happiness, together with motives to the faithful use of them; but on this faithfulness, on the free and full exercise of their own powers, their happiness depends. There is thus a fixed, impassible limit to human benevolence. It can only make men happy through themselves, through their own freedom, and energy. We go further. We believe that God has set the same limit to his own benevolence.

Channing's essay is the first systematic study in American literature on voluntary associations. For this reason it is surprising that more attention has not been given to this treatise. Max Weber, the German sociologist, was deeply impressed by Channing's conception of spiritual freedom. By reason of his stress on freedom and autonomy, Channing stands much nearer to Wayland than to Beecher. Likewise, he recognizes the threats to autonomy provided by associations. Channing's essay reads very much like a document written today. He is aware of the relation between voluntary association and the modern technology of transportation, communications, and coalition. He even speaks of "the principle of association" as "a mighty engine." "An impulse may be given in a month to the whole country, whole states may be deluged with tracts and other publications, and a voice like that of many waters, be called forth from immense and widely separated multitudes."

His essay is replete with psychological as well as sociological, ethical, theological, and political observations and analyses. Recognizing that man is an associational being, Channing takes a view quite different from that held, for example, by sociologist Ferdinand Tönnies, who a generation later in Germany wrote that voluntary associations represent a force of depersonalization in modern society issuing from rationalism and contractualism. "Men not only accumulate power by union, but gain warmth and earnestness. The heart is kindled," says Channing. Moreover, he sees the principle of association as a great releaser of energy. "By the feeling and interest which it arouses [union] becomes a creative principle, calls forth new forces, and gives the mind a consciousness of powers, which would otherwise have been unknown."

Channing does not overestimate the significance and value of voluntary associations. He gives priority to what we have called the nonvoluntary associations and to what he calls "those associations formed by our Creator, which spring from our very constitution, and are inseparable from our being." These associations are "the connections of family, of neighborhood, of country, and the great bond of humanity, uniting us with our whole kind." He clearly distinguishes these associations from "those of which we are now treating, which men invent for particular times and exigencies"—"missionary societies, peace societies, or charitable societies, which men have contrived." He then proceeds to "illustrate the inferiority of human associations," by contrasting the pervasive and perduring benefits of the family "among the masses of men" with the limited number of people served by "asylums for children." Since he places the churches among the associations created by God he does not consider them under the rubric of the voluntary association (though he does of course favor the ecclesiology of the voluntary church—considered as established by God through Christ); and he contrasts the church with missionary societies, whose work he does not aim to discourage. The latter are not to be preferred to the church with its concern for "the common daily duties of Christians in their families, neighborhoods, and business." He notes that "the surest way of spreading Christianity is to improve Christian communities; and accordingly, he who frees this religion from corruption, and makes it a powerful instrument of virtue where it is already professed, is the most effectual contributor to the great work of its diffusion through the world."

STRENGTHS AND WEAKNESSES OF VOLUNTARYISM

If we now take a bird's eye view of the development we have traced, we must speak of it as an organizational revolution. It may be viewed as an aspect of modernity, of rationality and technology (that is, the technique of forming social organizations). As such it represents the creation of space in modern American society for associations, loyalties, and activities the like of which have not appeared anywhere to the same extent in previous history. These voluntary associations are significant not only in themselves but also by virtue of their influence on each other and upon the nonvoluntary associations—for good or ill. In the context of the present essay, however, their principal significance is their import for the shaping of American religion. As Channing suggests, the voluntary principle is "a creative principle." It functions as a creative principle by making way for free interaction and innovation in the spirit of community. Thus the church may remain open to influence from its members, from outside the church, and from the Holy Spirit; at the same time it assumes the responsibility of exercising influence in the community. The organizational prerequisite for this kind of interaction is the separation of powers, a separation that combines independence and interdependence and which looks toward the achievement of unity in variety. When however, the voluntary principle is the sole principle, the question remains as to the source and character of the unity. To this question we shall return.

Not all of the churches adopted the voluntary principle without reservation. The Presbyterians and the Reformed, the Anglicans and the Lutherans in the nineteenth century rejected or severely criticized the principle insofar as it left the churches open to development in any direction that historical accident or the will of the members determined. Their resistance expressed itself in a variety of formulations. The voluntary principle, it was said, militated against any structured continuity within the rich organism of historical Christianity. For another thing, the heavy reliance, in the nineteenth century, of many of the voluntary churches on revivalism was viewed as a mixed blessing. Even where revivalism is now largely a thing of the past it has left a residue of subjectivity, erratic spontaneity, a mere sense of immediacy—with the consequence that many of these churches have shown little concern for theology or for history, for liturgical substance and form, for denominational structures, or for prophetic "social action."

These old-line churches, however, were not alone in adversely criticizing this kind of voluntaryism. Channing, as we have already observed, criticized the bad taste, the irrationalities, the highly organized forms of ignorance, which were perpetrated by the voluntary societies set up by some of the churches. Thus one can say that the bastions of bad taste, invincible ignorance, and wild varieties of so-called religious experience are to be found in many of these voluntary churches. We shall return to this point later, in another connection.

Nevertheless, the churches that have opposed these vagaries have not been able to remain immune to the voluntary principle, as is evident especially in the similarity of structures that obtains in the local parishes of these denominations and in those of the churches of pronounced voluntaryism. On the other hand, some of the "free churches," skeptical of the spontaneities and disruptions of revivalism, have been sensitive to the need for continuity and structure. Witness Horace Bushnell's critique a century ago of "the thunderclaps of grace" (the phrase comes from Jonathan Edwards) and his preference for "Christian nurture." Witness also his highly original analysis of language.

It would be exceedingly difficult to trace the influences back and forth in order to explain these varieties of, and changes in, religious consciousness and perception. Yet one can affirm that among the various types of churches, and in general in the pluralistic society, mutuality of influence obtains. This mutuality of influence appears not only between churches of different types but also between the churches and other associations.

The variety of voluntary associations, as we have already hinted, is almost beyond the power of unaided imagination to conceive. Their purposes have included prison reform, the prevention of cruelty to children and to animals, the establishment of schools and colleges, the conservation of natural resources, the protection of civil liberties, the attack on poverty, the improvement of race relations, the emancipation of women, church lobbies in Washington and at state capitals, the promotion of world peace, and so on. We have already mentioned the missionary societies, antislavery societies, and tract societies. Through participation in voluntary societies, members of many churches have been able to extend their perception of the social realities. Indeed, one can say that associations such as these provide the means whereby the churches achieve a knowledge of "the world." They are media through which the churches promote a vital relation between religion and culture. Like the voluntary churches, they serve also as the means for the achievement of skills of discussion and organization, and even the skills of listening. Consider, for example, the variety of knowledge and skills learned by church members, and especially by the women, in the missionary societies of the nineteenth century. In terms of skills these women might well be thought of as the spiritual ancestors of the League of Women Voters. The skills of which we speak were required initially by the men and women who were struggling for the right of freedom of association, the right to form a voluntary church. In the eighteenth century the Friends were conspicuous for their ingenuity in registering dissent and in bringing about changes in legislation. These expressions of the voluntary principle have provided the occasions for the churches not only to influence other associations (including the state) but also to gain new perceptions from them, and even to gain broader conceptions of Christian responsibility.

This whole development, including the emergence of the voluntary church, probably would not have been possible without the tremendous expansion of economic resources in the modern period. Indeed, one can argue that the voluntary churches in their emergence and growth accompanied the emergence into modern history of the middle class. If we view the long historical perspective that embraces the development of the voluntary principle in Anglo-American history, however, we must see more than the emergence of the middle class. The voluntary principle was in some degree taken over into the political realm to confirm the demand for the extension of the franchise (for "government by consent") and even to promote the idea of the loyal opposition and an extension of the protection, instead of the persecution, of minority views. From there the voluntary principle moved into the realm of private education; next, to the initiation of the labor movement; then, to the franchise for women, and in our day to the civil rights movement and the beginnings of a movement to promote black empowerment. The voluntary principle has operated also in the transformation of the authoritarian family into the consensual family. All of these movements were, to be sure, opposed as well as supported by the voluntary churches.

We have spoken of the voluntary principle as the dimension in which the churches have been able with some concreteness to move in the direction of a theology of culture and to attempt to fulfill the mission of the church in a new age. This process could not take place without cooperation between church members and nonmembers. In this process the voluntary churches have learned to some degree that social order and social justice require them to cooperate even with those who do not agree with them regarding theological presuppositions or specifically Christian norms. At the same time this cooperation again and again has served to prevent the churches from making absolute claims; indeed, it has promoted the recognition that God can work through secular people and even through "infidels." Equally significant is the fact that in the twentieth century, cooperation (in voluntary associations) between Protestants and Roman Catholics became possible. Indeed, one of the documents of Vatican Council II proclaims it to be the responsibility of the Catholic to work with others in voluntary associations concerned with the common good. The cooperation in voluntary associations among members of different denominations and between church members and nonmembers is of such long standing that we may claim that it represents the oldest ecumenical movement. Possibly the existence of this sort of ecumenism explains the relative absence of significantly organized anticlerical movements in regions where the voluntary church has prevailed.

THE PATHOLOGIES OF VOLUNTARY ASSOCIATIONS

However, there are negative as well as positive elements in voluntary associations. One can see also perversions of the human community, the alienation of person from person, and of humanity from the God who is the ground of human community. Here we have to do with the pathology of voluntary associations. This pathology is roughly twofold: the diseases of voluntary associations in their relations to the rest of the community, and the diseases within associations themselves.

One of the major misconceptions of the role of voluntary associations is the notion that they can in all circumstances provide viable forms of integration in the community. This view, in its extreme form, has been set forth by anarchism. A more restricted view has been held by the Liberalism which, in adherence to the theory of automatic harmony, assigns a mainly negative role to the state—the maintenance of freedom of association. Actually, this view has not been held without qualifications by the laissez faire economists. The major crises of the past half-century, whether in international relations or in face of impending economic collapse, have demonstrated that voluntary associations are not omnicompetent alongside a "negative state." In face of serious economic maladjustment, or of major structural social needs, the appeal for voluntary associational solution of the problem is likely to be motivated by a class ideology. For example, Richard Nixon's theory of "the voluntary society" leaves it to people of tender conscience to cope with pervasive maladjustments by means of voluntary associations, thus relieving government, or the community as a whole, of responsibility. "Back to the grass roots" here in actuality means, back to the more intractable power groups of the local or regional community. The first evil then, against which we need warning, is the evil of making too great claims for the competency of voluntary associations.

Other evils characteristic of voluntary associations in their relation to the community at large are not far to seek. Voluntary associations provide one of the most effective means for promoting narrow and particularist interests: the protection of special privilege for ethnic groups, for class groups, and for economic power blocs. Accordingly, they often solicit their membership from these groups. Whereas political parties try to mobilize majorities, pressure groups, as Schattschneider puts it, try to organize minorities. (Even voluntary associations that are not special-interest pressure groups are by no means universal in class provenance; today they still draw mainly upon the middle classes for membership). In a Nazi-like manner, pressure groups frequently coordinate interlocking memberships for purposes of collusion. Thus they impinge upon the effectiveness of other, weaker associations, exercise nonmarket controls over the "free" market, and "infiltrate" leaders into key positions in other organizations. They impede legislation intended for the general welfare or they promote special-interest legislation. To some extent, to be sure, the conflicts between associations are countervailing. In any event, the techniques of manipulation, deception, and domination appear to be almost part and parcel of associational "freedom." (Associations are prone to all of the evils to which flesh is heir.) The principal corrective to these special-interest configurations is exposure at the hands of public opinion, that is, at the hands of other associations. Unfortunately, the corrective is seldom promptly or substantially effective, and in many instances it is not effective at all.

Diseases in the internal structure of voluntary associations are equally frustrating and destructive. The larger an organization becomes the more it becomes subject to the disfunctions of bureaucratization, although it is surprising how quickly a "pecking order" can develop in even a small association. Robert Michels has succinctly characterized this disease by his term, "the iron law of oligarchy." A voluntary association, like any other, can readily come under the control of a power elite. This form of domination is aided by the default, the apathy, of the rank-and-file membership. Often the bureaucracy carries out policies that are contrary to those favored by the membership; the correction of the evil would require more energy on the part of the dissident membership than is ordinarily available. The situation is aggravated in those vocational and professional associations that are not really voluntary. In these associations membership is mandatory, and withdrawal from membership would be suicidal.

There are other ways in which membership in an association can severely restrict freedom. Adam Smith long ago pointed out that the individual gains a certain sense of dignity by being brought within a religious sect—a dignity that comes from the discovery that others care enough about him to wish to convert him; but that at the same time the individual member, in joining the sect, may find himself in a vise that crushes his individuality and freedom. Following essentially the same pattern, some secular voluntary associations repress minority opinion within the organization. If the individual in this kind of organization hopes to be selected for leadership, he will tend to "conform" and try to gain the "confidence" of the leaders already in power. Therefore, far from being a medium for the realization of freedom, a voluntary association may be a means for its constriction. An association that lacks a permissive atmosphere may contribute to the annihilation of privacy and inner integrity. Partly with this in mind, a wit has observed that "what a man belongs to constitutes most of his life career and all of his obituary."

But whatever the diseases to which these associations are subject, "we know," as Louis Wirth has reminded us, "that without belonging to these organizations we are paralyzed, we are impotent, we are negligible." Moreover, without these organizations the community too is paralyzed, as the sociologist, Emile Durkheim pointed out in his protest against the lack of voluntary associations in France.

PRESENT THREATS TO FREEDOM

One aspect of the competition of the associations for the attention of the individual deserves at least passing reference. A major study of "mass political apathy" in the United States has found that since 1892 the proportion of eligible voters participating in presidential elections has decreased by 40 percent. Bernard Barber argues that this decline of participation in politics is due largely to the pressures coming from the family and from occupational demands. Recognizing that the family shares the improved or unimproved status of the head of the family, the latter eschews associations that might interfere with the improvement of his economic status. One is reminded here of the view of Plato that the family is the enemy of justice; that is, it may be the occasion for the entire distraction of attention from the concerns and responsibilities of citizenship. Thus the middle-class family may in this fashion become a major sacrament for the bitch goddess, Success.

This problem of competing responsibilities is compounded if we now consider only two aspects of one of the most important associations (which we have scarcely mentioned), the association within which one earns his livelihood. First to be noted is the characteristic feature of urban society—the separation of the place of work from the place of residence and the separation of these from the places of recreation and from the places of instrumental associations. Fragmentation of existence is the inevitable consequence of this spatialization of life. This observation gives weight to the definition of secularism as fragmentation and incoherence of meaning. This leads to the consideration of the major, largely hidden source of "integration" (or is it disintegration?). In a technological society, in rural as well as in urban setting, the major corporations largely determine the patterns of authority, the definitions of success, the form and content of the mass media of communications, and even the perjuring policies of public government. We can look here only briefly at this last-mentioned phenomenon.

Ernst Fraenkel, a political scientist at the Free University in Berlin, in his widely used book *Die Amerikanische Regierung* has defined the American Congress as in the main a clearinghouse of the great pressure groups. Former Senator Paul Douglas in a study of these pressure groups has shown the geography of these associations: the cotton interests are rooted in the South, the lumber interests in the Northwest, the copper interests in the Rockies, the dairy and grain interests in the Middle West, the steel interests in Pittsburgh and Gary, and so on. The Ervin Committee has recently been attempting to expose the ways in which major financial interests support party politics. Class legislation promoted by these special-interest groups has become readily visible to the naked eye under the present Nixon-Ford administration by reason of the energy crisis and the revelations about hidden subsidies.

The coordinated power of the major corporations enables them to maintain affluent pressure groups at all levels of government, and these pressure groups exercise their power by means of coalition (or better called collusion). The lobbyist for the cotton interests at a particular juncture says to the lobbyist for the copper interests, "I know you are not at all interested in promoting or stopping this particular piece of legislation, but if you will assist me now, I shall repay you when you need similar support." Because of this feature of contemporary society our economy is called "interest-group democracy." The private economic governments, including the multinational corporations and even some of the professional societies, have become stronger than the public governments. One is reminded of James Madison's warning that a principal threat to democratic public government would be the inordinate power of a single faction. This warning represents one of the oldest arguments of democratic socialism against capitalism. In any event, relations between voluntary and nonvoluntary associations encounter acute crisis in the United States. In the halls of government the major conflict is between the voluntary associations concerned for the general welfare and the lobbies of the major economic power groups that aim to promote or protect their "interests." Considering the massive concentration of economic-political-cultural power, we may say that our condition today is not unlike that which obtained at the beginning of the modern period. Max Weber called it a cage.

ASSOCIATIONS TO COMBAT GOVERNMENTAL DISEASE

Considering the wide range and the effectiveness of the activities and lawsuits being promoted by Ralph Nader and his associates, we may expect that in the coming years policy-oriented voluntary associations will give increasing attention to the behavior of the major industrial corporations. Whereas in the past, organized dissent—the only kind that is ordinarily effective—has been directed against the state, in the future dissenting associations will be more and more directed at both the state and the economy. In addition to exposing the dubious relationships between private and public governments, these associations will increasingly scrutinize the internal structures of the corporations and their policies of deception in advertising and marketing. With regard to the internal structures, it will be recalled, Ralph Nader and his associates have been demanding that protection be afforded employees (and official auditors) who with integrity expose deception and other antisocial policies promoted by the employing corporation. This issue, as we have seen, was long ago faced in the Radical Reformation, when the protection of minority opinion was promoted by some church groups. This sort of protection for the individual citizen has been sanctioned by the Bill of Rights in the U.S. Constitution; an analogous protection is now sought for the individual in private governments. In this problem area we encounter what we might call the diseases that can appear in associations, public and private. Over a century ago, Channing set forth a warning about group pathology, pointing out that the very associations that promise new freedoms can also become the occasion for new tyrannies.

Taken together, these demands presuppose that effective accountability on the part of the economic sector requires more than the kinds of correction promised by free-market theory and practice. In "the Protestant Era," this sort of accountability has been late in coming. This belatedness is due partly to the inordinate independence accorded the economic sector, which R. H. Tawney documented long ago as beginning with the Puritan Reformation. But more than this must be said. The achievement of the integrity in public government requires the expansion of accountability to the private sector. The absence of this accountability is a major cause of the current, widespread skepticism that obtains regarding the effectiveness of citizen participation in politics. The lack of accountability, it is seen, has made possible the erosion of the moral limits to the legitimate power of private governments. Ultimately, moreover, the vindication of the claims made for the pluralist society as the free and open society requires a flank attack upon the private governments that exercise inordinate and hidden power in politics and in the society at large. The bloating of this power is a major ingredient in the now heralded "decline of pluralism." Today some of the impetus among youth toward privatization and "copping out" has been rooted in awareness of this decline.

As we look at the developing Third World, we see analogous issues coming to the fore in face of centralized political and economic power and in face of the multinational organizations that elicit obsequious obedience from local political authorities. Pluralistic democracy in the Third World is encountering in a shortened time span all the paradoxes and impediments exhibited in the West over a much longer period of time. The free spaces, rare enough in a traditional society, are not to be achieved in the Third World without dust and heat, if at all.

In order to check the diseases of government (public and private), new forms of coalition have been emerging. We have noted the composite constituency of many voluntary associations of the past century that amounted to a sort of ecumenism of church persons and nonchurch persons. In the present century collaboration has appeared in a different form, a coalition between church and nonchurch agencies. The earlier form brought *individuals* of differing orientations together. The new form effects collaboration between *associations,* religious and secular. A generation ago furtive efforts were made to bring into cooperation the churches and burgeoning labor organizations, a collaboration that began much earlier in England. More recently, local, regional, and denominational church committees, as agencies of the churches though not necessarily as official representatives, have been operating in this way. In Illinois, for example, a coalition calling for the impeachment of the president of the United States was active throughout the state. Another coalition, the Alliance to End Repression, has been centering attention on police and jail practices, even training "visitors" to serve on panels investigating deaths in jails and prisons. The Clergy and Laity Concerned have elicited cooperation in the effort to challenge industrial production of weapons for chemical warfare. The American Friends Service Committee and the Unitarian Universalist Service Committee, collaborating with the League of Women Voters and the American

Civil Liberties Union, have been promoting "court watching" and the training of "court watchers" to promote greater fairness in the criminal justice process. Other similar coalitions could be mentioned, especially those promoted by state and municipal federations of churches. Coalitions of this sort will presumably develop to attack other areas of performance in public and private governments.

The agenda is a heavy one, for example, in the areas of education, health, care for the aged, the eradication of poverty, civil rights, the conservation of the nation's natural resources and beauties, and race relations.

Here, then, we come to the pragmatic test. How well has this nation used its associations, its governments, private and public? What have been the consequences? The dark answer to these questions is the major reason for the heralded decline of pluralism. Fifty years ago Ernst Troeltsch had already predicted that the Western democracies would encounter disenchantment before the end of the century, that an increasing number of people would lose their enthusiasm for the promise of one man/one vote. As I understand Troeltsch's view, political democracy can remain viable only if it assumes responsibility for economic realities.

These considerations also pose the question of whether voluntary association has shown itself capable of eliciting sufficient social responsibility to correct the political and economic institutions. One may rightly say that the middle class initially was born in modern history largely by means of the voluntary association, that many workingmen's organizations found their niche in the society through the innovations of the voluntary association, and that ethnic minorities have made their climb in a similar fashion. But millions are still left out, and the cruelty and disease and deprivation are appalling, as are the bombings, kidnappings and shootings. The spaces available to the deprived are simply too cramped.

It may be that it is unrealistic to expect that a topheavy civilization such as ours can solve its problems through deliberate thought and action. It may be that a wider measure of social and economic justice can come only after the advent of a national or international crisis of mammoth proportions.

What, then, is the remedy? Certainly not the scuttling of the principle. That way lies tyranny. If the voluntary principle is to serve nourishing and prophetic purposes, the demand is for an understanding of the authentic ends of Christian piety and for the costly sacrifices that at least exhibit seriousness of commitment.

A special demand confronting the churches, then, is the demand for the reformation of reformation—the reformation of the voluntary principle. In the history of the church this function has been performed by a special kind of association, the *ecclesiola in ecclesia,* the small church in the large, which redefines Christian vocation in the changing historical situation. In the Middle Ages, the so-called Dark Ages, monasticism functioned as an *ecclesiola.* In the modern period the *ecclesiola* has been the small group of firm dedication that sometimes promotes the disciplines of the inner life, sometimes bends its energies to sensitize the church afflicted with ecclesiastical somnolence, sometimes cooperates with members of the latent church in the world to bring about reform in government or school or industry, or even to call for radical structural transformation.

To be sure, catastrophe can accelerate the process of reappraisal, but even then the commonwealth or the church cannot rise above the level of actual or latent spiritual integrity and power. The voluntary principle came to birth at the end of an era. In some quarters today it is held that we are approaching the end of an era. If we are, the increase in membership of the churches, especially the conservative ones, that is characteristic of our period gives little reason for encouragement, for it would appear in large part to bespeak the attractiveness of the "religion" of privacy.

In any event, the voluntary principle, insofar as it pursues worthy ends, requires sharp critical judgment of the actualities and vigorous, though serene, commitments that can make freedom of association, religious or secular, the salt that has not lost its savor.

Part II

SOURCES AND TESTS OF HUMAN ACTION

THE ESSAYS IN PART II stress the interaction of theological motifs and social engagement. These, for Adams, are the dual touchstones of all profound ethics. It is in the interplay, the dialectic, and the mutual correction of religious theme and concrete human relationship that Adams finds the sources and tests of all we know and do. In the three academic centers at which Adams taught, it is significant that he worked closely with the disciplines of sociology and/or social relations. Indeed, at Meadville/Lombard and the University of Chicago, at Harvard Divinity and the Graduate School of Arts and Sciences, and in the Andover Newton–Boston College Joint Graduate Program, he helped found departments of "Religion and Society" for advanced study in addition to personally influencing numerous students. Moreover, he was often the "theologian" to call upon when social scientists wanted a religious perspective, or the "sociologist" to call upon when theologians wanted to address or hear from a social perspective. In the following essay, writing as a theologian in the company of social scientists who were attempting to deal with the meaning of the word "love," he exemplifies the way in which theological matters are used to open up more profound dimensions of social experience and to relate that depth to practical social questions.*—M.L.S.

CHAPTER 6 · THE LOVE OF GOD

IN THE largely secularized culture and language of our time, the subject of this chapter is by no means one that elicits universal interest. To many serious-minded people phrases such as "the love of God," "God's love for us," or "the human response to God's love" are almost meaningless. Yet the subject is actually one of universal concern. This is obscured by the fact that we often discuss it without using theological language and perhaps even without being fully aware of what we are doing.

Even among people who think of themselves as having made a religious commitment, one may not discuss our subject without considerable difficulty. The variety of religious traditions and affiliations in our society create almost as many semantic problems as are confronted in face of the "unbelievers." In addition, the sharp differences of religious outlook that prevail among Jews and Christians present a host of difficulties with respect to both language and content.

* First published in *The Meaning of Love*, Ashley Montagu, ed. (New York: Julian Press, 1953).

Taking this situation into account, the ensuing discussion will assume no explicitly religious commitment on the part of the reader. Therefore, we must as it were begin at the beginning; and we shall go scarcely beyond that beginning.

At the outset an attempt will be made to show that, contrary to the rather generally accepted view, the basic concerns of religion are inescapable; indeed that some sort of religious faith is found among all people. Thus the most significant differences between people will be interpreted not as differences between religion and irreligion but as differences between conceptions of faith and also of the love of God; ultimately, the basic issue concerns the question as to what the most reliable object of human devotion is. Finally, an attempt will be made to show that the decisive differences between conceptions of the love of God become most clear when we determine the social-institutional implications of these conceptions.

The very title of the present chapter will arouse hostility in some minds. Love of family, of friends, of country—these are loves that may be, and often are, frustrated or perverse. No one, however, doubts the reality of these objects of devotion. It is not so with "the love of God." For some readers the word "God" is not the sign of a reality but of a powerful illusion; it epitomizes all that belongs to the pathology of love and dreams. From this viewpoint, the only appropriate intent of the present discussion should be to expose the illusion.

Such an attitude may not properly be brushed aside. The God that is rejected by the "unbeliever" may be an illusion and wholly worthy of rejection. After all, a multitude of conceptions of God, and of the love of God, has appeared in the history of religion; not all of them can possibly be true. Many of these illusions are doggedly tenacious. The absolute sanction of authoritarian faith (both religious and secular) and of the security it affords, protects it from radical criticism; and nonauthoritarian faiths have their own ways of ignoring criticism, too.

Those who are hostile to religion will not find themselves alone in their critical attitude. In much that they reject they bear the heritage of a venerable company of religious thinkers. From even before the times of Amos and Plato there have been prophets, philosophers, and theologians who have devoted a supreme effort to unmasking the illusions of uncritical religion.

But there is also such a thing as uncritical irreligion. The rejection of all belief in God as illusory may be the consequence of a failure to consider conceptions of God more plausible than those rejected. In some instances, moreover, the rejection of belief in God issues from the false notion that theology and religious faith are possible only because people indulge in speculation on questions for which no dependable answers are available. This view can often find cogent justification. But this rejection of so-called speculation is itself a spurious speculation. It may be tied up with an illusion, the illusion that religious faith as such may be dispensed with.

Actually, the nonreligious are not themselves without faith, even though they reject what they call speculation. There are many kinds of faith that may be dispensed with. But there remains one kind which no one can live without. We do not need to use the word "faith" to refer to it. The word "confidence" will serve just as well. No one and no culture can for long maintain a dynamic and creative attitude toward life without the confidence that human life has some important meaning either actual or potential, and that this meaning may in some tolerable fashion be maintained or achieved, in other words, that resources are available for the fulfillment of this meaning. This concern with the meaning of life and with the resources available is no merely optional luxury. It is a universal concern. It is the essential concern of religion. In its characteristic intention religion has to do with these inescapable issues and realities, and unless we are coming to terms with these issues our concern is not essentially religious. To be sure, what calls itself religion can be a means for attempting to evade these issues. Irreligion is often a protest against trivial or perverted religion; it may be a way of coming to terms with the serious and inescapable issues. Archbishop Temple perhaps had this fact in mind when he asserted, "It is a great mistake to suppose that God is only or even chiefly concerned with religion."

If we understand the word "religion" to refer to the concern with the inescapable issues regarding the meaning and the fulfillment of life, we may say that there is no such thing as a completely irreligious person. Both the "non-religious" and the "religious" person are concerned with these issues, and they are both somehow believers; they are people of faith, whether they use the word "God" or not. Indeed, the rejection of the word "God" may be only a sign that the word does not point to the ground of faith or confidence. The rejection itself may reveal confidence of some sort; it is a sign of devotion.

We live by our devotions. We live by our love for our god. All alike place their confidence in something, whether it be in human nature, reason, scientific method, church, nation, Bible, or God. This confidence finds explicit or implicit expression in belief and disbelief. As Emerson observed, "A man bears beliefs as a tree bears apples."

To equate the devotion one lives by with the love of God may seem at first blush to be questionable. Is this not a mere playing with words? Does not this imply, for example, that an atheist who is utterly devoted to his atheism is thereby expressing his love for God? And is this not absurd?

The absurdity lies only on the surface. It is no mere word play to assert that the convinced atheist loves God, particularly if the atheism grows out of a total attitude toward life. Whoever with seriousness rejects belief in God (as that word is understood) expresses loyalty to a standard of truth or of goodness on which the judgment is made. The rejection implies that this truth or goodness is valid and reliable. For that person this truth or goodness is sacred; it may not be violated. The atheist rejects what appears to be sacred and sovereign for the theist; but in doing so recognizes something else that is sovereign and even holy for him or her. This recognition of something as sovereign, in practice if not in theory, appears in both the serious atheist and the serious theist. The one rejects the word "God," and the other accepts it. But both believe something is sovereign and reliable.

Sacred, sovereign, reliable. Just these are the qualities that have always been associated with deity. It would appear that even when belief in God ostensibly disappears, the attributes of deity remain and are attached to something that is not called "God." Religion therefore might say to the unbeliever, "When me you fly, I am the wings." In other words, if we discover what persons really believe to be sovereign, what they will cling to as the principle or reality without which life would lose its meaning, we shall have discovered their religion, their god. This sovereign object of devotion is not always readily discernible, but it can sometimes be detected by what we might call the "temperature test." When the temperature of a person's mind or spirit rises to defend something to the very last ditch, then generally that person's sacred devotion is at stake. The test is as revealing when applied to the believer in God as when applied to the unbeliever. It may show that the God avowed by the believer is not really sacred to him or her. It can show also that a serious rejection of belief in God may be a form of the love of God in the sense that it is a giving of oneself to, an identification with, something cherished above all else.

This kind of atheism is really a happy, confident atheism. It is in its way an affirmation of meaning. There is another kind of atheism, however, which is far from confident or happy. It denies that there is anything worthy of ultimate loyalty, that there is anything sacred or sovereign. This kind of atheism is nihilism, it takes nothing (not even itself) seriously; it holds that nothing is worthy of love and that love itself is meaningless. This is the anomie that leads to suicide. This perhaps is the only consistent atheism. It asserts that nothing dependable remains.

Whether people call themselves theists or atheists, the issue comes down to this: What is sacred? What is truly sovereign? What is ultimately reliable? These are the questions that are involved in every discussion of the love of God. And even if we do not like to use the words "the love of God," we will nevertheless deal with these questions in any discussion of the meaning of human existence. These are the questions to which we are always giving the answers in the embracing patterns and the ultimate decisions of our existence. Indeed, the struggle between the different answers constitutes the very meaning of human history.

Nihilism, the sense of complete meaninglessness in life, has been vividly depicted by the French existentialist Jean-Paul Sartre in his play *No Exit*. The setting of this play is hell, the hell of isolation. The author depicts the inferno of human loneliness and despair, the alienation of three souls—a man who had in life been a fascist collaborationist, and two women, the one a strumpet and the other a Lesbian. They are all three imprisoned and condemned to the eternal torture of keeping each other company. For them there is *no exit* from the torture of loneliness even though they are together. They share no common values that can give them dignity either as individuals or as a group locked in their room in hell. The souls in Dante's Inferno retain some human dignity; they seem to be at least worthy of punishment. But the souls in Sartre's hell have lost even that dignity. The three people struggle for each other's attention but without believing they have anything worth giving and without believing the others would really esteem anything worth giving. In the end, the man cannot decide whether his own spiritual leprosy allies him most closely with the woman who has been and still is a strumpet or with the one who can only give or receive affection from a duplicate of herself. And yet all of them are to remain for eternity without any other companions and without any affectionate, human interest in each other. Finally, in desperation the man says, "There's no need for hot pokers in this place. Hell is—other people." The "hell" represented in the play is the "hell" of sitting out eternity in common isolation from one another, again and again making abortive attempts at forming tolerable relationships, or at destroying one another.

The anti-heroes of *No Exit* live in the void of meaninglessness, for meaning is a shared and enjoyed relatedness. They participate in nothing that forms community. The only thing human that remains in them is the longing for community. Humans are made for relationship, and without it we are of all creatures the most miserable. In this play, then, we have a parable of the human condition, a parable of an inescapable reality. The condition of being human—of being made for community—is a fact that we cannot elude. We belong to a cosmos that is social. Only the despairing nihilist has lost the sense of belonging to it. The confident atheists, in finding some meaning in life (even though it be partly expressed in "atheism"), have the sense of belonging to a community. They even place their confidence somehow in that community. But in doing so they do not characteristically think of themselves as people of faith. They simply take the community, and also its possibilities, for granted.

The theists believe of course that they belong to a community of meaning; but they believe also that this community is not ultimately their own, either in its actuality or its possibilities. They believe that as human beings, they possess some freedom to choose the ways in which they will participate or not participate in the social cosmos in which they find themselves. But for them, the human condition as creatures longing for fellowship and as creatures possessing some freedom is a gift. In religious parlance, it is a gift of divine grace. Fulfillment of freedom is seen also as a divinely given task—and peril.

Here a positive parable of the divinely given community of meaning, the parable of the prodigal son, may with profit be added to Sartre's parable regarding the negation of community. The latter is a parable of the lost community; the former a parable of the community lost and found again.

The parable of the prodigal son is not primarily an ethical parable teaching right behavior. It is, we might say, a metaphysical parable, a picture of the social cosmos of divinely given community, of the divinely given human freedom, and of the divinely given task to fulfill that freedom in all its venture and risk. In short, this is a parable of the nature of existence and meaning, and of the love of God—of His love for humanity and of the human response to that love.

It is not possible or necessary here to spell out all the significant details of the parable. But we should observe that its principal religious import resides in the parable as a whole—in its assertion that the total human condition is to be understood as a manifestation of God's love and that participation in community is our responding love for God. Each of the elements of the parable must be understood in this context, the dignity of the creature by virtue of its participation in the social cosmos, the community of relatedness in freedom ("Give me my portion," says the son), the isolation and frustration that issue from the breaking of fellowship, the possibility of new beginning, the enrichment and fulfillment of community that comes from reconciliation. And we should add that this whole picture depicts not only the loss and the regaining of community on the part of the son; it presents, in the image of the father, the attitude of love which all must take toward each other in the re-formation and transformation of community.

It is just at this point that our earlier questions become pertinent. We have suggested that we may determine anyone's conception of the love of God (including the atheist's) by answering the questions: What is sacred for him? What is considered sovereign, what the reliable object of devotion? If we pose these questions in relation to the parable of the prodigal son, we may secure highly significant answers. But this will require that we take note of another figure in the story. So significant is he in this parable that it has been often suggested that the story should be named "the parable of the elder son."

The elder son in the parable corresponds to the antihero of

Sartre's play. He manages not only to lose participation in community; he also fails to regain it. But here the resemblance stops. His failure is due to the fact that he is a "good" man. He does the evil as well as the good that "good" men do. He does remain at home, and (unlike the prodigal) he helps to maintain the fabric of the community. But when the prodigal returns, the brother becomes the defender of morality, of law and order. He makes his ethical principles sacred and sovereign. But they turn out to be unreliable, for they would make the community exclusive; they have in them nothing that goes out to greet the prodigal who has come to himself and wants to be a part of the community again. In the mind of the teacher of the parable, the sovereign good, the sovereign reality, is not an ethical law. It is the outgoing power that transforms and fulfills the law; it is the creative element in the law that prevents justice from becoming self-righteous and unjust. But it cannot work here because it is resisted by the "good" man. And the consequence is that the "good" man is undone; he becomes alienated in isolation from the affectional community. He depends upon something undependable.

The love of God, then, is the giving of oneself to the power that holds the world together and that, when we are tearing it apart, persuades us to come to ourselves and start on new beginnings; it is not bound to achieved evil, and it is not bound to achieved good. The prodigal escaped from the one, the elder brother was bound to the other.

And why is this sort of love alone reliable? Because it alone has within it the seeds of becoming, even in the face of tragedy and death—when it keeps confidence, saying, "Into thy hands I commend my spirit." This love is reliable also because it alone can engender respect and love for the necessary diversity of men. Through this love which is a self-giving to a process of transformation rather than to a "law," all persons, in their relation to each other and in their diversity, become mutually supporting and enhancing rather than mutually impoverishing. Here the antagonism between egoism and altruism is transcended in the devotion to the good of others, which is at the same time the fulfillment of the good of the self. In the fellowship of the love of God one loses life to find it. And yet the loss and the finding are more than the process of self-realization. We become new creatures. This is the work of God that brings the self to something more than and beyond the self, beyond even the "highest self."

This kind of love, however, promises no rosy path. It may lead to what Thomas à Kempis calls "the royal way of the cross," a way which God as well as man traverses, not for the sake of suffering in itself to be sure, but for the sake of suffering, separated mankind. A comprehending mutuality rooted in immemorial being stirs and allows itself anew to heal and unite what has been wounded and separated.

I have never seen this re-creative power of love in its full orb portrayed more tellingly than in a sixteenth-century woodcut titled "The Prodigal Son," which used to be kept in the Dürer Museum in old Nuremberg. In this picture the father and the son, with joy and suffering in their faces, are almost at the point of reuniting on the road that leads home. Their arms are extended toward each other, but they have not yet embraced. Yet out beyond them we see their shadows extending as it were into the depth of being. And there they are already embracing. The two had always belonged to-gether. They belonged together in something antecedently given, as on the day of creation when the morning stars sang together and all the children of God shouted for joy. The reuniting of the separated is a re-creation, and thereby a new creation.

The love of God, then, is a love that we cannot give unless we have first received it. Ultimately, it is not even ours to give, for it is not in our keeping. It is in the keeping of a power that we can never fully know, of a power that we must in faith trust. Humanity's expression of it is a response to an antecedent glory and promise, the ground of meaning and the ever new resource for its fulfill-ment.

"By their fruits shall ye know them" is obviously a test that must be applied to love for God. We learn what is meant by any conception of the love of God by observing what sort of behavior issues from it. Indeed, the principal way to make a religious-ethical idea clear is to show what differences it makes in action. This test of the meaning of an idea we commonly apply in the realm of personal behavior. Love for God, we say, which does not issue in individual integrity, in humility, and in affectionate concern for others, is counterfeit.

But the meaning of love for God must be clarified in another realm besides that of personal attitude and behavior. It becomes fully clear—and relevant—only when we know what it means for institutional behavior, when we know what kind of family, or economic system, or political order it demands. The decisive differences between the old Lutherans and the Quakers, for example, may not be immediately discerned from their words about the love of God, but they become sharply clear in their different conceptions of the family. The one group sanctioned a sort of patriarchal family in which the authoritarian father was the vicar of God in the home, and love of God among the children was supposed to produce instant, unquestioning obedience; the other group preferred a family in which a more permissive, persuasive atmosphere prevailed. Yet both groups avowed the love of God as proclaimed in the Gospels. In general, then, we may say that the meaning of a religious or ethical imperative becomes concrete when we see it in relation to the social context in which it operates. Often the meaning of an ethical generality can be determined by observing what its proponents wish to change in society or to preserve unchanged.

Recently in Greece I visited the remarkable Byzantine church of the eleventh century at Daphni, situated on the ancient Sacred Way from Athens to Eleusis. As one emerges from the vestibule into the main church and as the eyes meet the imposing and striking mosaics on the walls of the old monastic church, one senses immediately in this monumental style of Eastern Christendom a powerful feeling for the sacred and the sovereign, the majestic, and the commanding. The eye rises to the dome and one is awestruck by the grim King of Heaven, the All-Ruler (Pantocrator), surrounded by the cruciferous nimbus, holding in His left hand the Book and with His right hand blessing the worshippers. The commanding energy of Christ the Pantocrator in his high eminence above the mosaics of the Prophets and the Feasts of the Church recalls to the worshippers the familiar themes of salvation. But in its time this Pantocrator symbolized also a political idea, the absolute authority and the majestic unapproachability of the emperor. The authority of the Pantocrator was understood in terms of the rule of the emperor. The one buttressed the other. The church and its God have become a department of the absolute state.

Here was little freedom apart from that narrow and insignificant margin permitted by the Emperor-Pantocrator. To the modern man accustomed to the democratic way of life, or to anyone who esteems the community of mutuality and freedom reflected in the parable of the prodigal son, this Caesaro-papism is demonic. The contrast between the King of Heaven (and Emperor) in the mosaic and the Father in the parable highlights opposite ends of the spectrum of conceptions of the love of God.

All the more striking is the contrast if one recalls that the primitive church, the social organization that emerged from the Gospels (which, to be sure, was not a democracy in any modern sense), gave a new dignity to Everyman—to the fisherman, to the slave, to woman, and even to the prodigal. The new fellowship enhanced this dignity by eliciting a new freedom from its members and by assigning them unprecedented responsibility. But, as the Byzantine outcome illustrates, this new freedom and responsibility were soon to be threatened and were later to be submerged.

It is beyond the scope of our discussion here to attempt to apply the spirit and the norms of the love of God (as characterized all too briefly in these pages) to the contemporary situation. Our purpose at this juncture is only to propose that belief in God and the love of God must, as Whitehead has observed regarding the early Christian conceptions, become the basis for principles of social action and organization. This means that those who interpret the love of God as movement toward a community of freedom and mutuality will be able to vindicate the claim that they serve a power that is reliable, only by yielding to that power in the midst of a world that is suffering, divided by the cleavages of race, class, and nation. What is at stake is the creation of a world in which this kind of love of God becomes incarnate in a more just and free society.

SOCIAL ACTION is a term widely used by both religious activists and social scientists. In one usage it has often meant the mobilization of religious associations to accomplish political objectives. In another, it has meant intentional and reciprocal human behavior in interpersonal and group contexts. But whether the term has the specific connotations of moral reform or of structural and functional interactions, it presumes that action in decisive human communities involves both a common sense of meaning and the exercise of power. Seldom, however, do either the activists or the scientists articulate the meaning or the root possibilities of the power they wield. Both groups are thereby deprived of the capacity to examine more profoundly the bases of their social action. In the following chapter,* Adams suggests that the connecting link between meaning and power is theological and that denial of that connection destroys the credibility of both religious activism and secular analysis.—M.L.S.

CHAPTER 7 · THEOLOGICAL BASES OF SOCIAL ACTION

$\mathbb{T}$HE DECISIVE ELEMENT in social action is the exercise of power, and the character of social action is determined by the character of the power expressed. Power has always a double character: first, as the expression of God's law and love; second, as the exercise of human freedom. To understand power as God's law and love is to understand it as Being; to understand it as human freedom is to understand it as our response to the possibilities of being, a response that is both individual and institutional. All response is therefore social action in this broad sense. In this chapter we shall be concerned with social action in this broad sense and also in the narrower sense of group action for the achievement of consensus with respect to the shaping of social policy. Both types of social action are expressions of necessity as well as of freedom. The expression of power in the dimensions of both freedom and necessity at its most profound levels must be understood religiously, that is, in terms of its theological bases. The definition of the theological bases of social

* This essay first appeared in The Journal of Religious Thought, vol. 8, no. 1 (Autumn–Winter 1950–1951), and subsequently in Adams' Taking Time Seriously (Glencoe, Ill.: The Free Press, 1957).

action must be achieved in terms of the ultimate purposes and resources of human life; it must be achieved equally in terms of the threats to the fulfillment of these purposes. Taken together, divine necessity and human freedom operate for the creation of community, or for its destruction. According to the Judeo-Christian view of God's law and love, it is the destiny of humanity to love and to be loved; there is an interdependence of spiritual destinies; this is the "plan of salvation." All response on the part of humanity to God's law and love is thus social action in the broad sense, whether the response furthers community or perverts and destroys it.

Much social thought has misunderstood or ignored the dual character of power as God's law and human response. The misunderstanding has come from an exclusive preoccupation with the dimension of human freedom, which ignores the dimension of God's law. It is not enough to say with Henry Adams that "power is poison," or with Jacob Burckhardt that "power is by its nature evil, whoever wields it." The power that is law, understood as God's law, is not in itself evil; it is the ground for the possibility of human exercise of power for good or evil. Lord Acton's assertion that "power tends to corrupt, and absolute power corrupts absolutely" is true as he understood it—namely, as applying only to human freedom, the social-political dimension. But power can be understood to corrupt absolutely only when the social-political power is sundered from its theological ground, God's law and love. This was Acton's understanding of the meaning of his famous aphorism. Contemporary social thought has tended to lift the dictum out of its total context. When accepted so superficially, such dicta give plausibility to Candide's admonition that in a world of corruption we should simply cultivate our own gardens. This interpretation has given both religious and irreligious people a spurious rationalization for retreat from social action. Accordingly, the American temper has often been deeply antipolitical, dismissing politics as necessarily corrupt. It is as the American temper has lost its theological basis and has thus failed to understand power as limitation as well as freedom that it has retreated from political action. But the retreat does not give us freedom from power. Candide could not even cultivate his garden without exercising the human power of freedom. The power to reject or disregard power is itself an expression of power.

The idea of power is in no way alien to religion. Religion cannot be adequately described without employing the conception of power; likewise, power cannot be properly described without employing religious concepts. Power is both the basic category of being and the basic category of social action. The crucial question for both religion and social action is the question concerning the nature and interrelation of divine power and human powers. All social action is therefore explicitly or implicitly grounded in a theology, and all theology implies a fundamental conception of social action. Politics, therefore, must consider the theology of power as much as theology must consider the politics of power. When power is not considered in its proper theological character, but only in its political, it becomes demonic or empty, separated from its end. Here power in the end achieves little but its own creation and destruction, and thus virtually denies itself as creative. In the human order this is what the Bible calls hardness of heart. The creative element of power is divine. The destructive element of power appears wherever power is divorced from an understanding of its source in the divine.

DEFINITIONS OF POWER

Having conceived of power as human freedom under God's law and love, we must now consider the varieties of human experience of power. We must turn to an examination of the relations between the two ultimate poles of power.

"All power is of one kind," says Emerson, "a sharing in the nature of the world." We may take this to mean that all power is of one kind in the sense that all power is capacity or ability possessed or exercised within the context of existence as it is "given." One is reminded here of Plato's laconic remark, "And I hold that the definition of Being is simply power." Plato understood power as creative, as the condition and limit of all social existence. For Plato this definition considers power as primarily law; it is transmuted in the Stoic and the Christian tradition as God's law, *Logos*. Here power is similar to the typical modern generic definition, wherein it is simply the capacity to exercise influence. The modern definition is true so far as it goes. But it is true only with respect to the power of freedom, the power to influence others, the power to control one's own behavior (freedom). Plato observes in the *Sophist* that power is present equally in the capacity *to be influenced.* Power exhibits duality, but it is one in this duality: there is no adequate conception of power as freedom except as it is simultaneously conceived of as law and except as it is viewed in a context of interaction ultimately grounded in the divine power of being (with its possibilities in terms of free and also ambiguous response).

God is not to be understood merely as a rigid lawgiver, nor humanity merely in terms of freedom. As there is a dialectic between the two, there is also a dialectic within each. Plato suggests that power is twofold: it is both active and passive. In the Christian view the active and passive powers, in both God and man, are dialectically related. God is creative, a redemptive, active power. But God takes satisfaction in our free obedience; in this respect God is influenced by human behavior. We possess creative freedom to influence ourselves and others; this is active power. But we are also influenced by participating in God's power, that is, by being affected by God's law and love and by other people's behavior. This is passive power. Where mutuality of influence appears, both active and passive power operate; and, ideally, coercive power is employed primarily for the maintenance of mutuality.

This dialectic of power is sometimes overlooked by the definitions employed by the sociologists. The typical sociological definition of power as the capacity to influence the behavior of others, in accord with one's own intentions, is a truncated definition. It refers only to active power. Max Weber's much quoted definition, for example, makes explicit reference only to this active type of power. "Power," he says, "is the probability that one actor within a social relationship will be in a position to carry out his own will despite resistance, regardless of the basis on which this probability rests." This definition makes room for force (influence by physical manipulation or threat), for domination (influence by making explicit what is commanded or requested), and for manipulation (influence that is effected without making explicit what is wanted, as for example certain types of propaganda). But Weber's definition does not explicitly include "passive powers," the capacities possessed by those who yield to one or another kind of active influence. Chester I. Barnard's discussion of communication in *The Functions of the Executive* is at least more comprehensive in this respect, for he interprets executive power as requiring two-way communication, that is, as requiring the yielding to influence as well as the exercise of influence.

A contrast that cuts across the distinction between active and passive powers should be noted here. We may speak of "power of" as ability (for example, the ability to learn or the ability to express oneself) and of "power over" as the capacity to dominate. In the social arena, when "power over" increases in a group of people, "power of" diminishes among those who are dominated. When "power of" is possessed by the members of a group engaged in social action, they have power in the sense that they participate in the making of a group decision, though of course the decision itself may lead to the attempt to exercise "power over" another group.

In all of these definitions, it is emphasized, then, that power does not exist *in vacuo;* it exists in some relation in nature and in persons, and between persons or groups of persons, or between humanity and God as the limiting, creative, and redemptive power. As Locke observes, following Plato, "Power is twofold; as able to make, or able to receive, any change; the one may be called 'active,' and the other 'passive,' power. Thus power includes in it some kind of relation—a relation to action or change." Power is a relation and it must therefore always be stated in two terms: law and freedom. In the realm of individual psychology the two-term relation of power is readily evident. Perceiving, knowing, imagining, willing, and feeling, are expressions of freedom, the power to choose. But perception implies its object; otherwise, perception is itself the creator of its object. The object is thus the condition of perception, and necessary to it. Perception as an expression of freedom is united with the object as an expression of necessity or law. This interrelated, active and passive character of power must be taken into account in any discussion of human behavior. We turn now to a brief review of the development of the concept of power in the history of religion.

Explicit religion involves the belief that there are divine powers with which man must enter into relations for the maintenance or fulfillment of meaningful existence. (We must omit here a discussion of the question whether the divine power may properly be conceived to *a* being alongside other beings.) There is no notion of God, even among primitive peoples, in which deity is not power, or does not have power.

One of the most widespread primitive conceptions of power (which may or may not be associated with deity) is the idea of mana, a mysterious impersonal force that can be in anything and which makes that thing strikingly effective. Archbishop Söderblom has suggested that in its nature and working mana may be compared to electricity; it is impersonal, it can flow from one thing to another, and it can do a variety of things. It is a holy power in things, animals, persons, magical incantations, and events. As Söderblom says, "Numerous phenomena which we understand to be essentially different are explained by primitive man to be the operation of Mana: poison, the power of healing, the power of nourishment in plants, the killing effect of weapons, the growth of plants, success, luck, unusual events, mysterious impressions, the effect of a word, the course of heavenly bodies, everything depends on Mana or rather is Mana" *(Das Werden des Gottesglaubens,* p. 88). Since mana is sacred and is therefore considered to be dangerous, various taboos are established for protection against it.

This power may be inherited or acquired by persons. In either case, the possession of this "electricity" requires obedience—a primitive understanding of law—and can become the basis of authority and deference. In this fashion it can determine certain of the principal social patterns. In addition to being an active power (in the sense we have defined) mana sometimes is conceived to be also passive. Among the Polynesians, for example, ritual is performed partially for the purpose of regenerating or increasing the power of the gods themselves, so that while the people depend upon the gods, they are also able to strengthen the gods by their own exertions. The gods will run down if the people do not recharge them. In many traditions the giving of offerings to the gods involves, among other things, the replenishment of divine potency. When no one offers anything to a god, the god "dies." Here both gods and men have the power to do, and they may also be undone by the other. Both the gods and the men may dominate the other or be dominated by the other. In any event, the power of mana "as electricity" is neither law nor ethics as we understand those concepts. Mana can be captured by an individual, thus raising freedom above law.

Modern, civilized people consider quite fantastic any proposal that the conception of mana should serve as a basis for social action. Yet millions of "moderns" have quite seriously accepted as a basis for social action ideas that are not so very different. The "magic" potency of "blood and soil," "national interest" or "natural instincts" serve as the basis for "religions" that in effect consider biological, tribal-territorial or libidinal powers to be divine and therefore decisive for social action. Aggressive nationalism, "lily-white" Americanism, neo-imperialism, and anomic hedonism live on these powers. Arnold Toynbee has argued that American Protestants assimilated this kind of religion into a conception of themselves as the chosen people establishing a new Canaan in the Western hemisphere. Like the religion of mana, this modern tribalism is not in a universal sense ethical; it is pseudo-ethical because it is a law unto itself, thus contradicting the meaning of law.

PROPHETIC CONCEPTIONS OF DIVINE POWER

For a more adequate theology of social action the definitive conception of divine power is set forth in the biblical tradition—the conception of power as judging, forgiving, healing love working toward the fulfillment of the divine purpose of history. The law of grace is sovereign. This conception is a far cry from the primitive idea of mana and from the powers on which primitive (or "civilized") tribalism lives. Between the primitive conceptions and the biblical conception there stands more than a millennium of religious experience. This period of history is very familiar territory to the reader precisely because its ideas have been decisive for Judeo-Christian theologies of social action. Despite its familiarity, however, we may, perhaps with some warrant, view it in the light of our concern with a theology of power as the basis for a theology of social action.

Conceptions of divine power very similar to the idea of mana, as well as tribalist conceptions of divine power, are to be found in early Hebraic thought. But the power in which the ethical prophets placed their trust was of a different sort. Although this power was evident for them in miraculous event and in ecstatic (though not orgiastic) experience, it was a power that became peculiarly manifest in the corporate life of the People of God. It was a view of the divine that had its roots in an earlier deliverance from bondage and whose goal was a universal, ethical purpose. Here power is conceived of as the freedom of the Jews under the Law; they were chosen and they responded by choosing. All events are therefore both power as the freedom of humanity and power as the law and love of God.

This prophetic conception was not the result of merely abstract reflection. It appeared on the occasion of a power struggle, the struggle for domination undertaken by the military empires surrounding Israel. It was developed as a reaction to the military weakness of Israel in the face of the overwhelming strength of the great powers. As Max Weber points out, "Except for the world politics of the great powers which threatened the Israelite homeland . . . the prophets could not have emerged." In a previous interim of peace, the Palestinian "states" had appeared, and with them a sense of superiority in the Hebrews, a sense of pride in past achievement (freedom) under divine guidance (law), and a faith in a glorious future for the nation (freedom under God's law). The revival of oppression at the hands of the Mesopotamian and Egyptian empires raised the old mantic vision of the power of an ethical, national deity to the level of the international. The prophets were "political theologians" concerned with the destiny and the ethical significance of the state. They viewed the power of God (law)—as it operated through social and political institutions and in international relations—as an occasion for the expression of human freedom. This is a conception of divine power that in its magnitude staggers the imagination; indeed, it is the conception that the pietists, with their preoccupation with the immediate relations between the individual soul and God, always have great difficulty in comprehending or taking seriously. Yet the pietist, like anyone else, participates in the institutionalization of powers that society defines and redefines.

It is worthwhile to observe here, in passing, that the activity of the prophets was itself possible only because of a peculiar aspect of the social organization of the society in which they found themselves. The prophets could not have emerged had they not been able to appeal directly to the people. In this fact we may see implicit a principle of freedom that is indispensable for any Judeo-Christian theology of social action. The lines of political communication and activity were not held in monopoly by the monarchy. Unlike the "prophets" of surrounding countries, the Hebrew prophets were not an adjunct of the monarchy. Weber, in a slightly pejorative sense, calls them "demagogues." Within the social stratification of their society, they were able to be the spokesmen to and for the poor and the oppressed. In their tradition there was a separation between charismatic and traditional authority, which left the way open for prophetic criticism. In other words, the freedom of the prophet presupposed a separation of powers that in a narrow way bears comparison to the modern ideal of freedom of the press. This separation of powers, which permitted the liberty of prophecy, was related to the fact that the covenant between God and the People was not through the monarch; the covenants between God and the People and between God and the royal house were parallel convenants, and both were subject to prophetic criticism. The divine kingship was limited by this separation of powers. The will of God could be discussed by the prophets without license from the government; it could even be expressed through the mouth of the prophet against the monarchy.

Viewing the overwhelming power of the great empires and exercising the liberty of prophesying, the prophets elevated Jahwe to the Lord of history. In the course of time they claimed that God uses the great powers (for example, "My servant Nebuchadnezzar" —political power) as an instrument for the punishment, the purification, and the education of even the chosen people. This political god was raised above the gods of the world powers, and, finally, was said to be the one and only God.

The prophetic conception of the divine power was shaped, then, in the stress of power politics. Conversely, the conception of power politics was shaped under the stress of a new vision of the divine power. To the degree that the conception of divine power changed its character, Israel reacted differently to subjugation, indeed transcended it, and found a new meaning in it. The divine power was not only ethicized. It was also interiorized; it was interpreted as operating in the most intimate aspects of psychic experience and of divine-human fellowship. Both God and humanity were now seen to be bound together not only in the realm of politics but also in the inner life. This remarkable interiorization of piety represents the translation of the conception of divine power into a new dimension: it represents also a deeper conception of the conjugation of the active and passive powers. These two aspects of the divine and the human powers, the ethical and the interior, are so important for a theology of social action that they deserve closer scrutiny.

Since the present brief essay aims primarily to be a constructive statement rather than an historical one, we shall not try to express the Hebrew prophetic outlook exclusively in its own vocabulary. Rather, we shall try to present it in a way that readily lends itself to an appreciation of its perennial relevance for a theology of power.

I.   The power that is worthy of confidence is the Creator of the world and humanity. This is a mythological formulation; in essence it means that existence is grounded in divine power—the power of being, in law—and is therefore a divinely given realm of meaning. Christian theology has succinctly expressed this basic presupposition of the doctrine of creation: *Esse qua esse bonum est.* Being as such is good; it is of God. Good is possible only within being. God offers the possibility of good. The doctrine of *Imago dei* is an application of this view to anthropology. The human in freedom participates in this divine law and creativity. Recasting this affirmation in terms of a theology of power, we may say that to exist is to possess, or to participate in, the divine power of being; it is to be the beneficiary of the divine power which is the ground of order and meaning.

This means that the prophetic view renounces any radical asceticism in face of the material order. It rejects the cynic's notion that all power is evil, a notion that represents an extrapolation from the view that political power is evil. For the prophetic view, this false notion would imply that the perfect God should be perfectly impotent. On the other hand, prophetism rejects not only the fallacy that being is evil; it rejects also the fallacy that existence is simply good. There is a possibility of good or evil in existence. Both possibilities can express themselves in human action. Prophetism therefore laid a burden of responsibility upon humanity. Escape from action to contemplation was rejected as a mode of irresponsibility. Escape from the material for the sake of the spiritual, the renunciation of the finite for the sake of the infinite, constituted irresponsibility in face of the divine possibility and command. There is no freedom *from* the world that is not freedom *for* the world. Matter is not a demonic power; it is not the enemy of meaning. Sin does not derive from the fact that we participate in a material world but rather from our disobedience to the divine demand for love and justice. The fulfillment of meaning is inextricably related to things earthy, to soul *and* body, for both soul and body are God's creatures. It does not appear in spite of or in protest against the earthy. The order of nature, in us as well as beyond us, demands our care and love just as it receives God's.

Yet, the Judeo-Christian doctrine of creation asserts also that the divine power is not to be identified with the world or with any part of it. It is never capsuled anywhere in the world—not in a "superior" race or nation, not in a religious tradition, not in religious ceremony, not even in the prophet's word. The attempt to capsule the divine power is the attempt to control and manipulate it, to become sovereign over it; the attempt is blasphemous. "Thou shalt have no other gods before me." Everything finite stands under the divine judgment. "Religion" itself stands under this judgment. The basic threat to "faith-ful" freedom is the threat of idolatry—giving to the creature that which belongs alone to the Creator. This view is the basis of prophetic criticism. Prophetic religion speaks out of a religious vision; it is not first and foremost a movement for social reform. But the vision issues not only in prophecy against idolatry; it lures toward positive obedience to and fulfillment of the divine law.

II.   The power that is worthy of confidence, the power that alone is reliable, has a world-historical purpose, the achievement of righteousness and fellowship through the loving obedience of its creatures. As an ethical, historical religion prophetism is not mystical in so far as mysticism is interpreted as a flight above the temporal world into timeless communion with eternity. For it, time is not the enemy, as it is in much of Hellenism; time is not the order of deterioration. It is the arena of fulfillment through law and freedom, though it is also the arena of God's judgment. The divine purpose is manifest not in abstract, timeless entities but rather in historical events and patterns of events, in events and even in periods in the life of the people. Past events become necessity in the form of judgment where once they were only elements in the arena of freedom. On the other hand, they are interpreted as evidence of the faithfulness of God. In the past God had chosen Israel and made a covenant in order to carry out the divine purpose in a special way. Israel was delivered from bondage and slavery. Freedom from bondage is the working of a divine power, freedom from domination. But it brings with it the demand for a new commitment. The divine power, the reliable power in history, forms humanity into universal, righteous community. Where true community is being formed, there the divine power is working. Indeed, this is a way in which we may identify the divine power. Prophetic religion is an historical religion not only in the sense that it is concerned with the struggle between good and evil in history but also in the sense that it looks toward the creation of an historical community of memory and hope with respect to God's working in history. Toward this end, we may be unfaithful, but God will be faithful.

III.   The power that is reliable in history places an obligation to righteousness upon the whole community of the faithful as a community, though to be sure the fulfillment is in God's own time. The response to the divine power is responsibility. The covenant of God is with the community and the individual members of it; it imposes responsibility upon community and individual for the character of the community and especially for concern with the needy and the oppressed. Religious institutions, cultus, political and economic institutions must serve God's righteous purpose. There is no enclave that is exempt from this sovereignty.

IV.   The power that is reliable and sovereign in history offers itself as the basis of a community of *persons*. While working on the visible, outer side of history it generates the inner side of history and community; it manifests itself in the responsive, creative, healing powers of justice and love, of tenderness, forgiveness, and mercy. These qualities are not merely human devices. They are the capacities and feelings that express the fullness of the divine power. The interrelatedness of persons is seen to involve these interior qualities. When we do not exhibit tenderness, forgiveness, and mercy, we use our freedom to frustrate or pervert the divine power. Prophetism is not only a religion concerned with the divine power as it manifests itself in the outer events of history; it is also an interiorized religion of community between God and persons and between people under God. This feature of prophetism is conspicuous not only in the writings attributed to the prophets. Its literary precipitate appears also in the *Psalms*, the most intimate devotional literature of the race. Thus the power of God is strikingly personal in contrast to the merely impersonal, "electric" power of mana. It is a passive as well as an active power; and it looks toward the expression of "power of" and "power with" rather than of "power over" (domination). The significance of this emphasis can be appreciated if we consider another aspect of the problem of the theology of social action.

The theological bases of social action cannot properly offer a blueprint for social action. The attempt to make a blueprint and to give it a divine sanction always runs the danger of issuing in idolatrous legalism. Yet the relevance of any theology of social action can become clear only when one discerns the demands that it makes upon social action and organization. Right attitudes are never sufficient alone. They must find embodiment in social institutions. Indeed, one must say that one does not even understand the meaning of "right attitudes" or even of a theology until one recognizes their implications for social organization. If no particular demands ensue with respect to social organization, right attitudes can be a snare and a deception, a form of organized irrelevance.

Now, when we search in the prophetic writings for an explicit statement of the principles of justice and love on the basis of which one might devise a theory of social organization, we get a rather "dusty answer." As Ernst Troeltsch says, the prophets did not work out these principles. But this does not mean that they were vague and inexplicit in their specific demands. Taken altogether their specific demands for social change are extensive; the prophets cannot be accused of being otherworldly.

Just at this point Troeltsch makes a radical criticism of the prophets as social reformers, as promoters of social action. In effect, he argues that when they became specific they tended to become also irrelevant, for they were not very willing to grapple with the actualities of the new economic and political situation in which Israel found herself; they indulged a nostalgia for an irrecoverable past. Their demands were not practical for their times and, he argues, they are not practicable for any other society in so far as that society is urban or is becoming urban. Several, if not all, of the prophets idealized an old, simple, half-nomadic, agricultural, small businessmen ethic; they opposed the bigness as well as the luxury of cities; they deplored the violent force of the wars of empires, the precarious entangling alliances with foreign powers, the pomp and intrigue of the court, the loss of the simple, friendly justice administered by the elders, the impersonalism as well as the bribery of the courts of the princes, the officiousness of state functionaries, the oppression of officialdom, the law and usages and abuses that are characteristic of any urban economy. So far from being progressive radicals the prophets were reactionaries in the sense that they wanted to return to the good old days. To a large degree their social program was atavistic. As Troeltsch puts it, "The prophets are representatives of that strictly Israelite mentality in which the old customs of the fathers stand in closest connection with the Jahwe cultus."

Troeltsch appears to suggest that the antiurbanism of the prophets rendered their conceptions of social justice anachronistic even in their own time. But there is a sense in which precisely this aspect of prophetism is perennially relevant, especially in an urban economy. Stated in sociological language, the yearning of the prophets for the rural ways of the idealized past was a yearning for a society in which primary, affectional relations are dominant. In the urban economy, where division of labor is elaborate and social mobility is required, the total personality is not brought into play in most social relations. Secondary relations, segmented impersonal relations, tend to predominate. A certain alienation reflected in the individual's feeling of isolation, homelessness, restlessness, and anxiety is the consequence. The sense of alienation is created by the lack of intimacy, the impersonalism, the multiplicity of norms, the atomizing of obligations, the loss of communal solidarity. All of these consequences follow from the loss of primary ties. Luxury alongside neglected abject poverty, concentration of economic power, exploitation, callousness, intrigue, all produce alienation of person from neighbor, of individual from the convenanted community, of humanity from God; they pervert people and society; in short, they alienate us from the community-forming power of God. Alienation can appear, of course, where primary ties are strong (divorce is not unknown); but in recommending the return to the past the prophets were trying to cope with a fundamental and characteristic problem of urban life. They were trying to correct the evils of mass society by the restoration of primary relations wherein compassion, friendliness, intimacy, common responsibility could again prevail. They wanted the return of the power of mutuality as over against the power of domination. They saw that the power of God unto salvation can work only when people are not treated as things. They would have understood the Marxist protest against *Verdinglichung* ("thingification"). This term is perhaps as good a symbol as any that could be used to characterize the major consequence of the frustration of the power of God as understood by the prophets. At any rate, no word could better indicate the pressing relevance of the prophetic ethic for the dehumanized anonymity of contemporary fragmented life. The prophetic ethic may be atavistic in its details; in its essence, however, it is an ethic that is especially pertinent in the face of what John Stuart Mill called "the prices we pay for the benefits of civilization," the drying up of the sources of great virtues, "the decay of individual energy, the weakening of the influence of superior minds over the multitude, the growth of charlatanerie and the diminished efficacy of public opinion as a restraining power."

As against Troeltsch, we must say that the instinct of the prophets was sound. Taken together with the other aspects of their theology of social action that we have already noticed, their demand for the values—the powers that attach to intimacy and mutuality—is a perennially relevant demand to be made by every Christian theology of social action. Love and justice can prevail only where they are supported by the fellowship, the friendliness, the concern of each for all and of all for each, the sense of responsibility found in the community of primary relations. These qualities of psychic relatedness are at the same time the working of the grace of God and the medium through which the divine power grows into history like a seed that grows "of itself," for through them the active and the passive powers of sensitivity operate in mutuality.

CONCEPTIONS OF THE DIVINE POWER IN THE NEW TESTAMENT

The reference to Jesus' figure about the seed (employed by Jesus in parables that have metaphysical as well as moral depth) assists us to observe the way in which he continued, extended, and deepened the prophetic conceptions of the community-forming power of God. In his conceptions of Love and Law he emphasized, as did the prophets, the divine yearning and initiative for intimacy between God and each self and among people. But going beyond their eschatological hopes (which we have had to leave out of our explicit discussion), he stressed the idea that the Kingdom of God has already "broken in." Moreover, Jesus transformed the Old Covenant into a New Testament, implying a new basis and a new world mission. He envisaged a more intimate relation between himself (the spearhead and earnest of the Kingdom now breaking in) and his community than that between Moses and the prophets to the People of God. The God of Jesus also seeks out after the lost and the neglected. Besides, he presents himself as a new, tangible manifestation and medium of divine power. As W. M. Horton wrote: "Moses received and gave Torah; Jesus *was* Torah, together with the power to fulfill Torah."

We should notice here another important difference. In his conception of the Kingdom of God, Jesus shared with the prophets, as we have indicated, the desire for intimacy of fellowship. In many respects his mentality and that of his immediate disciples was similar to that of the prophets in the sense that it was conditioned by agrarian protest against urbanization. "The gospel," says F. C. Grant, "is, in fact, the greatest agrarian protest in all history." But the prophets do not appear to have formed continuing intimate groups in which their theology of power, their theology of fellowship, could find application. The Christians *did* form a social organization in which the power of the spirit, the power of love, could find organizational embodiment. Moreover, in the conception of the Body of Christ they found a new ontological basis for the working of the divine power that was in Jesus, namely, the *koinonia,* a group living a common life with Jesus Christ as its head and informing power. Participation in a believing fellowship became the soil for the working of the divine power. Again, we observe that the divine and human powers were interpreted as both active and passive; moreover, the noncoercive aspects of power were greatly stressed. The New Testament ethic is an ethic of sharing.

We must observe, however, that Jesus gave his primary attention to person-to-person relations. He was not a political theologian. He and the primitive church showed little direct concern for economic and political problems and institutions as such, the problems having to do with impersonal relations. This attitude is to be explained mainly by his sense of urgency with respect to the imminent coming of the Kingdom in fullness and power. St. Paul, however, gave impetus to a conservative evaluation of political and other institutions. "The powers that be are ordained of God." "I have learned in whatsoever state I am, therewith to be content." Despite these attitudes, the early church exercised an increasingly transformative power in institutions, partially as a consequence of the fact that the church itself provided an opportunity for people who had previously been excluded from exercising significant social-political power to assume responsibility in the exercise of power, that is, in participating in the divine creative-redemptive power and thus in making social decisions. The early church's very existence was, on the social, economic and political fronts, as significant as its teaching (as Christians say also of Jesus Christ). But beyond this, it surely must be recognized that the canon of Christian social action does not close with the New Testament.

POWER AND SOCIAL ACTION IN THE DEMOCRATIC SOCIETY

The attitude of responsibility appropriate for achieving consensus toward the end of shaping social policy in modern democratic society is better represented by the nineteenth-century British theologian, William Whewell: "Every citizen who thus possesses by law a share of political power, *is* one of the powers that be. Every Christian in such a situation may and ought to exert his constitutional rights, so far as they extend, both to preserve the State and the Law from all needless and hasty innovation, and to effect such improvements in both as time and circumstance require; using the light of Religion as well as of morality and polity, to determine what really is improvement." Although the fellowship of the *koinonia* is perhaps possible only in the church itself, the vocation it places upon the Christian in the world must presuppose the ongoing attempt to make its conception of the divine power applicable outside the *koinonia* as well as within it, in the latent as well as in the manifest church. The theological and ethical principles of Christian social action that are appropriate for the church are ultimately the criteria for judging and transforming society. The Christian looks for a society in which all may be treated as persons potentially responsive to God's redemptive purpose for history. And in working for it, we must perforce use that kind of community today called the voluntary association— where, within the church and outside it, consensus is formed and social action is undertaken.

But between St. Paul and William Whewell there stands a long period of development almost comparable in significance to that which separates the period of belief in mana from the prophetic period of the discovery of the Lord of history. Yet, the general framework of ideas provided by Jewish and Christian prophetism, together with its demand for responsible, communal fellowship, represents the orientation for the theological bases of social action that is imperative for any Christian who undertakes to fulfill the divinely given responsibility to participate in social action toward the end of offering loving obedience to the divine power, the Lord of history, and of the souls of persons. Christian obedience looks toward the kind of social action and the kind of society that can provide the soil out of which the creative, judging, healing power of God may like a seed grow of itself.

HAVING ARGUED in several ways for the importance of theology in understanding human action and sociality, Adams also never ceased to question the pragmatic human repercussions of theological ideas. Thinkers are known by what they oppose as well as by what they support. Thus, when theologians make affirmations of various kinds, Adams not only wants to know how their symbols relate to ultimate questions, he also wants theologians to spell out what their particular understandings mean in the human arena. What do they support, what do they oppose? More than one religious scholar, spotting Adams in the audience, has departed from the prepared text to say that "of course" what he is presenting needs to be spelled out in concrete terms, but "for the moment" and "for the sake of precision" attention will focus on theory. But for Adams, precision is not gained by narrow focus on one level of meaning, but by integrating levels of meaning in a way that relates to practice. Thus, in the following chapter, we see that theology must be a practical as well as a theoretical science; that is, it must imply an ethic. Indeed, the conviction that the ethic is a major test of the adequacy of any theology is the central thesis of this essay, first delivered as the presidential address of the American Theological Society and published here for the first time.—M.L.S.

CHAPTER 8 · THE USE OF SYMBOLS

IT WAS in the earliest seventies," Charles Sanders Peirce tells us, "that a knot of us young men in Old Cambridge, calling ourselves, half-ironically, half-defiantly, 'The Metaphysical Club'—for agnosticism was then riding its high horse, and was frowning superbly upon all metaphysics—used to meet, sometimes in my study, sometimes in that of William James. It may be that some of our old-time confederates would today not care to have such wild-oats-sowings made public, though there was nothing but boiled oats, milk, and sugar in the mess."

One of the residues of these wild-oats-sowings is what is called the pragmatic theory of meaning. We learn from Peirce that the theory was initially stimulated by the British psychologist Alexander Bain's definition of belief, as "that upon which a man is prepared to act." Peirce goes on to say that "from this definition, pragmatism is scarce more than a corollary." He gave his own formulation to this theory of meaning in two articles for the *Popular Science Monthly* entitled "The Fixation of Belief" and "How to Make Our Ideas Clear." Here he sets forth the view that the essence of a belief is a habit or disposition to act, that different beliefs are distinguished by the different habits of action they involve, and that the rule for clarifying the conceptual elements in beliefs is to refer them to "the habits of action." In extension of these ideas he says, "Thus, we come down to what is tangible and practical, as the root of every real distinction of thought, no matter how subtle it may be; and there is no distinction of meaning so fine as to consist in anything but a possible difference of practice." He wants to leave no uncertainty about this. He continues, "Our idea of anything is our idea of its sensible effects; and if we fancy that we have any other, we deceive ourselves." The rule for attaining clarity of apprehension of meaning is this: "Consider what effects, which might conceivably have practical bearings, we conceive the object of our conception to have. Then, our conception of these effects is the whole of our conception of the object."

Obviously, such a definition of the meaning of belief is a definition of only one kind of meaning. Peirce was fully aware of this limitation of the pragmatic theory of meaning. He made many attempts to express the pragmatic principle in a form that really satisfied him, in a form that would exclude nonsense without at the same time being a "barrier to inquiry." We need not here rehearse what Peirce considered the nonsense that should be excluded. We recall, however, that A. O. Lovejoy in his essay on "The Thirteen Pragmatisms" (1908) demonstrated that the pragmatists failed "to attach some single and stable meaning to the term 'pragmatism'." In face of this assertion James was actually enthusiastic. This was fine, he thought, for it proved how "open" pragmatism is—an attitude very different from Peirce's scrupulosities and soul-searchings. It must be emphasized that Peirce's pragmatic theory is not a theory of truth but a theory of meaning, one possible theory of meaning. William James carried the theory beyond this view when he asserted that it would enable us to come into better working touch with reality, and that the true idea is the idea it is best for us to have, best in the long run. Here truth becomes a subspecies of goodness. James at one time even made beauty a subspecies of goodness, for he wrote that an evening at a symphony concert has been wasted on a young man if on returning home he is not kinder to his grandmother.

More strictly within the province of the pragmatist theory of meaning is the question emphasized by the pragmatists. They asked regarding our beliefs, what difference to our practice and to our expectations it will make to believe this rather than that. William James was initially interested in the pragmatic theory of meaning as "a method of settling metaphysical disputes which might otherwise be endless"; and he held that if we examine many metaphysical hypotheses as we should examine scientific hypotheses—by considering what difference it would make to particular occurrences if the hypothesis were true—we find absolutely no difference among them. The basic intention of the pragmatic theory of meaning is to observe the relations between thought and action, or, speaking more precisely with Peirce, the relations between symbols and action. The life of man is viewed as essentially a life of action, action in the formation of symbols and action in bringing about practical consequences in terms of the symbols.

An extension of the pragmatic theory of meaning has been devised by the Oxford linguistic philosophers, under the influence of Wittgenstein. The Oxford philosophers define meaning in terms of linguistic use. The definition of meaning is put forward as a practical methodological rule. Thus, to ask how X is used, or in what context X is used significantly, is a device or "idiom," as Ryle calls it, to remind us first of the fact that words *mean* in different ways, and that the meaning of any word is always relative to the context in which it is used.

Now, it is not to my purpose, nor is it within my competence, to review even briefly the stages by which the Oxford philosophers have discriminated different meanings of meaning, descriptive and otherwise. Nor do we need to consider the utilitarianism that infects the thought of some of these linguistic philosophers. The important thing to note is that considerable emphasis has been placed on the idea that the meaning of a term is to be observed in the use or uses to which it is put, and also that expressions have meaning only in context. Thus, Nowell-Smith says that, instead of the question, "What does the word 'X' mean?" we should always ask the two questions, "For what job is the word 'X' used?" and "Under what conditions is it proper to use the word for that job?" Here, too, meaning is understood partly in terms of context. We shall return presently to this sort of question.

At this juncture I would like to refer to R. B. Braithwaite, who has formulated the pragmatic theory of meaning in a special way.

As a positivist empiricist he rejects theological statements at their face value, for example, theological statements in the Apostles' Creed; but he does not deny that they have pragmatic meaning. This meaning is to be observed in their implications for ethical behavior. Christianity, he concludes, aims to promote "an agapeistic way of life." Consequently, Braithwaite not long ago joined the Church of England, in the high-church branch. It is said that he sent out engraved invitations to his friends in Cambridge when his child was to be christened, and that following the service one of his agnostic colleagues asked him in puzzlement, "You say that you do not believe the Apostles' Creed as a theological affirmation. How, then, can you repeat it in church?" To which Braithwaite gave the ready answer, "That is simple enough. All I have to do is to omit the first two words." This response reminds one of the limitations Peirce placed upon the pragmatic theory.

Now, the central idea contained in the pragmatic theory, namely, that the meaning of a symbol is to be observed in its effect on action, on habits, is the principal, or at least the initial, text of my discussion of one approach to method in the study of Christian ethics. But I want to extend the application of the theory. We may say that the pragmatic theory of meaning is already implied in the New Testament saying, "By their fruits shall you know them." Ordinarily, however, this New Testament axiom is interpreted in terms of personal or interpersonal behavior and not in terms of institutional behavior. Probably this interpretation is wrong, for the admonition in the New Testament runs, "Thou shalt love the Lord thy God with *all* thy heart and mind and soul." In any event, the early pragmatists appear to have restricted the application of the theory. They did not use it in such a way as to include an examination of the institutional consequences of belief. William James in *The Varieties of Religious Experience*, for example, shows extremely little interest in the institutional consequences of religious experience and belief. He confines attention to consequences for individual behavior. This is true also of Braithwaite's interpretation of what he calls "the agapeistic ways of life." It is true also of many a systematic theology. Sometimes the only place where one is shown the social-organizational consequences of religious symbols may be in the section on the doctrine of the church. Otherwise, one is not shown what difference the belief or the theology makes for institutional behavior.

Here a distinction made by Ernst Troeltsch becomes pertinent. In his critique of Kohler's work on *Ideas and Persons* in Christian history he says that Kohler entertains the illusion that one can understand the history of the faith without studying the role of institutions. In his *Problems der Ethik* Troeltsch explicates what he calls the distinction between subjective and objective virtues. Subjective virtues appear in the immediate relations between the individual and God, the individual and the neighbor, and the individual and the self (in interior dialogue). Objective virtues, on the other hand, appear in those relationships that require institutional incarnation, though of course objective virtues presuppose subjective ones. From this perspective a person is not only good as such, but that person is also a good parent, a good administrator, a good citizen.

Roger Mehl of Strasbourg in his essay for the Geneva conference on Christian Ethics in a Changing World, comments tellingly on this differentiation:

> For a long time it was thought that social life was no more than the sum of relationships between individuals and that in consequence, social ethics was no different from personal ethics. . . . It is undoubtedly to the credit of the different socialist movements and ideologies that they have brought out (even at the price of indifference to the individual ethic and the virtues of the private citizen) the original character of social ethics. . . . Socialism discovered that the chief problems of social ethics are problems of structures. These are objective realities, which evolve in accordance with their own laws. (John C. Bennett, ed., *Christian Social Ethics in a Changing World*. New York: Association Press, 1966, pp. 44–45).

This statement, which points to the concern of Social Ethics with social structures, gives me occasion to present some basic presuppositions that must be borne in mind if one is to employ the pragmatic approach to the study of religious ethics. These are broad-gauged presuppositions that require more extensive consideration than is possible here. Yet, they must be mentioned at least briefly.

I.   The perspectives of religious ethics depend upon theological perspectives, and these theological perspectives are *sui generis*.

They possess their own intrinsic character, and when best under-stood they exhibit an inner coherence and consistency. To be sure, considerable variety obtains with respect to the formulation of the basic perspectives, a wide spectrum that includes different types of piety. A main task of theology and of theological ethics is to achieve clarity and consistency regarding the perspective and the formulation chosen, a clarity that reflects awareness of alternative possibilities. We have already indicated that the intrinsic quality of these perspectives is not the concern of the pragmatic theory of meaning.

Now, if theological perspectives are recognized as *sui generis*, then two false conceptions must be rejected. First, the view that the controlling perspectives may be explained as merely the consequences of psychological or social conditioning. And, second, the view that theology may be collapsed into ethical demands. This reduction is illustrated by Braithwaite's conception of the meaning of Christianity as an agapeistic way of life. An analogous reduction is to be observed in the Marxist attempt to transform metaphysics into social criticism. In this view, metaphysics is only a hidden social theory; more precisely stated, it is only ideology. Even though these views must be rejected insofar as they claim to be adequate, we should add, however, that the theology that does not examine the social consequences of belief is in this respect meaningless from the point of view of the sociological pragmatic theory of meaning.

II.   In the study of religious ethics a major purpose is to discern the "ordering" or the type of ordering that reflects the impact of its characteristic symbolism. This symbolism may exercise a positive influence upon the general cultural ethos, upon the structure of personality, and upon the institutional sphere. Or it may reveal the influence of these factors. Actually, the social-ethical as well as the personal-ethical content of the religious symbolism may in large measure be taken over from the immediate social milieu. In the institutional sphere, for example, both of these processes can be discerned. The symbols in the long run may exercise a clearly positive influence, even to the extent of changing the power structure; on the other hand, the power structures within which the symbols function may determine or deflect the interpretation of the symbols. The use made of a symbol may vary according to the social status or frustration or demands of particular social groups: the use made of a symbol by a ruling group will be different from the use made by a deprived group. In this whole area of analysis both substructure and superstructure must be taken into account. Both can affect the perception of the situation.

These differentiations also appear in the study of the history of Christian ethics, so much so that the history must again and again be reconceived in order to take into account new perceptions. Consider, for example, the marked changes that have taken place in the past century with respect to the definition of the Renaissance. Once the Renaissance was defined in the contours proposed by Jacob Burckhardt, the study of the symbolism and its influence was markedly affected. But when Konrad Burdach redefined the Renaissance in terms of renewal movements of the Middle Ages, the study of the symbolism and its influences changed considerably. During the past generation or two analogous differentiations have appeared with respect to the definition and influence of the Protestant ethic. Max Weber constructed his conception of it in a special way. By concentrating attention on the economic sphere and by excluding the political sphere from attention he arrived at an ideal type of Protestant ethic quite different from the type that emerges if one takes seriously into account the theocratic, political motifs in Calvinism and Puritanism. Indeed, his construction is extremely lopsided. He ignores precisely those elements in Puritanism that presented a much broader conception of vocation than the Puritanism he constructs. This broader conception of vocation, which included a political, reformist activism, not only supplemented but also brought under radical criticism the narrower conception that Weber stresses.

These problems of analysis are perennial, and thus the study of influences is bound to be tentative and even ambiguous in outcome. Nevertheless, one can say that symbolism when effective provides some sort of ordering of experience and its sanctions. Indeed, if one is to find out the meaning of religious symbolism in past or present, the pragmatic theory suggests that one must ask the believer what he in the name of the symbolism wishes changed or not changed; and one should ask also what aspects of existence are a matter of indifference. If the religious symbol does not call for change or interpretation of social structures, then to this extent it is meaningless (from the pragmatic perspective).

III.   As the Oxford linguists remind us, a variety of meanings may be attached to or be latent in a particular word or symbol or in a particular complex of symbols. This variety of meaning becomes evident when one examines the contexts within which the symbol appears. The pragmatic meaning of a belief may be interpreted in differing ways in different times and places, partly because of the great diversity of nonreligious as well as of religious conditions (or contexts) at various stages of the social process. Besides this consideration one must take into account what Schelling called "the infinity of the idea," the fact that any fundamental symbol is pregnant with, latent with, a variety of implications or connotations. This variety almost inevitably appears in time, for symbols belong to history, that is to the temporal sphere. This aspect of symbols is a mystery. Why, for example, should one have to wait until the twelfth century for a Joachim di Fiore to use the doctrine of the Trinity to devise a periodization of history according to which society was moving out of the current period, the period of the Son, to a third period, the period of the Spirit, a period of new freedom in which there would be a transfer of power from the secular to the religious clergy? That question is simply unanswerable. Nevertheless, one can say that the Joachites and their descendants exemplify the changing meaning of symbols as understood in relation to context. Presently we shall consider some other examples of change of pragmatic meaning in terms of change of context or in terms of change in purpose.

IV.   This consideration leads to a fourth observation. Certain symbols lend themselves more readily to application in the area of subjective virtues, others to application in the area of objective virtues. *Metanoia,* for example, has generally been symbolically powerful in the realm of subjective virtues, although in primitive Christianity this change of heart-mind-soul resulted in membership in a new community and thus brought about some change in the realm of objective virtues. It is worth noting here that the conservative Lutheran jurist Friedrich Julius Stahl in the nineteenth century held that the concept of conversion (as well as of redemption) must apply to society and social institutions as well as to persons. A similar duality appears in the concept of the demonic. In the New Testament the concept refers not only to a psychic phenomenon of possession but also to a social-cultural force in the world, that is, to the corruption of the culture and its institutions which is to be overcome by the Kingship of Christ. It can no longer be said that Augustine was the first to relate the concept of the demonic to both the psychological realm and the sphere of culture and institutions. This scope of reference appeared earlier in the New Testament.

The symbol, the kingdom of God, is likewise the type of symbol that readily lends itself to pragmatic meaningfulness in both the psychological and the institutional sphere. It is a metaphor drawn from the area of politics, and just as it is drawn from this area so it repeatedly finds application in the social-institutional sphere. In this respect it is like the concept of the covenant, a major integrating conception in the Bible and one of the most powerful in the Reformed tradition for the shaping of both ecclesiological and political theory. In the Old Testament the political symbols king and covenant point to the societal demands of Jahwe. Men are responsible for the total character of the society. "God hath a controversy with *his people.*" On the other hand, an interpretation popular in the past century held that "the kingdom of heaven is within you." This is a false translation and a lamentable reduction. Joel Cadbury has suggested that the saying should be translated, "the kingdom of heaven is available to you (among you)." This translation at least can avoid the reductionist interpretation that stresses only the interiorization of the kingdom which itself, to be sure, is an integral aspect of the symbol.

The broader scope and application of the concept of the kingdom is strikingly formulated by Talcott Parsons in his recent extensive article on "Christianity," in the new *International Encyclopedia of the Social Sciences*:

> the Christian movement crystallized a new pattern of values not only for the salvation of human souls but also for the nature of the societies in which men should live on earth. This pattern, the conception of a "kingdom" or, in Augustine's term, a "city" of men living according to the divine mandate on earth, became increasingly institutionalized through a long series of stages, which this article will attempt to sketch. Later it became the appropriate framework of societal values for the modern type of society.

The symbolic powerfulness and societal relevance of these political symbols have been made markedly evident in Paul Lehmann's *Ethics in a Christian Context* and in Martin Buber's *The Kingship of God*. Another political symbol should be mentioned here in passing, the concept of the warrior, which figures largely in certain sections of the Old Testament and which came to the fore again in the Middle Ages and in the Renaissance and in some measure also in Puritanism.

There is another symbol that possesses as great a variety of connotation as any of the symbols already mentioned. This is the domestic type of symbol which of course lends itself to elaborate conjugation, the concept of the family, of God and his children, of bride and groom, of brothers and sisters. The domestic symbol can point to more intimate interpersonal cathexis than the political symbol (as, for example, in Hosea's use). At the same time it can replace or serve as a surrogate for the political metaphor, to be observed especially in patriarchal theories of societal order. It is fascinating to observe the use of domestic symbolism by Friedrich Julius Stahl, a principal shaper of the Throne-and-Altar tradition in Germany in the nineteenth century. Stahl connects the patriarchal symbol with the doctrine of justification by faith: God's relation to man is personal, it is that of the father. Then by analogy he infers that the Christian state is an authoritarian one in which the emperor as father directly concerns himself quite personally for the sake of his people. The basic principle then becomes "authority, not majority." This combination of ideas he calls "the Protestant principle."

The Roman Catholic political theorist Carl Schmitt in his work a generation ago on *Politische Theologie* attempted to show the ways in which domestic symbols of a patriarchal character have figured in religious interpretations of the political order. Here he contrasts patriarchal authority that is majestically above the law and the trivial democratic leveling that issues from the rule of law. Perhaps it was the influence of his own application of the pragmatic theory of meaning that led him to support Nazism. In any event, for him the crucial struggle in the modern period is the struggle between the conception of *law* and the conception of the transcendent *person* of God and of the ruler. Here he approaches the position of Stahl with his "Protestant principle." He overlooks, however, the ways in which individualistic philanthropic liberalism has used domestic symbolism—the Fatherhood of God and the brotherhood of man—to articulate a religious conception of democracy. It is a striking thing that when the promoters of the Social Gospel wished to give a broader scope to religious and social responsibility under a sovereign God they placed a new interpretation upon a political (rather than a domestic) symbol, the Kingdom of God. This symbol was no longer to be interpreted as pointing only to the kingdom that is within (cf. Rauschenbusch's corollary, the Kingdom of God and the kingdom of evil—a societal, institutional conception).

At this point we should observe in passing that the biological or organic symbol, the body, must rank as one of the most powerful and persistent metaphors in history. It appears recurrently in both the Orient and the Occident. It figures as a psycho-political symbol, for example, in Plato, determining a hierarchical form of social organization. In this way it functions as one of the major symbols of conservatism in the history of political theory (comparable in this respect to the conception of "the chain of being"). The jurisdiction of the organic metaphor reaches from Plato and St. Paul through the Reformation and Romanticism to Vatican Council II, a span that suggests the wide range of possibilities. A similar variety of interpretation obtains with respect to the symbol of the covenant.

This variety of interpretation, obviously, is a major characteristic of the basic symbols, political, domestic, and organic, that have been used to indicate the societal consequences of respective interpretations of the divine mandate for man not only in secular society but also in ecclesiastical polity. Accordingly, one can find most of the spectrum of social theories under the rubric of each of these types of symbol, the spectrum from spiritual anarchism to monolithic authoritarianism.

The symbol that has exhibited a greater consistency of interpretation is the psychological symbol, the Holy Spirit. We have already referred to Joachim di Fiore's conception of the Third Era, the period of the new freedom under the aegis of the Holy Spirit. In general, the sanction of the Holy Spirit has been appealed to in order to break through rigid bureaucracy and to promote individual freedom. We think here of the outpourings of the Spirit in the sixteenth- and seventeenth-century Radical Reformation, in eighteenth- and nineteenth-century revivalism, and in contemporary charismatic leadership and in glossalalia. Radicalizing Rudolf Sohm's conception of charisma in opposition to law, Max Weber constructed his typology of authority, making charismatic authority the innovating power that repeatedly in history breaks through traditional and legal structures. The societal impact of conceptions of the Spirit is thus shown to be a fundamental and recurrent factor in the history of social organization.

The crucial roles that societal images play gives us reason to assert that in employing the method suggested by the pragmatic theory of meaning our typologies of religious perspectives are quite inadequate if we do not take into account the implications of these various perspectives for the spheres of both the subjective and the objective virtues. It is unfortunate that such a fruitful typology as that of H. Richard Niebuhr in *Christ and Culture*, with its articulation of the different types of piety—Christ above Culture, Christ in Culture, Christ Transforming Culture, etc.—does not examine the different kinds of social organization promoted by these different types of piety. Similar types of social theory appear under the different rubrics of Niebuhr's general typology. Insofar as this is true, we may suspect that a full application of the pragmatic theory of meaning cannot be effected in terms of the types as Niebuhr defines them. But no one knew this better than Niebuhr himself. Indeed, if one wishes to find an exemplification of the pragmatic theory of meaning in the sociological sphere, one finds it ready to hand in his volume, *The Kingdom of God in America*, where he gives explicit attention to what he calls "institutionalizing the kingdom." But the point I am stressing is that typologies should include the spectrum of social-organizational, that is, of institutional consequences of the various types of piety as they find expression in integrating images. In large degree these consequences, as we have seen, are related to metaphorical images.

Whitehead, in speaking of metaphors, asserts that the fundamental choice for the metaphysician is the selection of a ruling metaphor to express his conception of reality, and he makes a strong case for the claim. He calls this procedure the method of imaginative rationality, the devising of hypotheses whereby pervasive elements and structures may be discerned. He shows, for example, how metaphors drawn from mathematics have dominated in one period and from biology in another. His own metaphysics is based upon metaphors drawn from the spheres of psychology and biology, metaphors that he explicates in his panpsychic organicism. Insofar as these central symbols play a role in his ethics, the pragmatic theory of meaning raises the question as to the psychological and sociological consequences of the use of these metaphors.

The reference to Whitehead's method reminds us that the great integrating metaphors of Christian ethics that have influenced human behavior may not properly be studied or understood by means of a narrow conceptual analysis. They by no means have alone influenced behavior. Two things we have already hinted at must be mentioned here again. First, the metaphor has to be understood in the context of convictions about the nature of man and God, the nature of history, the nature and content of faith. Indeed, the entire Gestalt of Christian theology and piety must be taken into account if the inner meaning of a particular metaphor is to be properly understood. This consideration makes the application of the pragmatic theory of meaning much less simple than the formulation of the theory at first suggests.

The second consideration is, as we have already indicated, that in order to be effective an integrating idea or metaphor possessing social-ethical implications must be given articulation in a particular historical situation. It cannot be adequately explicated in a social vacuum. Let us take an example from Ernst Troeltsch, namely, the historical situation in which a reigning conservatism is faced with protesting movements. Troeltsch's characterization of conservatism is a masterly one. Conservatism, generally employing an organic metaphor, emphasizes above all, he says, the "natural inequalities" of men. Ethical values are derived from the *acceptance* of these inequalities. For these values conservatism claims the support of a realism that is not blinded by optimistic enthusiasm. The power structure, the separation of the classes, the need for strong leadership, the fundamental skepticism regarding the wisdom of the populace, are taken to be the dispositions that God has given to men; only in the context of this hierarchical structure does the conservative expect to achieve the good life. The powers that have historically evolved are to be regarded as God's ordinances to which one must submit as to a divine institution. They exist by the grace of God and demand submission. The recognition of sin should engender humility, readiness to be obedient and to be faithful to assigned tasks. A struggle for power on the part of the lower classes in order to change the system is the consequence of sin. Those in control of power maintain it by force in the service of God and the community. Through their service the natural process is to be purified and ennobled. Freedom for the average Christian is inner freedom. It can never become the principle of a political structure. The maintenance of the system is itself taken to be the will of God.

Now, in the face of this philosophy of conservatism a protesting movement must select symbolically powerful concepts if success is to be expected. The countersymbols selected will be calculated to undermine the religious sanctions claimed by the conservatives and to provide sanctions for fundamental social change. This means that the countersymbols must serve a dual purpose: first they must reconceptualize the conservatism and thus show its injustice; and second, they must point in new directions. In both of these processes a pragmatic theory of meaning will attempt to function; first to show the inadequacy of the previous symbolism (largely by reason of its institutional consequences), and second to provide symbols that point in the direction of new institutional forms. A characteristic bifurcation can appear in this process. It may be that the countersymbols employed will serve primarily as radical criticism of the old régime and will be somewhat irrelevant or ineffective for purposes of positive construction. Moreover, a new constructive symbolization may in turn lend itself to opposite or at least to divergent interpretations. Here again bifurcation appears. Both of these types of bifurcation can be illustrated by the familiar example of the Declaration of Independence in relation to the constitutional convention that followed the Revolution. The symbols of the Declaration for the most part were effective in making attack upon the old régime. But additional symbols were required "in order to form a more perfect union." And then division appeared again. Indeed, the same symbols were appealed to in order to define the more perfect union in varying ways. In these processes differing applications of the pragmatic theory of meaning came to the fore. In all of this we see a general feature of social change; namely, that new symbols and their pragmatic meaning always take their shape in face of a particular historical situation and in face of a previously regnant symbolism. History is made by latching onto what already has happened and onto what is occurring. Accordingly, the study of the pragmatic meaning of symbols cannot be adequately undertaken merely through the analysis of concepts, as though history proceeded from book to book or from theorem to theorem. It requires analysis of concepts in their contingent social situation and in terms of the social functions of the symbols, old and new.

There is no evidence that Peirce or James or Wittgenstein or Braithwaite has been concerned about this kind of analysis, particularly as it relates to the institutional consequences of belief or of symbols. Here we may observe that in general two kinds of answers have been offered by others, and not only by Christians. Each of those answers gives a special twist to the notion that the consequences of religious belief should appear in the realm of institutions. The first answer is that the demand for institutionalization requires the slow transformation of institutions. This is the answer of gradualism, of piece-by-piece transformation. One may call this the meroscopic answer, the attack upon crucial parts or segments of the problem. The second answer is that the entire system must be transformed. This second is the revolutionary or systemic or holoscopic answer.

It must be recognized, however, that institutionalization has an ambiguous character. It may give order to social existence, but it may also impose intolerable fetters. A certain type of religious belief may in a given situation only serve to increase rigidity, to sanction petrification. Religious belief of this sort may simply redouble the intensity of adherence to the Establishment, where improved means serve unimproved ends. Here nothing fails like success. The outcome may exemplify Howard Becker's definition of primitive religion: that set of motor habits that induces automatic resistance to change. This kind of religion finds illustration in the use that, alas, has been made of every one of the symbols we have discussed. Often the outcome represents an ethos quite contrary to that which prevailed at the beginning of a movement. Max Weber had in mind this kind of exploitation of symbols when he said that the Protestant Ethic began with a doctrine of freedom in the demand for freedom of vocation and has ended by imprisoning us in the iron cage of "specialists without spirit."

Despite the ambiguities of institutionalization, we must be wary of the claim that social change simply requires a change of attitude. Attitudes do not necessarily find expression in institutional criticism and change. At least they do not do so soon enough. Something of this sort must be said about the currently burgeoning theology of hope. A theology of hope that does not indicate the specific institutional changes that are required is not yet a theology that follows through to the consequences of religious belief. It can leave us in the mood of Augustine when he prayed, "O God, make me chaste, but not yet." White suburbia today is bursting with new attitudes and with new hope but not with importunate demand for social change.

Troeltsch's description of the theology of conservatism may seem at first blush to be of something far away and long ago. But it is a transcription not only of the eighteenth-century *ancien régime*. It is a transcription also of the system of apartheid in South Africa. And for certain contingents of the Black Power movement in the United States it is a description not only of the racist system of discrimination but also of the system that keeps almost a quarter of the nation in poverty and dependency. Further, contemporary feminists can easily recognize the contours of this theology in everyday patterns of male-female relations.

If we ask the question how we are to get out of the cages in which we live, cages that are gilded with racism and sexism, we all recognize that a crucial question is that of the redistribution of power. The means to overcome our "unconquered past" of racism and sexism brings us to two fundamental aspects of our problem of the consequences of religious belief.

I.   The consequences of religious belief will depend largely upon the distribution of power and whether or not the consequences are intended. If the social system is monolithic, the prevailing religious belief will have monolithic consequences. A different sort of consequence can issue only from a separation of powers that opens the space for new religious belief and for new consequences. It is a striking fact that already in the Bible one can discover this sort of shift again and again taking place. The late Henri Frankfort discerned this separation of powers in the advent of the idea of a double covenant. The prophets, he pointed out, stood on the covenant of Jahwe with the people, and they attacked the monarchy for its betrayal of its own covenant with Jahwe. Max Weber has suggested that the Hebrew prophets, by not being attached to the court, represent an anticipation of the modern free press.

Likewise, the early Christian community broke with the Establishment, and as much with the Roman as with the Jewish Establishment. They insisted that religious organization must be independent of the civic power. These early Christians also made membership in the community transcend class, ethnic, and familial status. In short, the Christians formed a new kind of association as the proclaimer of a new freedom in Christ and an exhibition of the institutional consequence of their belief in this freedom. Thus the association could be at the same time the bearer and the institutional exemplification of its own message. An analogous outcome is to be seen in the institutional consequences of Athanasian orthodoxy at Nicaea. The Athanasians rejected the idea that the emperor, along with Christ, was a mediator: they forbade the emperor to sit in the chancel, restricting him to the nave; the arrangements were institutional consequences of religious belief. We can trace this pattern down the centuries as it recurrently challenges a monolithic Establishment—in the conciliar movement, in the abolition of the monolithic idea of "Christendom" (the dependence of civil rights upon religious confession), in the struggle for "comprehension" and for Nonconformity and Independency, in the *ecclesiola in ecclesia,* in the idea and institutional implementation of the priesthood of all believers, in the autonomy of pietistic groups, in the encouragement of freedom of inquiry, in the development of dissenting academies, in the encouragement and defense of trades unions, and in the current civil rights and womens' movements. Analogous tendencies have appeared in Roman Catholicism—initially in the emergence of religious orders, later in the principle of subsidiarity, in the responsibilities assigned to collegial configurations, and in the lay apostolate. All of these institutional consequences of religious belief have served to disperse power and responsibility. The divisions of power were at the same time consequences and causes, consequences of religious conviction and conditions for the emergence of new convictions in new situations, in short, for the emergence of mutual criticism. In the main they presuppose that no one configuration of authority and power can be trusted.

II.   What we have said of the significance of the division of power for the sake of the freedom of religious belief to find new

institutional incarnation, may also be said regarding the importance of this division for the sake of the criticism of ethical ideals.
If no single configuration of power may be trusted, so also no
single ethical idea or virtue may be adopted as final or trustworthy.
William Hazlitt once said that the trouble with the man with one
idea is not that he has an idea—that is rare enough. The trouble is
that he has no other. That way lies demonry. "In my father's house
are many mansions." Accordingly, the consequence of religious
belief under a sovereign God must always be a rejection of idolatry
before any *one* ethical idea and a promotion of "free trade" and
tension among ideals. Following Pascal, we might call this the
ethos of opposite virtues. According to him, the Christian has the
obligation to exhibit opposite virtues and to occupy the distance
between them. That is, we confront the obligation to pursue
simultaneously the opposite virtues of freedom and order, freedom
and equality, participation and privacy, and justice and mercy.
Because of the tension among the demands in the open situation, it
should be clear that either in the sphere of subjective virtues or in
that of objective, institutional virtues any attempt to deduce
precise pragmatic judgments from a given creedal position is likely
to be overzealous in intention and to reveal ideological taint—the
desire to protect special privilege. Nonetheless, it is generally
possible to advocate various social-ethical emphases or pragmatic
meanings that derive from differing creedal positions. But the
divisions and tensions of which we have spoken remain.

These divisions and tensions have never been more nobly or
more powerfully depicted than by Giotto in the murals of the
Arena Chapel at Padua. This chapel is a brick box, barrel-vaulted
within. Over the chancel Giotto painted the Eternal, surrounded by
swaying angels, and listening to the counterpleas of Justice and
Mercy concerning doomed mankind; the Archangel Gabriel is
serenely awaiting the message that should bring Christ to Mary's
womb and salvation to earth. This is the Prologue. Opposite on the
entrance wall is the Epilogue—a last judgment, with Christ
enthroned as Supreme Judge and Redeemer amid the Apostles.
These tensions within the divine economy bespeak the tensions
and contrarieties that belong to the human condition as well.
Without them, religious belief and the consequences of religious

belief are doomed to degenerate into deformity, disillusion, and destruction, and to call forth from the Stygian depths both hybris and nemesis. For, ultimately, the consequences of religious belief are not in our hands.

THE SOURCES OF human action are not only rooted in the theological and the social dimensions of life. Nor are tests of human meaning limited to the symbolic and the pragmatic; there are personal and aesthetic touchstones of meaning as well. But, contrary to much contemporary psychology and art criticism, these sources are not a realm apart. Adams would agree with those who argue that the personal is real, but he would say that it is also inseparable from the social dimensions of existence. He would agree that art has intrinsic purposes "for its own sake," but would also affirm that every artistic expression of greatness involves a pertinence to the life situations of real people. In these regards, he sees the deeper aspects of aesthetic experience as profoundly similar to religious experience, for both involve interpretations of the fundamental meanings of life. The next two chapters illustrate the interactions between personal and social dimensions of reality and between religious and aesthetic interpretations of life.*—M.L.S.

CHAPTER 9 · ART, PSYCHE, AND SOCIETY

THE GREAT ARTIST is capable of grasping and depicting in imaginative fashion the various dimensions of the human condition. In doing so the artist may point to something universal in the human situation, express something characteristic of the period in the history of culture, or give utterance to some peculiar perspective or vision of life, form, or color.

The Swiss sculptor and painter Alberto Giacometti in his depiction of the human person presents all three of these perspectives, but especially the perception of a pervasive element of experience in our time—man's alienation from an oppressive social order. Giacometti portrays the human figure as a lonely entity, extremely slender and elongated, rough and attenuated. A small head is connected to small feet by means of a very thin line of body.

There was a time when I all too casually assumed that the elongated thinness of these figures was simply an arbitrary mark of Giacometti's style, conditioned by his use of clay on a metal armature. But one day on a visit to the Tate Gallery in London I

* The essay in this chapter appeared in the *Perkins Journal*, vol. 26, no. 1 (Fall 1972), pp. 17–24. It has been edited somewhat for its inclusion here.

found in the catalogue a more authentic interpretation. "The thinness," we are told, "is to emphasize the space around the figure, which seems to press in upon it." Most of Giacometti's figures are "tensely vertical and motionless, as if they were vibrating in their stillness." Their "rigid frontality" gives them a "curious feeling of remoteness and isolation." Others too saw deeper meanings in his work. Writing of the distance that surrounds each of the sculptor's figures Jean-Paul Sartre once said:

> What is this encircling distance . . . but that negative notion, the *void*? Giacometti sees the void everywhere. Not everywhere you will protest. There are objects in contact. But that's just it, Giacometti is sure of nothing, not even of that; for whole weeks together he has been entranced by the legs of a chair; they did not *touch* the floor. Between things, between men, the bridges are down; the void creeps in everywhere, every creature secretes its own void.

Here, then, the sculptor depicts the almost unendurable pressure of society on the cramped psyche, bespeaking an acute hostility between the psyche and society and also an awareness of the absurdity of the alienation. Because of the alienation evident in his work Giacometti has been called an existentialist sculptor. He interprets human existence as a conflict of spaces, a conflict between psychological and social space; the individual yearns for an ampler space, both psychological and social.

At this point, you may be tempted to say that these interpretations are too heavy a load for these little sculptures to bear. But we should remember that by working in stone or wood or clay every sculptor inevitably deals with spatial relations, no matter what the subject. He is obliged to say what he has to say by ordering or interpreting space. Modern abstract painting and sculpture have centered attention almost exclusively upon spatial relations without reference to any specific subject, thus starkly presenting spaces in tension and in coordination with each other. We may recall here that the eighteenth-century dramatist and art critic Gotthold Ephraim Lessing defined the arts of painting and sculpture as confined to the use of signs (or lines) in spatial relations.

I would like to suggest that implicit in Giacometti's sculptures are the rudiments of a theology of psychological and social space. Moreover, if we go beyond his conception of the conflicts between these kinds of spaces, we may encounter cosmic space, and even the transcendent that lies beyond and within all spaces—beyond and yet impinging upon them.

This reference to the transcendent leads us beyond the perspective of Giacometti insofar as a theology of space is concerned. The first or the last word of a theology of space is not the word conflict. In any theology we look for a unifying, integrating perspective that not only informs the spaces in themselves but also appears in the voids before they existed and after they cease to exist—in the proton and the eschaton. Here a transcendent reference is given to both space and time. While we cannot at the moment explore the temporal perspectives, let us consider briefly the spatial dimension in its relation to the transcendent. This relationship is familiar in the history of religions, and specifically in the multifarious mythologies that tell the stories of the actions of the gods.

RELIGIOUS IDEAS OF SPACE

In the mythology of the Achilpa of Australia, for example, a divine being initially gave order to space. In Mircea Eliade's phrase, this divine being had "cosmicized" their territory, giving it a place in the cosmic order; it also created their ancestors and founded their institutions. At the center of the territory was the cosmic axis, and around it the land became habitable. Thus the very fact of being in the world of space possesses a religious value stemming from its relation to the cosmic axis. To *live* in space is to participate in the cosmic axis. If contact with the axis, the transcendent, is broken off and the spatial orientation is thus disrupted, the Achilpa "let themselves die."

I once visited the large city of Tenri in Japan, which is entirely under the control of the Tenri cult, one of the "new religions" of Japan. In the major shrine is a representation of the cosmic axis; the center of the world is believed to be right there. Again we discern an integrating, unifying, transcending power. In this cosmic perspective, however, conflict is not ignored. Often the sacred cosmic space or axis is believed to have been created after a struggle between a divine and an evil (or demonic) principle. One is reminded of the Old Testament myth of the creation of spatial order, which occurred only as a consequence of God's overcoming chaos. And we also recall that in the New Testament the Kingdom of Heaven is viewed as a dynamic power still engaged in a cosmic struggle against demonic powers.

In contrast to these primitive attempts to find and express meaning by reference to a center of social space, Giacometti perceives contemporary humanity as having no reliable basis on which to order and delineate the space around us. Hence, the space invades and presses in upon us unchallenged. Giacometti's humanity is oppressed by social space and yearns for the ampler space of individual freedom. This struggle for social space against contending powers is one of the oldest themes of our history; one of the earliest examples is the story of the Exodus from Egypt. This striving initially takes the form of protest, as echoed in American black folklore:

Go down, Moses,
Way down in Egyptland
Tell old Pharaoh
To let my people go.

These are fighting words: "Go down, Moses, and tell old Pharaoh . . ." But Moses does not go down alone; God is on his side, or rather, he is on God's side. He is emboldened by a transcendent reference (a burning bush) that not only gives him the courage to be but also the courage to struggle for emancipation.

According to the biblical narrative, the power of God was working in its most characteristic and decisive way when the children of Israel were being liberated from bondage in Egypt. In the biblical conception, this evidence of the power of God in history recurs innumerable times. Hence, the Exodus of the Old Testament has been called the first Exodus, and the appearance of Jesus Christ and the primitive church, the second.

The theme of Exodus is not only that of release from slavery; it is also the theme of being led through the wilderness into freedom; it is liberation from an old space, "the house of bondage" and also the conquest of a new and ampler space. The Exodus leads to the conquest of land, of a land that is to be called the Holy Land. Just as oppression requires space, so also does emancipation and consolidation. Moreover, the release from bondage is powered by self-determination, in obedience to the Lord of history. In this story we see a multiple conflict of spaces—first the conflict with Pharaoh, and later the conflict with the Canaanites. In this connection we should observe that the word "Hebrew" may be derived from a name for a social class of displaced persons (including political refugees), a group of people rising from oppression within a society, or even a sort of pressure group. All of these from time to time have sought to win fellow travelers in support of emancipation.

This aspect of Hebrew experience can be traced back to the patriarchs, to Abraham's response to God's call to leave the land of his fathers—Ur of the Chaldees—where (scholars tell us) he and his clan may have been oppressed at the hands of an idolatrous moon-god cult. The theme of release from bondage is also familiar in American history, beginning with the Pilgrims who were escaping from an old space of tyranny and seeking a new space of freedom. The blacks in America for over a century have been singing, "Go down, Moses," and some radical contemporary feminists are seeking an Exodus from the present religious establishments in a search for "sisterhood." This search for space is the fundamental thrust of freedom, of self-determination.

THE SOCIALITY OF SPACE

Now there are four features of freedom that should be stressed here. As we list them we shall assume that the relation between the psyche and society is not merely the relation of a lone individual to society; for psychological space is meaningless and ineffectual if it belongs to and is used only for the benefit of the isolated individual. Freedom for the individual is tied necessarily to the freedom of other individuals; the very act of defining freedom is a social process and action, and the achievement and maintenance of that freedom requires not only space for the individual but also shared space. The individual in a Giacometti sculpture cannot alone recover or extend space. Thus, psychological space requires social space. If freedom does not have a shared space, it will—if it exists at all—be a vanishing space. Unshared space is precisely the space that totalitarian society assigns to the individual as a way of boxing him in.

The first criterion, then, of freedom for the individual in relation to society is that it requires the creation of a space; it requires its own turf, its own toehold, its own *terra firma* in face of dominating powers in the surrounding territory. In our day this means economic resources and political and economic rights—a dwelling, a job, freedom to move and to associate—enabling the individual to occupy a space in which he or she can make choices, choices that concern not only the individual's privacy but also a concrete relationship to society. The title of a recent book by Robert Ardrey asserts this requirement in a succinct phrase, *The Territorial Imperative.* For all the problematic character of certain aspects of his argument, his imperative reflects an Old Testament theme known as the motif of "the conquest of the land."

The first criterion involves a second. Since a viable space is a shared space, effective freedom must be a collective phenomenon. In a territorial system, neither freedom nor emancipation from tyranny is possible for the isolated individual. Giacometti seems to recognize this fact when he depicts the isolation of the individual as a form of social impotence. In his sculpture entitled "Four Figurines on a Tall Stand" the relationship between the figures is, as Sartre pointed out, "a purely formal one like that between strangers in a street." Psychological space, if unsupported by social space, is an illusion. Psychological space supported by social space and social space supported by psychological space gives power to freedom—power in the sense of capacity to participate in the making of social decisions regarding public policy.

But the effectiveness of freedom in power is not a casual, ad hoc affair. The third criterion of effective freedom, therefore, is that it requires an institutional framework or space. The history of effective freedom in the relation of the individual to society is not the history of individuals asserting self-descrimination. It is the history of the institutionalization of freedom, the institutionalization of the process whereby freedom is defined, protected, redefined and extended in the changing historical situation. It is through this process that abuses perpetrated in the name of freedom can be exposed and corrected. Repeatedly the struggle for freedom is a struggle against an institutional system that oppresses; and the goal of the struggle is not to abolish institutions as such but provide new social and institutionalized space for those who have been deprived of it. Often the struggle takes place with those who are fighting to prevent others from sharing their freedom. In a system oriented to justice, however, no one is free until all are free. In the institutional arena the good will of the isolated individual is not sufficient. Adopting the current idiom used by blacks and women, we may say that both oppression and freedom from it are "systemic"; accordingly, blacks speak of the built-in racism of our institutions. The geography of the self in society is determined by the creative involvement of the individual in groups concerned with the criticism and transformation of institutions.

Fourth, from a religious perspective, authentic freedom is not the opposite of being under oppression, domination, or alien control. It is response, as with Abraham and Moses, to a call, to a divine initiative. Freedom at its most profound levels is, ironically, closer to responsibility and purpose than to license and anomie. Both the ability to respond and the sense of purpose are perceived as deriving from sources beyond and proceeding to immediate empirical realities. The appropriate response is participation in a "divinely given" creative process that makes for a social order of justice and mercy. Effective freedom, then, has a transcendent reference.

These four features are manifest, as we have already suggested, in the Hebrew experience. The liberation from bondage—the first Exodus—was a collective enterprise leading to the formation of a nation. With the emergence of Christianity, however, a new interpretation came to birth, a demand made by a subgroup within the territory rather than by a nation. That was the second Exodus. In order to find living space, the early Christians had to struggle for space within the Roman Empire. Initially, no legal space was available to them; there was no room for them as an association, as an institution. According to Roman law, no legitimate association could exist without license and control from the state. The Christians were unwilling to meet the requirements; that is, they were unwilling to worship Caesar and the gods of the civil religion. Tertullian tells us that as a consequence the churches were viewed as illegal. Moreover, their members were considered blasphemous, for they appealed to a sanction and authority transcending the state. Here, then, we see the four features I have mentioned. The primitive church, seeking a new space, was a collective enterprise; it demanded institutional, systemic space; and it claimed a higher sanction than the territory—a transcendent sanction. This new principle found expression in later centuries when the struggle for separation of church and state was renewed.

OBSTRUCTIONS TO HUMANE SPACE

Our central concern at the moment, however, is the relation between the individual and society. Having examined the demand for a cooperation between psychological and social space, we should raise the question of the principal impediments to such cooperation; and I think we may venture a fairly simple answer to the question. One principal obstruction is the cult of privatization, which, is by no means to be viewed only with lament. If, on the one hand, the achievement of justice in a territory involves the institutionalization of freedom in the public sector, the achievement of integrity for the human person requires the interiorization of a value system, the interiorization of piety in the individual. In a highly organized, technological society engineered by the mass media, the struggle for psychological space, for a private inner life, is acute. The overadjusted man knows only the public life; he is bent on being a marketable personality, a good mixer. Robert Frost used to tell about his problem as a college student. He was awaiting admittance to a student fraternity and was told confidentially that only one factor was delaying his entry: the fact that he took long walks in the woods by himself. He had been "caught redhanded engaging in solitude."

Yet, it would be false to assume that the inner life of the individual can be significant if it is only a form of isolationism. Martin Luther once said that when the Christian is in the closest of prayer Christ and the church are there with him. So the cultivation of the inner life itself requires community and discipline if it is to be a means of grace.

But it is not this community of the devout life for the individual and the family and the prayer circle that gives the cult of privatization its bad name. It is rather the identification of piety with merely personalistic religion; that is, it is the identification of piety with Pietism.

Pietism is the restriction of religion to the immediate relations between the individual and God and to interpersonal relations. In Pietism the relation to God is a one-to-one relation between the individual soul and God and between the individual and other individuals—that is, with the other "saints." Whether in the Orient or the Occident, Pietism of this sort wrongly assumes that if the individual is on the path to Nirvana or is devoted to personal meditation or gives his life to the Jesus of personal piety, he does not need to be concerned directly with institutional existence. The problems of institutions, we are told, will take care of themselves if everyone would only adopt this religion of personal salvation.

This view of piety amounts to religious spatialization. On its ethical side, religion has to do only with personal behavior; it is not concerned with, or responsible for, the analysis and transformation of institutional behavior—as though the two could be separated! This spatialization puts God in a box, and he is told: so far you may go, but no further. This spatialization is a denial of the sovereignty of God over the whole of life, and thus it is a form of idolatry. It confines God to our personal existence and in effect leaves the rest of the world, the suprapersonal public life, to the principalities and powers of this world. Indeed, it often makes close alliance with these powers of nation, class, and race. (We are reminded of how Nixon summoned a serviceable chaplain to the White House for "personal ministry.")

Malcolm Boyd speaks of this alliance as "the cult of the Potomac." By this cult, he says, "salvation of the 'soul' is given priority over the bodily condition of men, women and children. . . . The Second Coming of a white Christ is a more pressing reference point than Jesus in the streets, on battlefields, or inside prisons." In the cult of the Potomac as well as in that of existentialist narcissism, the new sharing of space is deferred indefinitely. The proponents tend to be well-fed.

Let me give another example or two of the spatialization of piety. If you look at the famous book by William James entitled *The Varieties of Religious Experience* you find that James restricts his attention almost entirely to the type of religion and also of conversion that changes only the life of the individual. Very seldom does he deal with the type of piety or of conversion that makes an impact upon social institutions—upon the economic or the political order. Not long ago I had occasion at the Harvard College library to make use of a volume from the private library of William James; it was a copy of Baron Friedrich von Huegel's *The Mystical Element of Religion.* Folded into this volume I discovered a long letter from Von Huegel, thanking James for having sent to him a copy of *The Varieties.* After expressing grateful indebtedness for this work, Von Huegel goes on to speak of his "dissatisfactions." "I continue to feel," he says, that "your taking of the religious experience as separate from its institutional, historical occasions and environment to be schematic, *a priori*, not what your methods so concrete and *a posteriori*, seem to demand." Von Huegel concludes by saying that if James in *The Varieties* had presented this broader, institutional dimension of religion, "the result, I think, would have been of greater permanent value and instructiveness." We must add that James' book does not really deal with the varieties of religious experience, for it is highly selective; it scarcely recognizes the existence of prophetic religion. It deals with the impact of religion upon personal vices and virtues. With regard to prophetism, Ernst Troeltsch has observed that the Old Testament prophets rail not so much against personal sins as against sins of institutions. From their perspective, the covenant with the Lord of history entails responsibility for the total character of the society (though, as in the Psalms, it includes also the interiorization of piety). The cult of privatization is a pious form of turning away from the Lord of history. And to the adherents of this cult, the Old Testament prophets of that Lord would say, "Return ye."

One must recognize, however, that privatization is in part a revulsion against the enormous, seemingly unmanageable, uncontrollable powers of the economic or the political or the ecclesiastical sphere. Nonetheless, this explanation does not relieve anyone of responsibility for the correction of the institutional system in which the individual is caught. Nor does it justify the sort of "copping out" that is frequent among certain segments of the youth culture. Nor does it justify the secularized form of Pietism that is manifest in the psychiatric practice that practices psychotherapy to the neglect of sociotherapy—that is, the therapy that leads directly to a sense of responsibility to transform the builtin diseases of institutions. Here we see the imperialism of a psychology that crowds out sociology and social ethics.

Freud and Jung, Kierkegaard, Heidegger and Bultmann, Billy Graham, and Norman Vincent Peale—all promote the cult of privatization. Each in his way "secretes his own void"—alas, at the same time making alliance with strange half-gods, either directly or by default. This is not the path of the authentic liberation that creates new psychological and social-institutional space. The modern novel, insofar as it is concerned with interpersonal and family relationships, is similarly inauthentic. The same thing may be said of much pastoral psychology and practice. The military-industrial-university-church complex has nothing to fear from these truncated, narcissistic conquests of space.

THERAPY AND PROPHECY

In the nineteenth century transition from Pietism to Prophetism is to be found an instructive example of a more positive relation between the self and society, in the transition from the perspectives of the Pietist Lutheran pastor Johann Christoph Blumhardt— father of modern pastoral care in Germany—to the perspectives of his son, Christoph Blumhardt the Younger. As a result of his studies of the Gospels, the elder Blumhardt concluded that Jesus' concern to cast out the demons of psychological pathology was a mandate for the kinds of pastoral care that, through faith and faith-healing, promotes the mental health of the individual. Later (in 1899), his son came to the view that the demonic element in the personal life of the individual must be understood in relation to demonic elements in the political and economic sphere, not only for the sake of mercy but also for the sake of social justice. In his view, the whole world, and not simply the individual soul, is the arena of the battle of the Kingdom of God against the principalities and powers of this world. The powers of darkness, the demonic powers, inhabit and "possess" nations, economic and political institutions, and even churches. The realm of the demonic, Blumhardt saw, belongs not only to the psychosomatic realm but also to the social-institutional sphere of class tensions, where men are struggling for bread and justice, and where others—in the name of God and Christ—oppose this struggle or are indifferent to it. These men, he saw, were struggling for social space, for a share in the territory.

Here I am reminded of the words of Frantz Fanon. In his book, *The Wretched of the Earth* (1968), he says: "For a colonized people the most essential value, because the most concrete, is first and foremost the land: the land which will bring them bread, and, above all, dignity."

Blumhardt the Younger asserted that the Kingdom of God may at times find itself obstructed by the churches and that God may be working incognito among the atheists and the Marxists. He therefore shocked his contemporary Lutherans, and especially the

Pietists, by joining the Social Democratic party, the first pastor in Germany to do so. And in doing so he at least in principle showed the authentic way of the psyche to society. For him (and why not also for us?) the Kingdom of God is a call for the transformation of the whole of life. To the social activist who has no inner life, no personal commitment to the God of the inner temple, and to the Pietist who has no commitment to the promotion of righteousness in the institutions of the public sphere, he would say: A plague on both your houses; each of you has spatialized the work of God, and thus has reduced the God of all life to a demonic and dangerous idol.

Both these gospels—for example, that of Kierkegaard and his heritage (both religious and secular) and that of the "vulgar Marxists"—is lopsided. In a formal sense, what the Marxists possess the Kierkegaardians lack, and vice versa. The geography of the self must embrace the self, not only in its immediate relation to God and to other persons but also in its relation to the social-institutional space in which our lives are cast. Only when these spheres are taken together can authentic Christian vocation find its place under the God who is sovereign of all. This vocation, then, is the way from the psyche to society and back again.

Giacometti epitomized contemporary man as an isolated being pressed upon from all sides. Pietism, both religious and secular, seeks out this alienated, lost man to offer him salvation in a restricted territory of restricted humanity and restricted responsibility. The young Blumhardt realized that the way of the Kingdom of God is through the larger dimensions of humanity's nature to the finding of a transcendent identity in the geography of the institutions that impinge upon us and our fellows.

The thrust of liberation from perversion and oppression is toward a commonly shared space, and it succeeds not without dust and heat in the wilderness, and even then only partially. We can only dimly see the Promised Land. Yet, in solidarity, we are no longer merely isolates, victimized and oppressed by the voids pressing in on us.

IN ESSAYS addressed to different audiences, Adams has spelled out what he believes to be the sources and tests of human action, often with specific reference to social behavior and social or political situations. Cultural actions involving both "projections" and "introjections" are properly understood as genuine actions by him. Action, indeed, involves the capacity to receive, to absorb and appropriate things that are beyond us, as well as the capacity to reach out and alter the world around us. Perhaps no essay captures this dimension of Adams' thought better than the sermon on music that follows.*—M.L.S.

CHAPTER 10 · MUSIC AS A MEANS OF GRACE

> When the morning stars sang together, and all the children of God shouted for joy.   Job 38:7

> And round the throne are four living creatures, and these four living creatures, each of them with six wings, day and night never cease to sing, "Holy, Holy, Holy."   Revelation 4:6–8

IT IS STRIKING that the authors of these two passages cannot conceive of the beginning or the end of the world without music—at the beginning the morning stars sing together, and at the end the living creatures never cease to sing, "Holy, holy, holy." Music in all ages and cultures has been closely associated with religion, with primitive religion and with the higher religions. But it has a special connection with high religion.

No theologian in the history of Christianity has given a higher place to music than did Martin Luther. "I most heartily desire," he said, "that music, that divine and most precious gift, be praised and extolled before all people. I am so completely overwhelmed by the quantity and greatness of its excellence and virtues that I can find neither beginning nor end nor adequate words or expressions to say what I ought." "A person who does not regard music as a marvelous creation of God, must be a clodhopper indeed and does not deserve to be called a human being; he should be permitted to hear nothing but the braying of asses and the grunting of hogs."

* First published in the *Crane Review* (Fall 1967), pp. 42–45.

"Next to the Word of God," he said, "the noble art of music is the greatest treasure in the world. . . . There is no art its equal."

In Luther's view, the corrupting influence of Satan is helpless against this power, for "music alone can do what otherwise only theology can accomplish, namely quiet and cheer up the soul of man." Indeed, he says that music cannot be explained as an achievement of men but only as a gift, a creation of God given to men.

Luther even ventured to set forth a theology of music. Moreover, he helped to maintain the study of music as an integral part of education. "Those who have mastered this art are made of good stuff; they are fit for any task. . . . A teacher must be able to sing; otherwise I will not so much as look at him." Luther was the author of thirty-seven chorales. We do not know how many or for which of them he also wrote the music. But one could say that Luther sang the people into the Reformation. Certainly, Germany's accomplishments in music cannot be understood apart from him. Partly under his influence the organ became closely associated with the chorale, "Der Tanz im Himmel."

Music has been associated not only with religion, but also with work, with play, with love both erotic and spiritual, with war, with Bacchanalian revelry, with wine, women, and song, and with all celebration whether solemn, festal, or inebriated. There are no strangers to music. Moreover, the question can be raised as to whether there is anything intrinsic in music that makes it religious or secular. What any people consider to be religious music is largely a matter of custom. The late Dr. Archibald Davison of the Harvard faculty used to remind us in the Harvard Glee Club that Händel's *Largo*, one of the most widely accepted pieces of so-called religious music, was originally incidental music for a scene in the opera *Xerxes*, a scene in which a man who has just eaten a heavy dinner sleeps it off sitting under a tree out in the garden. What is called religious music, or any other kind of music, is a matter of cultural conditioning. That proposition, I suppose, has become almost axiomatic for the musicologist.

Must we be content then to let the matter rest there? Plato, for one, would not accept such a view. Although he would by law exclude certain types of melody from the well-regulated state, he held that in authentic music there is an order that comports with ultimate reality, that consorts with the metrical harmony of the cosmos, and also with the order of the good. "The gods," he says, "who have been appointed to be our companions in the dance, have given us the pleasurable sense of harmony and rhythm; and so they stir us to life, and we follow them, joining together in dances and songs."

For Plato, authentic music also possesses a dimension of freedom. Through it men are freed from bondage to the pressing environment with its immediate claims. By means of music an ordered world, a higher and divine reality, is posited as a standard-giving environment. Whatever one may think of Plato's philosophy or metaphysics of music, he does suggest that something intrinsic, something more than merely culture-bound association, is to be encountered in music.

What a mysterious, almost fantastic, action is the creating and appreciation of music. In its purest form music is not a representational but rather a nonobjective, nonverbal world. It is a world of its own, almost a *creatio ex nihilo,* an occasion for immediacy of experience, a nonreducible mode of beauty, of contrast and resolution, of order and of ecstasy flowing through and beyond the order. Order, and ecstasy rooted in order: that sounds like the relation between law and love, law and gospel. In these qualities of music there is something more than pleasant and ordered sound, something transmusical. How is one to express this extramusical quality? Often the question is asked of an artist, what is the meaning of this piece of music? And the artist is tempted to reply simply by playing the music again. Is the playing and the listening to the music only a game, the enjoyment of contrast and its resolution? I think not. But, in a time of the breakdown of old myths and symbols, the answer perhaps communicates little that is persuasive. One could speak of a music of the innocence of creation, the music that reaffirms the song of the morning stars at the beginning of creation. One could speak of the music of the Fall, the music that expresses a sense, a metaphysical sense, of man's alienation from the innocence of creation. One could speak of the music of redemption, the music of the third movement of Stravinsky's *Symphony of Psalms,* when alienation and tragedy are overcome, yet with the sense also that there always will be alienation and tragedy and suffering. It is not hyperbole to suggest that at times the music of Bob Dylan combines these dimensions, giving utterance to the joy of creation and to the protest of youth against social evil, and also summoning one to participation in "The Times, They Are A-Changing." The same dimensions appear in the martial music of the civil rights movement: "We Shall Overcome."

The music that rouses to a new sense of promise and to new resolve serves as a judgment upon the actualities of the present and at the same time as a contemplation, a harbinger, of future fulfillment. It can also make one "calm of mind, all passion spent" if it is the music that says "Hallowed Be Thy Name, Thy Kingdom Come." The sense of frustration is the sense that humanity is made for fulfillment, that alienation, and the separation of person from person, the sad music of inhumanity of man to man, is a shadow that reminds us of the sun and of a Presence that both judges and sustains. With a special sense of immediacy and inwardness, authentic music redefines, illumines, refreshes, orders our experience. It is not escape from reality; it is rather the rediscovery of a center of meaning and power, of a center that is a symptom and sign of faith—ultimately not a human achievement but a gift of grace. In short, the authentic music of high seriousness elicits what cannot be put into words. It is a "joyful creation" that enables us to sing without words, "Holy, Holy, Holy, is the Lord who was and is and is to come."

Part III

REFRACTIONS OF MEANING

IN THIS PORTION of the volume, we turn to those figures whom Adams most consistently finds problematic and promising as he attempts to identify the themes that carry particular meaning in the modern era. These are also the thinkers to whom Adams often turns in his teaching and who owe their impact on American religious thought in part to the ways in which Adams and Adams' students have integrated their work into the training of pastors, scholars, and laity. To be sure, each of the figures treated below has his own advocates, disciples, and detractors in his own special field. Marx, the subject of the first essay,* is known for political and economic analysis; Weber is known as a sociologist; Sohm as a jurist; Troeltsch as a philosopher; and Tillich as a systematic theologian. Adams, however, is interested in that juncture where all of their work touches three issues: the nature of human existence, the center or core of all genuine religion, and the interpretation of society. Whatever the force or frailties of other dimensions of their thought, all these figures in varying ways see the interaction of the three elements, and they have set forth their views in ways that have continuing significance. Thus, by looking at these matters through the prism of each of these thinkers, Adams presents us today with refractions of meaning that can and need to be mediated into the present.—M.L.S.

CHAPTER 11 · SOCIALIST HUMANISM AND
RELIGION: KARL MARX

IN THE CONTEXT of reflections on religion and human nature, it is impossible to omit reference to the form of humanism that currently governs more countries and the lives of more people than any other. Further, it is of special importance to religion, for it is a form of humanism that is most aggressively antireligious in several respects. I refer, of course, to socialist humanism, rooted in the thought of Karl Marx.

The traditions of Western religious thought produced two great social philosophies: Thomism and Calvinism. These systems found their ultimate sanctions in a theological orientation. Both the residues of these systems and the sanctions to which they turned remain powerful in many quarters. But it is surely not wrong to

* The essay was presented at a conference at Notre Dame in 1967 and was published in Nicholas Lobkowicz, ed., *Marx and the Western World* (South Bend, Ind.: Notre Dame University Press, 1968).

suggest that Marxism is the major social philosophy that has emerged in the era of post-Christian secularism (and which has in part contributed to it).

Karl Marx apparently attributed such power to the theological sanctions of the Protestant and Catholic establishments that he was convinced that these traditions could not be radically altered without his coming to terms with theology; this he did by appealing to antitheology, that is, to atheism. For him the beginning of all criticism is the criticism of religion.

It is obvious that in important respects Marx cannot be understood without taking into account the Western religious tradition, the Judeo-Christian background. Likewise, contemporary Christianity, and particularly prophetic Christianity, cannot today be understood without recognizing the stimulus and challenge it has received at the hands of Marx and the Marxists. Because of these relationships, the question of the *relevance* of Marx for Christianity is a question that is closely bound up with a consideration of the similarities and dissimilarities between Christianity and Marxism. The similarity and dissimilarity have been given cryptic formulation in the familiar assertion that Marxism is a Christian heresy. This is only a way of saying that the one cannot be properly understood apart from the other. Still another way of expressing it is to observe that Marx himself promoted a humanism that had some of its roots in previous Judeo-Christian outlooks. Marx's humanism—his intention to promote the full realization of the potentialities of humanity—cannot be viewed as something completely unique that bears no positive relation to the previous Judeo-Christian humanism.

Certainly it is misleading if, in speaking of Marx as a materialist, one thereby assumes that his materialism is the direct opposite of everything that belongs to Judeo-Christianity. In face of this false assumption, the late Archbishop William Temple was wont to say:

> Christianity . . . is the most avowedly materialist of all the great religions. . . . Its own most central saying is: "The Word was made flesh," where the last term was, no doubt, chosen because of its specially materialistic associations. By the very nature of its central doctrine Christianity is committed to a belief in the ultimate significance of the historical process, and in the reality of matter and its place in the divine process.

We do not need here to survey the familiar delineation of the different meanings of the word *materialism*. Marx himself distinguished between dialectical materialism and the old materialism of "crude communism." It is more to my purpose to point to one of the most significant similarities between Christianity and Marxism and, in this connection, to take note of one of the most fundamental of the differences between them.

This similarity and this difference involve the biblical doctrine of creation. Here one must distinguish between the original mythological formulation of the doctrine of Creation—the narrative about the Creation of the world in six days—and the implications of the doctrine, which have been scrutinized again and again in the myth research of cultural anthropology. In its cultural implications, the biblical doctrine of creation is presupposed by Marxism, as well as by most forms of secularism in the West. In the biblical view, creation (nature and human nature) is essentially good. According to Genesis, God looked upon creation and saw that it was good. The evil in humanity or in nature does not issue from materiality. The true destiny of humanity is not to escape from flesh and time. No matter how evil we may become through the abuse of our freedom, our restoration or our fulfillment is held to be a realization that fulfills creation.

The ancient doctrine of the resurrection of the body is a mythological expression of this view, as is also the doctrine that "the Word became flesh." This positive evaluation of the material order is not something that one may simply take for granted. It had to be fought for in the earlier centuries, as against dualistic conceptions emanating from Greece and from the Orient. Even after the mythological formulations of the Book of Genesis have been abandoned or "broken," this positive evaluation has remained. In this respect we may say that modern secularism is a Judeo-Christian secularism, and this is also true for Marx.

Another aspect of the Genesis myth is worth mentioning here. From ancient days the doctrine of creation has also borne the implication that humanity is not only to subdue but also to care for, to love, the creatures of earth. Nature is not merely to be used, to be exploited, by us. This Judeo-Christian view of creation appears by implication in the view of the Yugoslav Marxist philosopher Gajo Petrovic, who rejects the idea that nature is "only a possible object of subjection and exploitation" and who asserts that true humanity requires that we shall "participate in the blessings [of nature] in a human way." This view, from a Christian perspective, is a form of Judeo-Christian secularism.

Bearing all of these things in mind, we may say that Marx presupposes the cultural implications of the Judeo-Christian doctrine of creation. But in this connection, we also encounter the most significant difference between Christianity and Marxism. The Christian doctrine of creation asserts that men, women, and nature are creatures—they depend upon a divine Creator. Not only our bodies but also our freedom and the very possibility of meaning are gifts of God's grace. If we use here a category of philosophy of religion, we may say that humanity is oriented ultimately to the transcendent. The modern Protestant does not accept literally the Old Testament myth of Creation. It is a broken myth. We do not view God the Creator as a divine being who as a separate entity brings creation into existence. The formulations of the transcendent reference have varied greatly. Indeed, one must concede that a clear and readily plausible conception of transcendence is not easy to come by. Since the time of Kant and also of Feuerbach, the popular, traditional conception of God and of transcendence has been increasingly brought into radical question by Christians themselves. This skepticism has been in part the consequence of Marx's critique of religion as ideology. By now, however, the sophisticated Marxist is aware of the fact that something more than "ideology" is in question here.

At this point, two rather obvious considerations must come into play with respect to the relations between Christianity and Marxism. On the one hand, the Christian cannot accept the secularism, the self-sufficient finitude (as Tillich called it) of Marx. On the other hand, the Marxist offers a vigorous challenge to the Christian, the challenge to give a cogent restatement of the "ground" or "object" of his faith. The issues at stake are relevant for the discussion of every major dimension of the confrontation between Christianity and Marxism, though varying formulations of the issues can be found in different branches of Judeo-Christianity. Face to face with each other, then, Christianity and Marxism have some unfinished business to conduct with regard to their respective presuppositions.

One may give historical reasons for the atheism of Marx and of dialectical materialism. One may say, for example, that atheism is an understandable and rationally or psychologically justifiable response to the *Realpolitik* of ecclesiastical powers in collusion with economic and political privilege; in short, that atheism, not only in Marxism but also in much of secularism, was a reaction that was passionately promoted for the sake of human values. In face of this situation, prophetically minded theologians have felt constrained to give positive theological significance to atheism. For example, the German pastor Christoph Blumhardt in the 1890s asserted that the Kingdom of God was being promoted better by the Marxist atheists than by the churches.

A similar transvaluation may in the end accrue to atheism within the context of Marxism itself, particularly if Marxism should live to be as old as Protestantism. The atheism of Marx himself may not be an inextricable element in Marxism. Atheism may be viewed simply as a *Kampfbegriff* contrived by Marx in order to promote revolution in face of entrenched ecclesiastical powers. The intrinsic merit of this sort of atheism may be discerned from its utility to a revolutionary movement at a given moment in history. There is a profound difference between utility and truth.

I have spoken of the disposition of the Protestant theologians to revise their own theology and even to discover positive theological significance in atheism. Marxism too has not been immune to change and to revaluation at the hands of Marxists themselves. In this connection, we should recall that the Marxist system of ideas, like the ideas of religious groups, almost inevitably changes somewhat according to the success of the movement. When Marxism was struggling to get a toehold in history, its system of ideas, including its atheism, assumed the stance of a *Kampfbegriff* promoting revolution. But in the course of time, after the revolution was successful and a new order of society was being established, Marxist ideas had to perform a new function. They figured more as a sanction for the ruling powers and for hope than as a sanction for radical criticism. This kind of shift is thoroughly familiar in the history of religion. It is usually referred to as the shift from a sect-type to a church-type of religious association (Troeltsch). The shift is somewhat analogous to the sort of change that Weber characterized as the routinization of charisma in the direction of bureaucracy. Thus in Marxism, as in other social movements, the function of ideas may change from serving as a means of protest to becoming a means of domination. The reverse trend is also possible, as for example in the current use of the Marxist concept of alienation as a basis for criticism of the communist bureaucracy. The Marxist can readily appreciate these observations because of his conception of the relation between theory and practice. Ernst Topitsch, the Heidelberg social philosopher, has pointed out that change in the social situation can bring about the transformation of a revolutionary idea into "empty formulas" *(Leerformeln)*. With the change of situation it becomes more and more difficult to connect these formulas with specific norms and with decrees being promulgated.

Not only does this process of change occur but we also encounter ideas previously overlooked or suppressed. The new concern with the concept of freedom, evident in the writings of Garaudy, Schaff, Petrovic, Rubel, Supek, and others, illustrates this trend. Moreover, one can observe in certain Marxist circles an increasing concern with metaphysics. Given freedom of discussion, one can conceive of the eventual development of concern for a revision, or deepening, of the concept of immanence that has characterized Marxist thought.

Already in the writings of Adam Schaff one encounters the recognition that an economic interpretation of history is incapable of adequately interpreting the meaning of death or even of human life as a whole. Thus we see the emergence of a new humanism in Marxism. Likewise, a Marxist might appear who would raise the radical question as to whether atheism is self-evident or is scientifically demonstrable. Science is capable of re-examining its presuppositions, insofar as its method is that of freedom of inquiry; thus Marxists might be expected eventually to raise the radical question as to whether atheism is an indispensable and integral ingredient of Marxism. Accordingly, we must take account of the possibility that atheism will not forever remain a category, or a dogma, in Marxist thought. A new and transitional crypto-metaphysics might take the form of a revised articulation of atheism issuing in what might be called neo-atheism.

Every Marxist today will perhaps view the prognostications just set forth as utterly ludicrous. But a Protestant theologian cannot properly take a rigid view of Marxist antitheological concepts any more than he can do so with respect to Christian theological concepts. The modern Protestant theologian recognizes, even with gratitude, that certain fundamental concepts of Christian theology have been subjected to radical criticism and transformation, such as the ideas of revelation, miracles, and divine providence. Many Protestant theologians would insist, with the modern scientist, that for empirical scientific investigation no attempt should be made to identify the specific action of divine agency in natural and social processes. Among some of these theologians, the doctrine of special providence has practically disappeared. More than that, in certain quarters, Protestant philosophical theology does not view theism as an acceptable solution of the problem of transcendence. Paul Tillich, for example, interprets the concept of the infinite as referring not to a being called God (alongside other beings) but rather to the infinitely inexhaustible resources in the depth of Being that are both a support and a threat to man. This disposition of some theologians to reinterpret the doctrine of transcendence contained in the doctrine of creation may be taken as an earnest of their willingness to enter into dialogue with the Marxist at the most fundamental level of presuppositions and implications.

Here we must in part reject the view of the Polish Marxist philosopher Leszek Kolakowski, who seems to define the proponent of religion ("the priest") as the "guardian of the absolute who upholds the cult of the final and the obvious contained in the tradition." Greater discrimination than this is required to achieve empirical acquaintance with the theologians. There are priests and priests. On the other hand, Kolakowski has defined a philosophical stance that the radically Protestant theologian could in part accept. In his characterization of "the jester"—whom he sees in contrast to "the priest" defined above—he desiderates the inquirer who, "although an habitué of good society, does not belong to it and makes it the object of his inquisitive impertinence; he who questions what appears to be self-evident . . . one who detects the non-obvious behind the obvious and the non-final behind what appears to be final." Kolakowski does not appear to recognize that a radically Protestant theologian views the transcendent as precisely that which stands beyond and against human self-projection into the absolute. Moreover, he lamentably gives to his "jester" a Faustian flavor. This jester comes short of displaying ultimate seriousness if he retains the Kolakowski principle of promoting a philosophy that "has no foundations and desires no roof." Apart from this limitation, the spirit of the jester, as characterized by Kolakowski, is the spirit that should inform the dialogue between

Christians and Marxists who are willing to forego the security of absolutes and are willing to question the allegedly self-evident. "The philosophy of the jester," Kolakowski says, "is a philosophy which in every epoch denounces as doubtful what appears as unshakable; it points out the contradictions in what seems evident and incontestable; it ridicules common sense and reads sense into the absurd." This spirit might tease us into admitting that our discourse, whether it be Christian or Marxist, is *human* discourse, never final in its findings, never exempt from criticism, never absolutely unified. I would say that the challenge of the jester is relevant for both the Christian and the Marxist. At the same time, the Christian must concede the view expressed by Lucian Gruppi —one of the Marxist philosophers who, in April 1965, participated in the international conference on Christianity and Marxism in Salzburg, Austria—that Marxists have the right to their philosophy and no one is justified in expecting them to abandon their positions. This view, however, does not preclude the possibility of open-ended dialogue between Christians and Marxists. In such a dialogue, Marxism will make itself peculiarly relevant by insisting that crucial consideration be given to the question of the practical significance of any theory of transcendence in the struggle for justice and for the fulfillment of man.

Before turning now to consider other aspects of the dialogue let me summarize: the Marxist and the Christian share a common presupposition that is rooted in the Judeo-Christian doctrine of creation; namely, the view that materiality in its essence is good. Neither Christianity nor Marxism is fundamentally ascetic in its evaluation of nature and human nature. On the other hand, the Christian and the Marxist differ with respect to another aspect of the doctrine of creation: the Christian emphasizes a doctrine of grace or of transcendence—man is a creature—and the Marxist is oriented to a philosophy of radical immanence. Neither of these views is subject to scientific demonstration.

The remaining portion of the present discussion will focus attention upon three additional points of connection at which socialist humanism is relevant to Protestantism. Especially important are certain structural analogues between major aspects of Christianity and Marxism. These connecting points are to be observed in the doctrines about humanity: that we are historical beings, that we are fallen creatures, and that we are socially associating beings.

In a letter Marx once wrote of the annoyance he suffered from the fact that his wife and daughters were in the habit on Sunday mornings of dressing up in their best clothes and attending church. He reports that one Sunday morning he reproached them for going to church, telling them that for the sake of their religion they should stay at home and read the Old Testament prophets. The Marxist interpretation of history does presuppose in important ways the Old Testament prophetic conception of history. In a fashion comparable to what we have already indicated regarding the Judeo-Christian doctrine of creation, there is a structural analogy between Marx's conception and the prophetic view of history.

Permit me to recall here the principal features of the Old Testament prophetic conception. The Old Testament prophets rejected both a naturistic view and a mystical view. They accent an historical rather than a nonhistorical interpretation of history. Nature is understood in subordination to history, and history is oriented to time rather than to space. Moreover, history consists of group formations and not merely of the aggregate of individual experiences, though the individual in later prophetism assumes an intrinsic status and significance. The driving force of history is the struggle between ethical monotheism and polytheism (naturism), the struggle between justice and injustice. God makes a covenant with a people who promise to be faithful in the pursuit of righteousness, justice, and mercy. This covenant involves collective responsibility before God. The people are responsible for the character of their society, and especially for the poor and the neglected. When the nation is unfaithful, God has a controversy with his people as a people. Thus their responsibility is for institutional as well as for individual behavior. This ethos, however, is not a purely externalized, institutionalized one. It is rooted in inward commitment of the individual as a party to the covenant. It is significant that the Ten Commandments are couched in the second person singular.

The reference to the covenant gives us occasion to emphasize that the dominant metaphors of the Bible are political metaphors. The idea of covenant was drawn from the realm of international relations (treaties). Along with king, kingship, kingdom, and messiah, the concept of covenant permeates the whole of the Bible. These political metaphors suggest that God is sovereign over the whole of life, inner and outer.

Political metaphor in the Bible possesses cosmic scope, and it includes also the sphere of the family. But it prevents the scope of responsibility from escaping out of the institutional or collective sphere in the name of the cosmic. It aims also to prevent any escape into a mystical sphere that is beyond time and history. Finally, political metaphor aims to prevent the reduction of the social-ethical sphere to the exclusive realm of the individual, to the inner life alone, and to the sphere of merely interpersonal relations. The domestic metaphors—father and child, bridegroom and bride, brother and brother—are essentially political, in the sense of being broadly institutional and in the sense of being subordinate to the wider sovereignty of God. In the New Testament, political metaphor reappears in the ideas of the kingdom of God and the kingship of Christ.

The historical interpretation of history does not view history and responsibility in merely abstract, timeless fashion. It presupposes that historical events possess a certain singularity. Faithfulness and unfaithfulness to the covenant become manifest in particular events and in institutional malpractices. The Old Testament prophets constantly specify the sins of the people, manifest in the social distance between the monarch and the people, in the callousness of the ruling and propertied powers, in the special privileges of the elite, in the grinding of the poor.

The historical interpretation of history, in its emphasis on the particularity of the historical situation, becomes especially evident in theories of periodization that articulate the various stages of the past and epitomize the particularities of the present. The first period is in the Garden of Eden. This period comes to an end when man is expelled because of his disobedience, his misuse of a God-given freedom and responsibility. In the first period, man and nature enjoyed an original innocence or wholeness. But man, created in the image of God, occupies a special position in relation to nature. Moreover, mankind is envisaged as a whole and in unity. But in the second period differentiation appears and eventually the perspective tends to be that of one nation. This nation in a later period is subjected to slavery in Egypt, and then its people are delivered from their slavery. Thereupon ensued a new covenant. But throughout, the people are enjoined to adhere to a law of righteousness in history, in the here and now. God does not offer escape from history, but rather demands righteousness in the present historical situation.

Not only the Creation and the Fall are understood structurally in terms of periodization but also the drive toward the future. Eschatology thus becomes a crucial ingredient of this historical interpretation of history. Indeed, one might say that a historical interpretation of history is one that by definition requires an eschatology. On the one hand, the divine promise is to be realized in the messianic period; but, on the other hand, the human voluntary response and responsibility of obedience is a condition of human fulfillment. The fulfillment is viewed at the same time as the work of God and as something for which social-ethical striving is a preparation. With the appearance of apocalypticism, however, the work of God is emphasized to the detriment of human responsibility. Moreover, the End or the fulfillment is projected more and more beyond history. In the New Testament a paradoxical view comes sharply to the fore—the kingdom is future and present, is immanent and transcendent. But even here the doctrine of the kingship of Christ expresses the conviction that fulfillment is not merely for the individual but is also for the political and economic institutions. Here the universal dimension reappears, for the fulfillment hoped for is intended for humanity. Indeed, nature is to enjoy the redemption, since it has also suffered in the fall.

This expectation of the kingdom is not to be realized without dust and heat, for the divine power demands a response that is willing to struggle. Indeed, the response entails a severe struggle with pervasive demonic powers, the principalities and powers that seduce and enslave men. Space does not permit our dealing here with the special kind of social responsibilities, somewhat truncated, that characterize the early Christian community. But special historical considerations do have to be taken into account. These truncated conceptions, which appear in peculiar circumstances, unfortunately have been accepted as normative by some Christians.

Looking forward in history, we may observe that the eschatological tension and the dynamic theory of periodization reappear in Christian history. They sometimes appear in a revolutionary proclamation of a coming, new era, when there will be a new social structure and even a new church and a new art. Of special interest to Marxists is Thomas Muentzer, the most violent of the revolutionaries, who has demanded that economic transformation must be accomplished by force, indeed that this economic revolution must be achieved first if the religious reformation is to have validity. Here the special place assigned to suffering (depicted in the paintings of Grünewald) is peculiarly significant. According to this view, the new era can emerge out of despair and suffering, and out of a daring resort to violence. The book on Muentzer by Fr. Engels makes it unnecessary to dwell any further upon this figure and his significance for Marxism. Much new light has been shed upon Muentzer which of course makes the Engels volume of limited value today.

Dynamic theories of periodization emerged in great variety in the century after Muentzer. New eschatologies accompany and motivate the struggles of the seventeenth century, struggles that anticipate the democratic, political revolution. Here the rational and systematic use of propaganda and agitation appears for the first time. In this many-pronged movement one can see many of the features of an historical interpretation of that which have been already noted above.

Now, it must be recognized that a considerable variety of interpretation obtains among Protestants with regard to the framework that has been adumbrated here. Some scholars, for example, would insist upon a greater degree of discontinuity between the Old Testament and the New. On the other hand, there are many aspects of this framework with which Marxists would disagree. We have already noted the most obvious difference, the difference of attitude regarding the transcendent powers. The Marxist would charge the Christian with mystification; he would also claim that this framework as presented is scarcely the basis for revolutionary action. The Christian for his part would find the Marxist lacking in an awesome and reverent sense of the gift of life. Nonetheless, the Marxist and the Protestant Christian should find some degree of agreement. They could agree, for example, that the historical interpretation of history is decisive, that the meaning of history is to be seen in the struggle between justice and injustice, that these are universal values, that the fulfillment of human life requires active criticism and participation in transformation of social institutions. They would also agree that a tripartite periodization is pertinent—the Christian interpreting individual and institutional behavior in terms of creation, fall, and redemption, and the Marxist positing a sociological and perhaps also a philosophical conception of an original wholeness, a subsequent rise above nature, and a "fall" into divison of labor or private property and a development toward a fulfillment of human nature. The modern Protestant and the Marxist would agree that scientific investigation should be the basis for the determination of historical origins (the question, for example, of primordial communism). And what shall we say of the end of humanity? When stated in the broadest terms, the ideal of human fulfillment would find Marx and the Christian in significant agreement. Indeed, through Feuerbach, Marx adopted the idea that God the Creator is really man whose essence is creativity. The means of fulfillment through violence is of course radically rejected by the Christian.

But when it comes to the discussion of the nature and cause of alienation, profound differences appear. From the Christian perspective, alienation can never receive adequate explanation in terms of sociological structures alone, and certainly not in terms of property alone. So long as freedom is possible, humanity will abuse it no matter what social system obtains. Moreover, even if property is held in common, the administration of it and of other resources will provide the opportunity for the abuse of power. If class struggle comes to an end in the classless society, new struggle will ensue unless monolithic power prevents it; and monolithic power requires unyielding violence, a requirement that itself violates the fulfillment of human nature. From a Christian perspective, such a perduring violence would be a demonic power of enslavement. We do not need here to examine Marx's own ideal of complete spontaneity and of the dissolution of the division of labor. There are two crucial deficiencies in traditional Marxism: first, that it presupposes that there is one, and only one, system of society that accords with the essence of human nature; and, second, it assumes that when the prehistory of mankind is finished, there will be no conflict of powers, and real communism will be identical with ideal communism. But before such a state of affairs could exist for the test, the transitional stage of the dictatorship of the proletariat would have to show that it is not a permanent stage, in short, it must show that the promise of ideal communism is not simply another ideology for protecting entrenched power. For all of these reasons the merely sociological concept of alienation promoted by Marxism must be abandoned; and the vision of the future entertained by Marxism must also be rejected as largely utopian.

At the same time the Protestant who accepts the conception of the sovereignty of God over the whole of life must assess Marxism as presenting a valid challenge to those types of Christianity that interpret salvation in purely individualistic terms. The criticism directed against Kierkegaard by Georg Lukacs may be accepted as a valid challenge in this context. Lukacs, in *Die Zerstörung der Vernunft*, is correct in his claim that Kierkegaard in the name of *Innerlichkeit* both desocializes and dehistoricizes mankind, and that he shows himself also to be an apostle of monarchist elitism. In its maintenance of the historical interpretation of history as demanding responsibility for the criticism and transformation of institutions, in its concern for the poor and the neglected and the exploited, in its claim that the criticism of religion is the beginning of all criticism, Marxism (perhaps even in its atheism) is an ally of an authentically Christian interpretation of history.

However, on two points I would like to interject a challenge of a sort to the Marxist. In some quarters, one can observe the disposition of certain Marxists to enter into dialogue with contemporary philosophy. It is surprising to note that the philosophy of Heidegger is attracting attention. But Heidegger seems in effect to reject the historical interpretation of history and thus to be indifferent to social structures and social responsibility. One might hope that Marxists would also attempt to enter into dialogue with philosophies and theologies who are concerned with institutional analysis and criticism and transformation. I recall recently hearing an account of a conference with Heidegger in Switzerland. One of the members of the group ventured to ask Heidegger why he does not concern himself with a broader scope of problems than that of the individual in relation to ontology. In response Heidegger said, "You are quite right. I am not concerned with institutional problems. If you are interested in that sort of thing, you should not be reading my works. I recommend that you turn to the writings of Martin Buber." It is significant that Buber was a man who was oriented to the historical and prophetic interpretation of history found in the Old Testament.

Second, it is rather unfortunate that Marxists did not continue the study of the left wing of the Reformation after some attention to Muentzer, as mentioned earlier. It is possible that the problems of effective freedom in speech, the arts, and related areas in Marxist countries derive from a failure to analyze the realities of the social system as they developed out of the left wing tradition. Here a major perspective of one type of Protestantism deserves mention. Neo-Calvinism, along with Spiritualism, fought for and established a high degree of freedom of association in English and American society. To be sure, if freedom is not to issue in anarchy, there must be an overarching loyalty or covenant under the roof of which freedom of association is exercised. Morever, freedom of association may become an ideology that tries to prevent the total community from remedying pervasive social or economic malad-justment. On the other hand, the practice of gradual revolution, or even of sudden revolution, is possible only where freedom of association obtains. Marxism as a movement could not have succeeded at all if such freedom of association had been completely suppressed. Freedom of association, we may say, is the institutionalization of evolution and revolution.

But there is a profounder justification for freedom of association. The strength of a society does not depend upon universal conformity. Universal conformity produces deformity, a pernicious form of alienation. The strength of a society depends upon the capacity of its members to be heard and to exercise an influence. It depends upon the capacity of the member of the society to participate and to make their several contributions. Without some such conception of the theory and practice of freedom, any society is monolithic. It produces Hobbes' Leviathan in which free associations are considered to be "worms in the entrails" of the sovereign, and only an entrenched elite (afflicted with ankylosis) will be responsible for the character of the society. By this means humanism, whether Marxist or Christian, suffers from organized frustration and suppression. However, it may be that Marx had in mind a similar sort of freedom of association when he expressed preference for the commune, for the localized microcosm.

In any case, surely a genuinely liberated humanity requires both liberty and justice. Socialistic humanism has pressed the case for justice, especially as justice involves material equality, more dramatically than have the great philosophies of Catholicism and Calvinism. But it has often sacrificed freedom. Similarly, many religious philosophies have carried the torch for freedom but without an adequate sense of justice. For both Marxism and Christianity, the fundamental social problem is the combining of a radical concern for a just society and the freedom to organize differentiation. If justice and freedom are to be achieved, we shall require a new birth of dialogue and joint action. In this way Marxism can be relevant to the Christian, and Protestant experience may become relevant for the Marxist.

AMONG SOCIAL THEORISTS, only Max Weber can be ranked with Karl Marx as a prophetic voice in the modern era. Adams viewed Weber as both corrective and supplement to Marx' perspective in charting major features of modern social existence that are directly pertinent to an understanding of both (1) the contemporary human condition, and (2) the relationship of religion to the forms of rationality governing much of our lives. The continuing pertinence of Weber is derived not only from his theoretical struggle with the problem of the relationship of fact and value, but also from his scientific recognition of both the necessity and the dangers of "institutionalization" and "bureaucratization," his intellectual objection to single-cause interpretations of history, and his encyclopedic command of the data of social life available in his time. It also derives from his ethical, even spiritual, protest against certain trends that seemed to accompany modernization. It is perhaps this protest that allowed, perhaps forced, Weber to press the question of "meaning" and "understanding" *(Verstehen)* in the interpretation of social existence and brought him to lay the social scientific grounds for the recognition of religion as a relatively autonomous force in human affairs. The "Protestant Ethic" in its relationship to modern capitalist society is the central thesis of his work. Subsequently, the Protestant Ethic has itself become more and more the object of protest and even contempt. In the following essay, Adams identifies the limits and the continuing importance of Weber's treatment of this powerful legacy of the Reformation.*—M.L.S.

CHAPTER 12 · THE PROTESTANT ETHIC
AND SOCIETY: MAX WEBER

IN MUCH OF current usage the term "Protestant Ethic" is associated with the widely influential book of Max Weber first published in Germany in 1904–1905. No book of its kind has elicited such a wide range of scholarly discussion, much of it a vast misrepresentation. One of the cruder oversimplifications is offered by William H. Whyte who, in a discussion of Weber, asserts that thrift and the survival of the fittest represent "the Protestant ethic in its purest form." Another

* This essay first appeared as a lecture delivered at the University of Mainz, published in the *Zeitschrift für Evangelische Ethik*, 12, Heft 4/5 (1968), pp. 247–67. It was revised for inclusion in B. Landis, E. S. Taulber, and E. Landis, eds., *In the Name of Life* (New York: Holt, Rinehart and Winston, 1971), pp. 174–90, a *Festschrift* for Erich Fromm.

misconception epitomizes Weber's thesis by the formula, "Protestantism—or Calvinism—produced capitalism." By others, the slogan "Capitalism produced Calvinism" is recited as an incantation, as if to imply that Weber was a Marxist. As summaries of Weber's thesis these formulas are, at the most, quarter-truths. They overlook the fact that Weber vigorously rejected any monocausal theory of history, whether idealistic or realistic (Marxist).

It is, of course, not my purpose to recapitulate and assess Weber's entire intention and accomplishment in his studies of "the Protestant ethic." That task has already been undertaken by a host of scholars. My principal concern here is twofold: (1) to remind the reader that since Weber's study was concerned with "ascetic Protestantism" in its relation to economic behavior, he by no means intended a complete account of the Protestant ethic; and (2) to show that in Weber's presentation, even within this limit, he fails to take into account important aspects of "ascetic Protestantism," and that correspondingly he does not give attention to a significant influence of the Protestant ethic, particularly with respect to an indispensable feature of Anglo-American democracy, the voluntary association. In view of the fact that Weber with tears laments the end-result (as he sees it) of "the Protestant ethic," the import of this essay is to qualify his conception of that ethic and its influence, and therefore to view it with fewer tears. This evaluation must take into account Weber's philosophical presuppositions and especially certain value judgments.

Weber is not a sociologist if by that term one refers to the specialist who examines human groups only by means of surveys and statistics. Weber must be classed with such seminal figures as Marx and Nietzsche, Adam Smith and Hegel. In a letter of his earlier years he wrote: "One can measure the honesty of a contemporary scholar, and above all, of a contemporary philosopher, in his posture toward Nietzsche and Marx. Whoever does not admit that he could not perform the most important parts of his work without the work that these two have done swindles himself and others."

Weber, trained initially in law and economics, was a man of strong moral convictions. He was fundamentally concerned with the values of civilization and the ways these values have been formulated and implemented or perverted. As a social scientist, however, he distinguished fact statements from value judgments, asserting that the social scientist must confine himself to the former. Nevertheless, he not infrequently interrupts his exposition to render a value judgment, and then to apologize before returning to the matter in hand. Here we see an acute inner tension between commitment to scientific objectivity and the values of moral integrity and individual responsibility. A similar tension obtains between his concern for individual freedom and responsibility and his concern for a strong German state.

In examining civilizational values Weber presupposed a conception of man as a historical, social being. Indeed, in the end he developed a philosophy of history. Of crucial significance is his view that the sociologist, like anyone else who aims to understand human behavior, must be concerned with the *meaning* of that behavior. The sociologist, he says, examines behavior "when and insofar as the acting individual attaches a subjective meaning to it." For Weber, as for Wilhelm Dilthey before him, the concept of meaning—a sense of the relation between the parts and the whole—enabled him to probe beneath the symbolism of religious and cultural myths, in search of "a meaningful 'cosmos,' " that is, in search of fundamental social and psychological sanctions and ultimate loyalties. These ultimate loyalties he held to be "religiously conditioned" insofar as they inform "a whole way of life." Precisely because of his concern with meaning (and meaninglessness), Weber as an "objective" social scientist dealt with the most "subjective" aspects of the human venture. In a special sense, then, he was a theological sociologist, though he spoke of himself as religiously "unmusical."

In explication of a doctrine of man, Weber held that ideas are not merely epiphenomena of social conditions and struggles, but decisively affect human behavior and history. At the same time, of course, he recognized that a reciprocal relation obtains between ideas and conditioning factors. His total work is, therefore, full of tensions, and it is a paradox that, despite his rejection of determinism and because of his recognition of conditioning factors (such as the unintended consequences of ideas), he was, in contrast to Marx, pessimistic in his assessment of present and future possibilities.

In examining "the Protestant ethic" Weber was mindful of his previous studies of the despotism of the Roman slave plantations, of the monopolistic practices of medieval trade associations, of the narrow self-interest and political insensitivity of the Junkers, and also of Bismarckian authoritarianism. Indeed, in his view his own father was a well-kept lackey of Bismarckian authoritarianism as well as being an insensitive, domineering husband.

All of these features figured in Weber's decision to study "the Protestant ethic," but as the book title indicates, his exclusive focus was to examine the relation between that ethic and "the spirit of capitalism." In his view, both this ethic and this spirit represent unique features in the history of religions and in the history of capitalisms; moreover, these historical entities enter into reciprocal relations. Without the ethic of ascetic Protestantism the spirit of modern capitalism could not have become so readily widespread. On the other hand, "the spirit of capitalism," in turn, affected the development, indeed the transformation, of "the Protestant ethic."

The unique features of the modern situation, as Weber views them, can be seen by examining his conception of "rational capitalism" and of "the Protestant ethic." These features of modern culture were but two aspects of an all-pervasive Western rationalism, manifest also in the arts, the sciences, and the forms of social organization. Rational capitalism came into being by cutting the moorings from the political capitalism and patrimonial order of the previous period. Rational capitalism not only promotes the free organization of labor and the idea of the intrinsic merit of work, but rejects the notion that acquiring money is a necessary evil. Instead, it views the earning of money as an ethical obligation; rejecting the notion that limits should be placed upon living standards, it promotes innovation by emphasizing impersonal considerations in accomplishing economic tasks efficiently. In these respects it is critical of the inherited tradition. In short, rational capitalism requires a functioning bureaucracy involving impersonal devotion to the task, specialized division of labor, and a rationalized discipline. These ingredients call for, indeed they engender, a particular kind of mentality, which Weber identifies as "the spirit of capitalism."

The uniqueness of this spirit Weber sees epitomized "in almost classical purity" in Benjamin Franklin's esteem for thrift and hard work, incumbent upon men as a profound duty—and in his case "free from all direct relationship to religion." This sense of duty finds expression in virtue and proficiency in a calling. The calling demands rationality in the sense of relating means to ends, achieving a systematic, methodical performance, and subordinating personal to impersonal considerations. Rationality and calculation, then, become matters of duty. Moreover, ostentatious enjoyment of rewards of success must be eschewed; it can serve only to damage one's credit and one's standing. Similar characteristics are presented in Weber's essay "The Protestant Sects and the Spirit of Capitalism," in describing Americans he encountered in the United States who "used" the church as an accrediting agency in the business community and as a place to "make contacts."

Alongside the already developing spirit of capitalism a new conception of meaning, "the Protestant ethic," comes onto the scene. Weber musters evidence to show that Calvinist theology and Anglo-American Puritanism were conducive to rationalized, individualistic activity (particularly in the economic sphere), activity undertaken not for the sake of gain but as a religious duty—to glorify God *in this world*. This vision of human existence—this "ascetic Protestantism"—was supported by an ethic of vocation or calling which issued in vigorous methodical activity, thus releasing a tremendous energy. This ethic was motivated by a doctrine of salvation predestined through grace, a doctrine that gave rise to an anxiety that led to a redoubling of effort. At least initially, the dominant motive was "interest" in the salvation of the individual rather than the acquisition of wealth.

In Weber's view, the central motifs of this vision of life had an independent origin in an interpretation of the Bible and of the disciplines of the Christian life. Through the spread of these ideas in England when "the spirit of capitalism" was already developing, they present a new attitude toward worldly activity which, in essential features, is "congruent" with that spirit. Accordingly, the ideas of the Puritans provide a milieu that is both receptive to the spirit of rational capitalism and able to qualify that spirit in terms of the "interest" of the Puritan in individual salvation, wherein a sign of grace is righteous, industrious, methodical activity in the world—labor in a calling. In time, however, ascetic Protestantism lost its powerful religious orientation and sanctioned a simple doctrine of work in the pursuit of wealth; indeed it even sanctioned the doctrine that wealth is a sign of grace, and finally that "piety is the surest road to wealth." These changes might be called Weber's account of the devil's toboggan slide of ascetic Protestantism. To be sure, these developments are traced in detail and with considerable subtlety, but much of the evidence offered has been challenged by other scholars.

Three other aspects of Weber's intention remain to be stressed. First, Weber says that he is "interested . . . in the influence of those psychological sanctions which, originating in religious belief and the practice of religion, gave a direction to practical conduct and held the individual to it." In the main, therefore, he was interested not so much in sociological, structural features of the societal changes taking place as in the psychological sanctions for the legitimacy of a new pattern of the individual's conduct, that is, for the legitimacy of rational economic activity considered as a duty. To be sure, social-structural changes occurred, as in the emerging independence of economic and other activities from political control, a precondition of a pluralistic society. Weber focuses attention on the personality types attracted to the new patterns and their motivations. He also indicates ways in which individual conduct is constricted by social forces it has released.

Second, Weber attempted, as part of his method, to construct "ideal types." This method, he insisted, had long been used (indeed is inevitable in analyzing human behavior); but he felt that it required clarification. Here again the concept of meaning is of crucial significance. The ideal type is an intellectual tool, a unified analytical construct, devised by the historian or sociologist in order to characterize unique, meaning-oriented phenomena of human action, and in such a way as to give them a quality of generality whereby comparison and contrast with other meaning-oriented phenomena become possible. The concept of meaning is involved here in dual fashion. Being a construct, the ideal type in the first place reflects the value-orientation of the one who devises or uses it as a tool. In the second place, it selects and accentuates concrete, individual phenomena in a onesided way so as to achieve precision, a precision that combines generality with individuality in a context of meaning. Weber thus combines insights regarding generality and particularity which may be traced respectively to the Enlightenment and to Romanticism. Since ideal types are made up of highly abstract patterns, he speaks of their being "utopian" (not to be found anywhere in concrete detail) and also of their "artificial simplicity." They serve as "conceptual points of reference" for "experiments" in comparative cultural analysis. Major illustrations of these ideal types are such concepts as otherworldly and this-worldly asceticism; a patrimonial traditionalist social order and a rational, innovating capitalist order; and, of course, the Protestant ethic and the spirit of rational capitalism. In later writings Weber developed a whole series of ideal types, such as types of authority or domination (traditional, legal-rational, and charismatic) and types of prophetism (ethical and exemplary). It has been suggested that Weber's ideal types may be compared to Hegel's logically related concepts. Weber, to be sure, rejects any "emanationist" or dialectical theory of the sort espoused by Hegelian idealism. He was not only religiously but also metaphysically "unmusical."

Obviously, the particular form of an ideal type depends entirely upon the features chosen for accentuation. Hence, an ideal type is like a wax nose to be shaped in a variety of ways. Think of the protracted debate of the past generation regarding the question, What was the Renaissance? Similarly, Weber's ideal type of "the Protestant ethic," as we shall see, is not only made of wax, it is also a bone of contention.

Third, we must stress what we have already hinted at, namely that in Weber's view a crucial feature of Western culture is the element of rationality. He sees an anticipation of it in the universal ethical prophetism stemming from the Old Testament which in both Judaism and Christianity has served in principle to combat magic. Of course, he finds it in Greek science and logic. He also points out that, along with an ethos of work, it appears conspicuously in medieval monasticism in its methodical features.

Rationality "covers a whole world of different things." Moreover, for Weber it possesses a markedly ambiguous value: it is capable of obstructing as well as of promoting human freedom and fulfillment. If we spell out here its positive and negative aspects, we shall the more readily grasp the character of Weber's doctrine of man and his philosophy of civilization.

In its more positive aspects rationality appears in: the deliberate weighing of a methodical course of action; the process of intellectualization for the sake of clarity; self-control that overcomes instinct and "everything impulsive and irrational"; the rationalization of mystical contemplation; the shaping of means to ends; the method of scientific investigation (including the mathematization of knowledge); machine production, technology, and the mastery of the world; the division and coordination of activities for the purpose of achieving efficiency and productivity (which require, for example, rational bookkeeping); the stability and predictability of bureaucracy; the organization of free labor to create or appeal to a market; the rational-legal acquisition of wealth by virtue of one's ability and initiative; the limitation of occupational effort to specialized work; military training; the system of counterpoint in music; the establishment of rational-legal authority; the logical ordering and rearrangement of the contents of the law; the conceiving of different types of order in society; the carrying through of radical social change; and, of course, the construction of ideal types. In all of these forms of rationality we see the combining of order and meaning. Many of these expressions of rationality have appeared in modern "rational capitalism" in its conflict with traditionalism, while many of them antedate the modern period. But rationality appears in unique fashion in "rational capitalism" and in this-worldly "ascetic Protestantism" —in its methodical and ethical conduct of life motivated by a coherent system of doctrine and commitment that is able to overcome an inherited traditionalist system.

On its negative side, rationality can be severely restrictive. It can appear in the conservative philosophy calculated to resist social change; it can claim to understand everything under a single perspective; it can reduce almost everything to specialization and to the rigidity of bureaucratic system, thus stifling individual decision and initiative; and it contributes to the "disenchantment" of the world and to the elimination of any vital sense of meaning and depth in existence. In these ways it becomes a threat to, indeed the destruction of, belief in the supraempirical validity of an ethic rooted either in a humane sense of values or in a religious conception of the ultimate structure of things. Thus it can be the enemy of authentic personality and of commitment to "the daemon who holds the thread of its life." In these and in other ways rationality can lead to dehumanizing, compulsive behavior, to irrationality, and meaninglessness.

The positive aspects of rationality (along with individual freedom and responsibility) delineated by Weber are indispensable elements in civilization, and of course are cherished by him. The negative aspects, on the other hand, illustrate the axiom: the corruption of the best is the worst. It is no accident that the account given of the corruption of freedom and reason by Weber, a scholar learned in theological lore, should remind one of the Christian theologian's account of the corruption of the *imago dei*. In this respect one must say that Weber reveals a tragic view of history—in the Hebraic sense. Human freedom and reason are a heavy burden (as well as a gift) requiring constant vigilance; they are the pivot at once of meaning and of the possibility of the fall into unfreedom, irrationality, and meaninglessness. So fundamental for Weber is the negative dimension of rationality that it can be said to correspond to the concept of alienation in the thought of Karl Marx and Erich Fromm. Erich Fromm holds with Weber, however, that insofar as Marxism promotes monolithic bureaucracy it simply guarantees the continuation or creation of alienation. The dictatorship of the proletariat turns out to be the dictatorship of the bureaucrats.

Weber's most negative judgment on technical rationality and on the secularized, corrupted "Protestant ethic" appears in the famous passage near the end of his book:

> The Puritan wanted to work in a calling; we are forced to do so. For when asceticism was carried out of monastic cells into everyday life, and began to dominate worldly morality, it did its part in building the tremendous cosmos of the modern economic order. This order is now bound to the technical and economic conditions of machine production which today determine the lives of all the individuals who are born into this mechanism, not only those directly concerned with economic acquisition, with irresistible force. Perhaps it will so determine them until the last ton of coal is burnt. In Baxter's view the care for external goods should only lie on the shoulders of "the saint like a light cloak, which can be thrown aside at any moment." But fate decreed that the cloak should become an iron cage. . . .
>
> No one knows who will live in this cage in the future, or whether at the end of this tremendous development entirely new prophets will arise, or there will be a great rebirth of old ideas and ideals, or, if neither, mechanized petrification, embellished with a sort of convulsive self-importance. For of the last stage of this cultural development, it might well be truly said: "Specialists without spirit, sensualists without

heart, and this nullity imagines that it has attained a level of civilization never before achieved."

Then Weber goes on to make his usual apology for violating the principle that the social scientist should not inject value judgments into his presentation. "But this brings us," he says, "to the world of judgments of value and of faith, with which this purely historical discussion need not be burdened."

Despite the positive values of rationality, then, and despite the initial capacity of Puritanism to bring a new sense of meaning into life and to initiate a revolutionary process that displaced a restrictive social order, the outcome is an iron cage, a soul-less compulsive social system of specialization and bureaucratism without spirit and without heart—a nullity. This specialization and bureaucratism are closely linked with the joyless and impersonal character of work and with "its joyless lack of meaning." Moreover, capitalism, being today "in the saddle . . . is able to force people to labour without transcendental sanctions." The negative aspects of rationality have overwhelmed the positive.

In reading the long passage just quoted one is reminded of Nietzsche's prediction of the advent of "the last man," who will be a completely rationalized cog in a machine without creative vitality. This outcome, in Weber's view, is the working of the unintended consequences of initially noble impulses, and his comparative studies in the sociology of religion were intended to confirm this insight and to serve as a warning. In this connection one may think of Hegel's theory of "the cunning of reason." But whereas Hegel refers to the hidden instrument of the World Spirit unfolding and realizing a divine purpose, Weber's view is pessimistic—pessimistic also in contrast to the ultimate optimism of Marx. Weber leaves modern man in the iron cage; he questions whether there is a way out, hinting only at such ideas as "charisma" (see Chapter 13). Weber never loses his fear of perverted reason. It is strange, however, that despite his basic interest in economic forces, he says nothing here about poverty and the maldistribution of wealth. Nor does he explore the possible correction of bureaucratism. Yet, however dusty the answers he gives to the larger social issues raised, we must say with Benjamin Nelson that a major thrust of this whole study of "the Protestant ethic" is to be seen in his concluding protest against "conscienceless reason."

While appreciating the immensity of Weber's accomplishment and the stimulus he has given to the study of the relations between religion and society, I want to offer three critical comments on his presentation of "the Protestant ethic."

First, let it be noted again that Weber's ideal type of "the Protestant ethic" is by intention a restricted one, in that by means of it he aims only to set forth the essential features of the relation between that ethic and economic behavior. On the last pages of the book he emphasizes this point and specifies the large areas of investigation that remain to be undertaken. The ideal type constructed by Weber, then, is not an ideal type of the Protestant ethic as a whole. It excludes from consideration those types of Protestantism that do not belong under the rubric of ascetic Protestantism. Nor is it an ideal type of ascetic Protestantism as a whole.

Second, Weber stresses the point that the meaning of life in Calvinism and Puritanism was rooted in a belief in "a supramundane God" who is sovereign over the whole of life. Yet, due to his concentration on the "interests" and the conduct of the individual, Weber almost entirely ignores the Puritan concern for the social order as a whole. This deficiency in Weber's study is today receiving increasing attention. David Little, for example, has recast the Weberian thesis by directing attention to the Calvinist and Puritan demand for a new order of society (*Religion, Order, and Law*. New York: Harper & Row, 1969). In this connection we should add that Weber gives little attention to the internal life of the churches and the "pathos for order" rooted in the church fellowship. Thus he fails to take into account the Calvinist view that the church and its members have the obligation to work for the establishment of a society of justice and mercy. For Calvin and for many of the Calvinists of the period, the Christian bears a *general* vocation in the world as well as having a specific calling in his daily work. This outlook is today referred to as "the totalistic impulse" of the Calvinists, and a recognition of it has given rise to a new phase of the controversy over Weber's thesis. As a consequence of his not taking this "impulse" sufficiently into account, and of his centering attention on predestination and on the anxiety of the individual regarding his own salvation, Weber's finding with respect to "psychological sanctions" turns out to be inadequate.

The totalistic impulse of Calvinism is to be seen especially in the effort of the Puritans in England to take over the Establishment. When this effort failed, many of them became vigorous Dissenters, forming a variety of movements bent on reform. The totalistic impulse did not die. It was in wider commonalty spread (to adapt a phrase from John Milton). In this new situation sectarian doctrines of the church came to the fore, some of which developed into a protodemocratic doctrine of the free or voluntary church, but the demands for a new social order were not relinquished even though they were fragmented. In the middle of the century John Lilburne and the Levellers, for example, formed associations for political agitation, using rational techniques to appeal to public opinion. (Perhaps one can say that at that time "public opinion" as a factor in political life was born.) In some circles the idea of a democratic structure in the church was by analogy transformed into a demand for a democratic political order. Many of these efforts exhibit the continued working of the "totalistic impulses."

Of equal importance in this connection was another aspect of this development. The idea of the free or voluntary church, in order to vindicate itself in the face of the Establishment, called for a struggle for the freedom of religious association. In time this struggle was extended to a struggle for the freedom to form other voluntary associations. Even the Anglicans began to form religious societies for the reformation of morals. These societies flourished for fifty years after the Restoration and were able even to elicit cooperation from the Dissenters. The Friends early in the eighteenth century refined the techniques of agitation toward the end of effecting legislation extending their religious and political freedom.

Here we encounter, then, one of the most significant features of the Protestant ethic, which Weber ignored by reason of the limits of his study. Ernst Troeltsch has asserted that the Calvinists were given "to an organized and aggressive effort to form associations, to a systematic endeavor to mold the life of society as a whole, to a kind of 'Christian Socialism'." Protestants in England and America in the eighteenth and nineteenth centuries formed associations to promote philanthropy, educational reform, penal reform, factory reform, free trade, international peace, the extension of the suffrage, women's rights, the abolition of slavery and child labor, better working and living conditions, trade unions, cooperatives, the prohibition of alcoholic beverages, "municipal socialism," civil rights and liberties, lobbies, communitarian movements, know-nothing campaigns, and a multitude of other causes (including of course "antisocial causes" and "special interests"). Clearly, many of these associations have changed economic behavior.

In New England one can see the beginnings of these associations in the activities of the Friends in the seventeenth century, and later in the admonitions of Cotton Mather (*Bonifacius*, 1710) to form associations for philanthropic and moral purposes. Mather reports that he belonged to twenty such associations. Benjamin Franklin makes it clear that in forming voluntary organizations he was initially inspired by Cotton Mather's book. Early in the nineteenth century, when the United States was rapidly becoming a "nation of joiners," fairly elaborate theories of association came from the pens of leading clergymen.

These associational movements for social change, anticipated in principle in seventeenth-century Puritanism, may be viewed as activities that in varying ways expressed a sense of vocation broader than that which Weber presents with respect to the vocation of daily work. They provide the citizen with the opportunity to emerge from the "iron cage" of specialization and to join fellow citizens in bringing under criticism economic as well as political and other institutions. They have served in both church and society as a principal means to promote criticism and innovation, individual and group participation and responsibility, and thus the dispersion of power. Although subject to manipulation and to rigid, soul-less bureaucratization, they have been a source of vital tension within the Protestant ethic. In the positive Weberian sense they represent a major form of rationality in Anglo-American life, toward the end of "turning the flank of recalcitrant institutions." Moreover, for more than three centuries these associations have provided a continuing critique of what Weber calls "the Protestant ethic." They represent the institutional gradualization of revolution.

Why does Weber leave this whole dimension out of his delineation of "the Protestant ethic"? The answer is that in tracing the development of individualism he left out of account the residues of the "totalistic impulses" of original Puritanism. But there is an additional reason.

In a lecture of 1911 entitled "A Proposal for the Study of Voluntary Associations," delivered in Frankfurt, Germany, at an international sociological congress, Weber said:

The man of today is without doubt an association man in an awful and never dreamed of degree. Germany stands in this matter at a very high point. . . . America is the association-land par excellence. In America membership in some middle-class association belongs directly to one's legitimation as a gentleman. The prototype of these associations is the sect, a union of specifically qualified people. Today the association furnishes the ethical qualification test for the businessman, certifying that he is worthy of credit. American democracy is no sand heap, but a maze of exclusive sects, societies and clubs. These support the selection of those adapted to American life; they support it in that they help such people to business, political and every kind of success in social life. In these associations the American learns to put himself over.

No one can deny that this kind of association has existed in wild variety. But the association concerned with the public weal or with public policy, so far from legitimating the qualifications of those who worship at the altar of the bitch goddess Success, often elicits obloquy rather than enviable status for its members.

We have already observed that Weber views Benjamin Franklin as a manifestation of the spirit of capitalism "in almost classical purity," devoted as he was to frugality and industry for the sake of personal success. But Franklin was also the association-man par excellence. He probably formed more associations for the public good than any other American of his time: an academy for the education of youth in Pennsylvania, a voluntary fire department, the Pennsylvania Hospital, a society for the abolition of slavery, and the American Philosophical Society (which is still flourishing), and so on. If Franklin's secularized frugality and devotion to a methodical discipline of life and work were due to the influence of "the Protestant ethic," may we not say that his concern for the methodical discipline of associations calculated to promote the public good was also influenced by the Protestant ethic of "totalistic impulse"?

One might raise the question as to why Weber took such a narrow view of the voluntary association as we have just observed. The reason is perhaps that in Germany he could see few associations of the type concerned with public policy. In the lecture just cited he scores the singing academies for draining off the national energy into "warbling," thus distracting attention from public policies (a distraction that, he says, was much to the liking of the politicians in Berlin). Another reason is that in considering the sect as an agency certifying the qualifications of piety he selected characteristics belonging more exclusively to the *withdrawing sect* rather than to the Puritan *aggressive sect* bent on bringing in a new social order (the distinction is Troeltsch's).

We see, then, that "ascetic Protestantism" from the beginning possessed a more composite character than that which Weber attributes to it. No doubt it was because of the broad scope of the totalistic dynamic that Troeltsch spoke of Calvanism as the second social philosophy in the history of Christianity (the first being Thomism and medieval Catholicism). With similar perception Lord Acton was wont to say that the nerve of democracy as we know it was engendered in the small Puritan conventicles of the seventeenth century.

Weber has seen a different side of ascetic Protestantism. But by neglecting the features we have adumbrated here he has given us a lopsided conception of the Protestant ethic. With him we may properly lament the appearance of the degenerated, rationalized, "encaged" Protestantism he presents. But considering the vitalities he has failed to see, may we not be allowed to lament with fewer tears?

But that question is not the proper way to end this chapter. Nearly three-quarters of a century have passed since Max Weber published his study of the Protestant ethic and the spirit of capitalism. The nullity of which he spoke is more readily evident today than when he pointed to it. What Weber the prophet offers us is the shock of recognition—to enable us to see the cage of the so-called affluent society. And seeing it, we are freed to seek an exit.

THE FOLLOWING ESSAY is the most technical theological chapter in this volume. Some readers may find it necessary to read it slowly and in small doses. Yet it is included because of the importance of the issues that are brought to the surface and because it exemplifies an aspect of Adams' work that is too important to be omitted. The concerns that are the focus of this essay derive from much of what we have already read: our humanity, dependent on a Spirit that is larger than our own resources and purposes, is also shaped by the ways in which we organize our common life. In short, the understanding of humanity requires a theological and a sociological perspective. But precisely where and how do they join? How does Spirit touch organization, or does it defy form? Christians have often focused on this question by asking what is the nature of the church; for the church is thought to be, by definition, both a spiritual community and a decisive social structure. At the same time, of course, the spiritual community is not confined to any single empirical structure, and decisive social institutions are by no means confined to the church. How then are these two realities to be related? Much ink and nearly as much blood have been spilled over this issue. The scholarly work of Rudolf Sohm raised the questions again for modern Christians, and it is in the presentation, analysis, and interpretation of Sohm's work that Adams identifies both the affinities and the points of contention that "Liberal" theology has with classic "Evangelical" Protestant and "Catholic" views.*—M.L.S.

CHAPTER 13 · LAW AND THE
RELIGIOUS SPIRIT: RUDOLF SOHM

ACCORDING TO Luther's conception of the Two Kingdoms, the Christian believer belongs to two realms, "one of which is the kingdom of God under Christ and the other is the kingdom of the world under civil authority." These two realms exist under quite different kinds of authority, the one under the love and spirit of Christ, the other under legal restraints; the one under the guidance of the Holy Spirit in conjunction with Word and sacrament, the other under the rule of law. In Luther's view, then, "temporal government has laws which do not reach farther than over person and property and what is external on earth; for God will not permit any one to rule over the soul of man

* This essay first appeared in Walter Leibrecht, ed., *Religion and Culture* (New York: Harper and Row, 1959), pp. 219–35.

but Himself. Where temporal power presumes to give laws to the soul, it touches God's rule and misleads and destroys the souls."

This view, adumbrated in Luther's treatise *On Secular Authority*, has long been a subject of controversy—for example, as it relates to claims regarding the spiritual and political significance of the Lutheran Reformation and the influence of that reformation. A generation ago the controversy found sharp focus in the opposition raised by Karl Holl to Ernst Troeltsch's adverse evaluation of Luther's conception of the two realms, an evaluation that attributed to Luther abject subservience to the power of any state able to establish itself. This particular controversy necessarily involved a discussion of the relations between law and the gospel. Since that time the debate in certain quarters has assumed a more restricted scope having to do with the respective roles of law and Spirit within the church. This discussion, which was vigorously promoted before World War I, appears now to be gathering momentum again. The roster of the contemporary participants in this discussion includes a substantial number of Protestant scholars. Much of the controversy has centered in the questions: what is the role of the Holy Spirit, of charismatic authority, in the church? Is there any place for a sacrosanct legal authority in the church? Does not any rule of law, any legal order, in a Protestant church deprive it of its distinctive evangelical character and freedom, and does it not drive a Protestant church into an essentially Roman Catholic bondage to canon law? Does not law in the church lead to idolatry? Is not charismatic authority in essence incompatible with divinely sanctioned legal authority, whether the latter officially establishes "pure doctrine" or a particular, fixed ecclesiastical order?

A key figure for understanding this controversy is the eminent German jurist and church historian Rudolf Sohm (1841–1917), who viewed charismatic authority (in conjunction with Scripture and the sacraments) to be completely incompatible with any "divine church law." The German literature dealing with Sohm's thesis is abundant, and it continues to grow. Almost every month a new treatment of Sohm appears. The presentation of his outlook set forth in this chapter can provide only a partial background for the understanding of the issues of the current discussion.

At first blush the non-Lutheran Protestant may understandably show little positive interest in the questions that have been raised by Sohm, particularly in so far as they are concerned with the validity of canon law. Is not "divine church law" a matter for live discussion only in Protestant-Catholic polemics? Why need one bother to defend the authority of the Holy Spirit as over against that of canon law? Actually, however, Sohm's characterization and defense of charismatic authority bear affinity to conceptions of the Holy Spirit that are familiar in the free-church tradition and (still more) in the left wing of the Reformation, to which many Protestant denominations and sects trace their lineage. To be sure, Sohm never explicitly recognizes this affinity.

In the face of the history of ecclesiastical legalism and tyranny and of recurrent forms of rigidity in Christian belief and practice, Sohm raised a vigorous protest against any constitutional legalization of the church, whether this legalization be Roman Catholic or Protestant. Besides appealing to Luther's doctrine of the Two Kingdoms (whereby he found an avenue to a New Testament norm for authority in the church), he asserted that in Luther's doctrine of the invisible church the Protestant should recognize a norm that was implicit, if not articulate, in the primitive church's understanding of itself. In spelling out his conception of the New Testament and Lutheran norm, Sohm developed what we might call a theology of church history in terms of loyalty to or deviation from the norm. This normative theory of periodization offers a striking analogy to Anabaptist theories charting the periods of the creation, fall, and redemption of the church. Sohm sets forth a basic norm for the church; he then traces the stages by which the church "fell" away from the Gospel; and, finally, he discerns the recovery of the norm in Luther (and its subsequent perversion in the Protestant churches). Sohm's view of the norm and of defection from it differs in important ways from that of the Anabaptists. We need not consider here the difference between his norm and theirs. It is of special interest, however, to observe that, whereas the Anabaptists discerned the "fall" in the alliance of church and state (with the consequent coercion in matters of faith), Sohm placed the "fall" much earlier, in the advent of church law. In this connection, one should note also the contrast between Sohm's and Harnack's identification of the "fall" of the church; Harnack saw it in the "acute Hellenization" of Christianity, while Sohm identified it with the legalization of Christianity—the advent of a legally constituted church under the episcopate.

In accord with Luther's theory of the Two Kingdoms, Sohm was particularly concerned to dissipate every confusion between the kingdom of Christ and the kingdom of the world. In his view, the most disastrous confusion can appear when the Christian church admits into its structure the authority that belongs to the political realm, the alien principle of legal direction and restraint. The primitive Christian *Ecclesia*, under the charismatic authority issuing from Christ and the Gospel, had excluded this alien principle. But again and again the Christian church has adopted it. Instead of remaining the Body of Christ under the guidance of the Holy Spirit, the church has tended to become a worldly, secular authority and organization, a second state as it were, often exercising legalistic control, including coercion, over its members. The effect has been to secularize the church from within. Sohm epitomizes his view in the axiom, "Ecclesiastical law stands in contradiction to the nature of the *Ecclesia*." From Sohm's point of view, this axiom at the same time grasps the substance of Luther's theory of the two realms and presupposes the New Testament norm of pneumatic or spiritual authority, which is the charter of the freedom that belongs to the church of Christ. The enemy of this freedom is law, "divine church law." Christ has delivered us from law.

Coming from a jurist, this radically negative evaluation of law in the church sounds strange. A striking paradox lies at the center of Sohm's whole enterprise as a historian and interpreter of canon law. As a jurist he devoted much of his career to teaching the theory and history of law. In addition to his classic treatment of Roman private law, *The Institutes*, he published a number of learned studies of Germanic law; he was also concerned with the history of the law of associations. In an autobiographical statement prepared at the request of a law journal, Sohm speaks of choosing his profession of jurist because of his conviction that (secular) law is a great benefactor of mankind, a primary means of social control and human fulfillment. But when he turned his attention to the search for the characteristic authority of the Christian *Ecclesia*, he found that legal concepts were completely inappropriate. The Christian *Ecclesia* was informed by a power of a different order. This power he called charismatic, the power of the Holy Spirit. We shall presently observe that he connected this conception of authority with the view that Christian faith requires primary orientation to an invisible rather than to a visible church. Canon law belongs to a faith that attaches itself to a visible church. Before considering these matters, however, we should examine the concept of law in contrast to which he posits the charismatic authority of the *Ecclesia*. Without an awareness of Sohm's definition of law, one misses the peculiar character of the contrast he envisages for the two realms. An understanding of his concept of law is the more necessary in view of the fact that even his disciples sometimes assert wrongly that for Sohm law is "only the command sanctioned by physical coercion." It is much more than this.

What, then, is law according to Sohm? Law, he says, determines, defines, and distributes the relations of power in terms of justice. Its immediate task through the state is to promote human freedom and justice by bringing congruence out of the struggle of different wills against each other *(bellum omnium contra omnes)*. It achieves this through the formal definitions of rights and obligations. In thus attempting to bring order and right into man's power relations, the immediate purpose of law is to regulate *external* freedom. It does away with external hindrances (such as are characteristic of the kingdom of this world). But law also has a broader task, namely, the congruence of the human will with the divine will. It aims at external freedom for the sake of inner freedom. In this connection one must observe certain contrasts between legal regulations and moral law. The moral imperative is obligatory in terms of its content, which demands inner assent to natural, intrinsic authority; it gives rise to an ethical community that has conventional law but not legal rules; and it is oriented to the present, that is, to the situation of the individual case. On the other hand, the legal statute or the formally established right is rooted in a national community, and it is obligatory without reference either to the present consent of the individual or to special cases. In the realm of law, moreover, one confronts the power of previously articulated forms (statutes, laws, custom); the past appears as the impartial judge of the present. "The nature of legal authority lies not in its being carried out by force, but in this, that it is formal in nature—that is, that it rests on the basis of definite events of the *past,* without possibility of criticism, without consideration of whether or not it appears to be really justifiable in the present." In addition, law must be enforced; "it tends towards coercive realization." The state, as the instrument of the national community and as the executor of law, is accordingly the power

over power relations, the power that enforces law. At the same
time, constitutional and statutory law give realization to a moral
law or to an ideal of justice residing in a community through
mediating agencies and forces that find their ultimate source in a
belief in divine justice. In the general community life, law is
therefore at bottom a moral and religious necessity. In sum, then,
law is concerned with achieving external freedom in the context of
power relations, it defines abstract rights and obligations within
the framework of a national community, its validity is bound up
formally with precedents out of the past, it is ultimately oriented to
moral law and divine law, and it can legitimately effect enforce-
ment by means of coercion.

Now, church law shares these features of law, Sohm finds, but in
a special way. In its earliest stage Christian ecclesiastical law
identified the church with the bishop, giving him legal rights in
perpetuity. Later on (in the Middle Ages), canon law, adopting
categories from Roman law, defines the church as a corporation
possessing the power of the keys to bind and loose and to mediate
the divine life. This corporation is an external, superindividual,
compulsory institution whose leaders hold office by virtue of
formal rights and obligations. These authorities dispense salvation
through the sacraments and through penitential disciplines. The
canon law purports to guarantee legitimacy and continuity for
offices and doctrines. Thus the guarantee binds the church to the
past, and the regulations obtain without possibility of criticism. In
the Middle Ages this legally constituted church becomes a sovereign world power, and that in a twofold fashion: in the secular
imperial constitution and in the church constitution. As a consequence the canon law is a second law alongside the imperial
constitution, and both constitutions are under the aegis of a church
that claims ecclesiastical monopoly. This corporation in the last
resort enforces its multitude of legal regulations by resort to
coercion and with the claim to absolute divine authority. The
inevitable outcome of "the divine church law" is the doctrine of
papal infallibility; and, paradoxically, the papal authority *ex
cathedra* can in the name of tradition subvert both Scripture and
church tradition. Merely human law assumes the status of divine
law. The *Ecclesia* that was ruled by the Spirit and was thus a
spiritual entity has become a secularized corporation under canon
law and papal autocracy. (In the Enlightenment, Sohm observes,

the idea of the corporation persists in Protestantism, albeit under the aegis of freedom. Here again the *Ecclesia* of the Spirit has disappeared insofar as the church is viewed as a voluntary association created by human consensus or contract.) The whole process of legalization, according to Sohm, is a process of secularization. The church becomes simply a worldly organization, making a divine claim for its corporation law. In the name of Christ, who delivered the Christian from subservience to law, the church again subjects men to "divine church law." It loses the authority appropriate and peculiar to the *Ecclesia*. It adopts merely worldly authority, and it proceeds then to give this worldly authority an absolute, divine sanction.

Luther, with his doctrine of the Two Kingdoms and his doctrine of the invisible church, set out to liberate the church from its legalized Babylonish captivity. Returning to the spiritual concept of the earlier *Ecclesia*, he rejected the idolatry and the ecclesiastical monopoly of the "fallen" church, he cast into the flames the *Corpus Iuris Canonici*, and he assigned temporal power with its law to the state (under God and not under the church). The Reformation protest was not a legal protest. It was a religious protest toward the end of making the church the province of the freedom of the Word and of making it again a spiritual entity such as it was at its beginning.

In contrast to the church ruled by "divine church law," Sohm asserts, the primitive Christian *Ecclesia* was under the direction of the Holy Spirit effective in the Body of Christ. His description of the *Ecclesia* is probably the most familiar aspect of his whole theology of church history. It represents the essential norm against which the process of legalistic secularization has exercised its insidious power. The primitive norm is rooted in the Pauline faith that Christ has delivered the Christian from the law and has brought him into the glorious liberty of "the people of God," the Body of Christ. It is rooted also in Jesus' affirmation, "My kingdom is not of this world." The *Ecclesia* came into being not by law or might but rather out of faith in Christ; it is the outcome of the working of *agape*. As the Body of Christ the *Ecclesia* is one and universal. Every assembly, whether large or small, is a manifestation of the one *Ecclesia*, of the whole of Christendom. This view is supported by the words of Jesus, "Where two or three are gathered together in my name, there am I in the midst of them" (Matt.

18:20). Where the Lord is, the head of the Body, there is Christendom with all the promises made to her. As the Body of Christ the *Ecclesia* is constituted by many members who are called by the Holy Spirit to various tasks. It is organized in terms of the distribution of gifts of grace *(charismata),* which both call and qualify the individual Christians for different activities. It is an organization given by God, not a corporation emerging out of merely human consensus. The decisive bearers of *charismata* are endowed with the gift of teaching the Word—apostles, prophets, teachers. Other bearers of *charismata* exhibit other gifts. The activities of the *Ecclesia,* indeed all the fruits of the Spirit, are charismatic in origin. Those leaders endowed with the gift of teaching have the power of the keys: to preach the Word and to apply it spontaneously from case to case. In the course of time the teaching offices became closely related to responsibilities incident to the conduct of the eucharist, but in no case do these bearers of spiritual gifts have a right to their offices. They may be replaced as the Spirit moves, though the apostles enjoy a special status. The leaders depend upon the permission of the assembly, upon charismatic free recognition and obedience. The confirmation of leaders is not a "corporate" action of the assembly as if the assembly were sovereign or democratic. It depends upon the witness coming from God. The obedience to the Spirit is given as a response of love, not out of obligation to law. The efficacy of the Spirit is always connected with Word and sacrament. Under the power of the Spirit the *Ecclesia* is obedient to a living, not to a dead, Word. It is thus not bound to the past.

The question arises as to why this pneumatocracy waned in favor of a legal organization. The causes were many, in Sohm's view. Charismatic leaders became less and less available. Heresy, instead of being combated by the living, authentic Word, was fended off through increasing bureaucratization. The conduct of the eucharist, the administration of the Word, baptism, ordination, church property, and church discipline, gave rise to an officialdom. In this process the doctrine of apostolic succession emerged, the division between clergy and laity appeared. Authority passed from the charismatic leader, a *person,* to a monarchic bureaucracy of permanent *offices* less and less dependent upon the confirmation of the members. The offices took over the control of the elements of the eucharist. This development constituted the reification or "thingification" of piety. The decline and the legalization can be traced in this shift from the charisma of *persons* under the Word to the charisma of *offices* in control of *things*. Charisma becomes an object at the disposal of the hierarchy. Sohm does not explicitly describe the decline in this way, but this is the burden of his account of the transformation of charismatic into legal authority.

A description of institutional changes, however, is insufficient to explain the corruption of the primitive charismatic *Ecclesia*. Something spiritual lies back of this corruption, which despiritualizes, depersonalizes, and legalizes the *Ecclesia*. This spiritual corruption Sohm calls "small faith."

> Mistrust appears, that is, lack of trust in the power of the divine Spirit. Fear raises its head, fear of sin, fear that the power of sin may be greater than that of love. Small faith demands props, crutches, external securities for the conserving of right order in the *Ecclesia*. Small faith longs for legal regulation, formal limits, guarantees for the maintenance of Christendom. Out of this small faith of the Christian epigones, Catholicism came into being. . . . As soon as small faith won the upper hand, as soon as fear of sin became greater than trust in God, legal right followed as a historical necessity. Out of the power of sin, which won room even in Christendom, came the need for church law, and with it came Catholicism.

Sohm is not content to leave the explanation here. He states his position with unsurpassable sharpness. Catholicism—any Christianity dependent on divine church law with respect to doctrine or polity—is precisely an expression of original sin. It is man's pious, "divinely sanctioned" means of escaping from spiritual freedom into the visible security of the Grand Inquisitor, who adds to the "rewards" for piety the gorgeous lushness of worldly success. Why did the *Ecclesia* "fall" into "small faith," into the false faith of Catholicism? Sohm's answer is memorable:

> The reason is not far to seek: Because the natural man is a born enemy of Christianity. . . . The natural man desires to remain under law. He strives against the freedom of the gospel. . . . He longs for a legally appointed church, for a kingdom of Christ which may be seen with the eyes of the natural man, for a temple of God, built with earthly gold and precious stones,

that shall take the heart captive through outward sanctities, traditional ceremonies, gorgeous vestments, and a ritual that tunes the soul to the right pitch of devotion. . . . Before all, he longs for an impressive, authoritative constitution, one that shall overpower the senses, and rule the world. He desires, as the key-stone of the whole, a fixed body of doctrine that shall give certain intelligence concerning all divine mysteries, presented to him in literal form, giving an answer to every possible question. . . . He desires a rock which his eyes can see—the visible church, the visible Word of God. Everything must be made visible, so that he may grasp it. From these impulses of the natural man, born at once of his longing for the gospel and his despair of attaining it, Catholicism has arisen. Herein lies the secret of the enormous power it has had over the masses who are "babes"; it satisfies these cravings. *The natural man is a born Catholic.*

"The natural man is a born Catholic." He wants an absolutized, visible church to which he may attach himself and from which he may receive guarantees. In short, he is an idolator. The Christian needs something to protect him from the temptations of "small faith" and to maintain his trust in Christ and the Holy Spirit and in a living Word. Actually, the primitive *Ecclesia* by its "fall" revealed a limitation that may have been inherent in that *Ecclesia*. It left the way open for Christians to put their faith in a tangible absolute.

Here Sohm's conception of the significance of the Lutheran Reformation becomes decisive. According to Sohm, Luther offered a corrective to the primitive *Ecclesia* and also to legalized Christianity by his doctrine of the invisible church. Faith in a visible church is the "small faith" of the natural man, the natural-born Catholic. Faith in the invisible church alone protects one from the natural man's idolatry. This conception of Sohm's has elicited such vigorous debate that we should cite here at considerable length the passage in which he sets forth his most radical application of the doctrine of the invisible church.

The Church in the religious sense—the Church as the people of God on earth—is a matter of faith and "what one believes, that one cannot see"; it cannot be seen with the eye of the natural man. The existence of the people of God (the *Ecclesia*) indicates the existence of a new life, of a superworldly life in the midst of the world, of a life through Christ with and from God. That there is such a life cannot be demonstrated by the reason or comprehended by it. The Church of Christ, therefore, does not exist for the unbeliever. It exists only for him who is himself a partaker of this life. . . . He recognizes it by means of its signs of life (the *notae ecclesiae*), especially by the preaching of the divine Word, to forms of which the Sacraments also belong. The believer perceives and comprehends the communion of saints which supports and nourishes him. He experiences the power which flows out of the people of God, out of the living Word, into his soul and assures him that such a word is the Word of God directed to him. The signs of life of the Church of Christ *(externae notae ecclesiae)* are manifest in the external visible Christianity, the fruits of which are peace, joy, righteousness, and works of Christian love. But it is a fellowship of these things that outwardly appear not by virtue of an external common possession but only as the fellowship of the invisible spiritual life out of which word and work arise. Therefore no one is able to see this fellowship to which word and work belong unless it be a believer. . . .

The Church in the religious sense, the people of God on earth, is, even as far as it possesses the Word and Sacraments not an external corporate fellowship. It can therefore not have an objective, institutional existence founded in any way on the possession of holy things physically perceptible. The Church in the sense of the Lutheran Reformation is not a holy institution, but a holy people (Luther: a holy Christian people which believes indeed in Christ); further, it is not a people to which a certain (although not outwardly recognizable) group of persons belong, but a people whose members are determined by the presence of a spiritual stream of life continually active in it. The people of God, the Church of Christ, exists where the new life through Christ with and of God manifests itself, life of super-earthly strength—today powerful in you, tomorrow in another. The people of God is not in any way an institutionally or personally organized, corporate society. The people of God is invisible. . . .

The Church of Christ is invisible. Therefore there is no visible fellowship which as such might be the Church of Christ. Even in as far as it possesses and administers Word and

Sacraments the visible "bodily" Christianity is not the Church of Christ. It possesses Word and Sacrament only outwardly, apparently. Just to the extent that it is the true Word of God that is operative in the visible Christianity, it is an action not of the visible but of the concealed, invisible Christianity. . . . Visible Christianity does not have the Spirit of God, is not the people of God, does not have the Word of God. . . . It is only the Christian World, not the Christian Church. Even in as far as it produces a fellowship of Word and Sacrament, it is only world, and not Church at all. There is no visible Church.

Thus Word and confession of visible Christianity are always only word and confession of the Christian world, never word and confession of the Christian Church (the Church of Christ). The word of the Christian world, as is self-evident, is not religiously binding; it is the fallible word of man, not the infallible word of God. An externally visible confession (word) of the invisible Church of Christ cannot be formulated at all. There is no infallible church.

The Church of Christ is not a confessional church. Had it a visible confession it would not be invisible. Its nature is not that of formulated doctrine but of participation in a spiritual, divine, holy life, which can be associated with the most varied kinds and types of spiritual confession. Therefore, according to the unquestionable Protestant doctrine of faith, the Christian Church (the true Church, the Church in the religious sense) is spread over all confessions. It is super-confessional. . . . The word of the gospel, of the good news of the Kingdom of God in the hearts of men can never be comprehended in the word of men. The Christian faith must always strive for an expression by which it can make intelligible the content of its assurance. There is no Christianity that is not dogmatic. There must always be dogmatics, but never dogmas which with their fixed forms finally assume sway over the nature of Christendom. . . . There is no *one* dogma, nor *one* doctrine, which is the sole means of grace. Protestantism in general does not know a faith in a doctrine of the church, nor a faith in the Scriptures. That would be mere assumption. Faith in the Protestant sense is trust that triumphs over the world and death. We can believe only in a living personality; in Christ and through Christ in God. No doctrine of any kind saves. Faith alone saves. . . . No kind of visible fellowship based on doctrine, but only the invisible fellowship of the Church of Christ can be the fellowship in which alone there is salvation. There is no visible church which is the sole possessor of the power to save.

Sohm's interpretation of the Two Kingdoms has led him to make the earthly kingdom visible and the spiritual one invisible. Although he asserts at times that the invisible church is always becoming (ambiguously) visible, one may question with many scholars whether his concept of the church is in accord with Luther's. In any event, Sohm is well aware his is *not* the concept that obtained in the primitive *Ecclesia* itself (although he holds that the idea was implicit in the view that the *Ecclesia* is a stranger on the earth).

Luther's concept of the church is different from the concept of apostolic Christendom. But in our knowledge of the nature of Christendom we also are not bound by apostolic Christianity. Luther brought forth his church-concept out of the depths of his own life with God, out of the gospel which had not attained to the knowledge of the invisibility of the people of God. Therefore it became Catholic. The discovery of Luther, that the church is invisible, carried within it the dissolution of Catholicism.

"Out of the depths of his own life with God, out of the gospel" that had been newly experienced by him. These words point to one of the most important things at stake for Sohm in the appeal to the invisible church (and to charismatic authority): inwardness is the indispensable condition of the working of the Word and the Spirit. In Sohm's view, faith in the invisible church is a sign not only of the Christian's dependence upon a grace from beyond this world, but also of the interiorization of piety.

This emphasis on the inwardness of true piety is succinctly expressed in Luther's assertion that every man must do his own believing. It is made very explicit in the paragraph of his treatise *On Secular Authority* that we cited at the beginning of the present essay: "Temporal government has laws which do not reach farther than over person and property and what is external on the earth; for God will not permit any one to rule over the soul of man but Himself."

In his pursuance of this theme Sohm brings his constructive position to a focus. The motive that runs through his whole protest against "divine church law" is his pathos for inwardness. Ecclesiastical law is the identification of the divine with external, finite machinery. Again and again Sohm asserts in one way or another that "one apprehends the Word of God not in some *form* or other but in its inner power. Christianity has only to follow that Word which by the power of an inner, free assent it *recognizes* as the Word of God. . . . God is *beyond* all legal ordering. He is not the source or object of any kind of law; he is only the source and goal of the inner life of the individual. The relation to God is no legal relationship, it is never a substantial part of any sort of *external* common life. Indeed, it is a relation of *person to person*—that is the secret of religion. It is this which is expressed in the faith in the love of God and in the righteousness of God springing from love." Sohm goes so far in his emphasis on inwardness as to say that the polity of the Church, a merely secular concern, is a matter of indifference. Thus he appears to view everything ecclesiastical as externality, as institution, as tradition, as "world." The inwardness of the working of the Spirit delivers from all bondage to the finite order and to the past—even from bondage to "apostolic Christianity." It is the absolute opposite of law.

What shall we think of Sohm as a theologian of law and of the Spirit? Any adequate evaluation of the great jurist today, over sixty years after the publication of his first massive volume of *Kirchenrecht*, should take into account a host of writings dealing with Sohm's views pro and con. We can here raise only a few of the important issues. These issues have to do with historical questions, and they have to do with theological questions regarding his treatment of law and the Spirit and of the relations between them.

Despite the extraordinarily vigorous and extensive literature that has appeared on Sohm, the crucial historical questions he has posed (particularly with respect to the primitive *Ecclesia*) remain, as Bultmann has said, unsolved. Harnack's double-organization theory continues to stand over against the Sohmian view of the early church, for there are signs of "constitutional" as well as of charismatic authority almost from the beginning. Bultmann suggests that the difference between Harnack and Sohm issues from the fact that the former is concerned with historical and sociologi-

cal motifs, while the latter is interested in the *Ecclesia*'s self-understanding.

Sohm's work illustrates the opportunities and the perils that
attach to historical analysis, particularly when that analysis is
conditioned by a theological presupposition that is to be vindicated
at all cost. Sohm's Lutheran piety and his Two Kingdom theory
have sharpened his scent for data that otherwise might not be
taken sufficiently into account. Certainly, Sohm's work represents
a turning point, indeed a point of no return, in the development of
New Testament scholarship during the past century. Before his
time, as Olaf Linton has shown, the consensus of scholarly
judgment favored the attempt to understand the church, in antiq-
uity or today, in terms of corporation or association theory. Since
his time that consensus no longer exists. Sohm as a jurist in
command of the immense lore regarding associations and as a
theologian accepting the dualistic view incident to the Two Kingdom theory spent most of his effort to show, on the one hand, that
the primitive church (and any Christian church) cannot be understood as a corporation based on law, consensus, contract, or
voluntary association and, on the other, that the church must be
interpreted in its own terms. His singling out of charismatic
authority as a unique and decisive feature of the primitive *Ecclesia*
can never properly be gainsaid. By directing attention to the role of
charismatic authority Sohm has done much to stimulate in ecclesiological theory the reinstatement of the doctrine of the Holy
Spirit. Thus he has shown that a church that today makes no room
for charisma does not stand in continuity with the early *Ecclesia*.
Moreover, Sohm's description of the *Ecclesia* as being in principle
one and universal, rather than being a congeries of autonomous
congregations, is now generally accepted. And with respect to his
axiom that "legal regulation contradicts the nature of the Church,"
we must agree with Bultmann that this view is irrefutable if such
regulation is interpreted as constitutive and not merely regulative.
In this connection we should also observe that Sohm's periodization of the history of the church in terms of alternative attitudes
toward church law offers a highly instructive perspective.

These insights of Sohm are the valid increment that has issued
from his application of the Two Kingdom theory. Yet, Sohm's
search for a norm consistent with this theory probably caused him
to give a distorted account of the structure of authority in the

primitive *Ecclesia.* His characterization of the *Ecclesia* is unquestionably lopsided. In presenting the evidence for the role of charisma he centered attention on the Pauline churches, and he thereby ignored the predominantly monarchic system of the Jerusalem community and of the congregations of the pastoral Epistles. He failed also to consider the Oriental background of the primitive community's conception of authority. This failure is understandable in the light of the state of research in Sohm's time. The current investigation of the Qumram community promises to reveal much regarding Oriental and Jewish conceptions of "constitutional" authority. Here, and also in the primitive *Ecclesia*, one finds signs of a complex, organic constitution where, as Bo Reiche has shown, "inclinations toward monarchy, oligarchy and democracy were present together, without being mutually exclusive or even in conflict." Apart from these considerations, however, we must observe that Sohm gave no attention to early Christian theological thinking about law. He allowed his own juristic conceptions to dominate his analysis. He even ignored the kerygmatic or charismatic interpretation of law implicit in the judicial procedures of the *Ecclesia* itself, procedures that were sanctioned by St. Paul's admonition that Christians should eschew the civil courts (I Cor. 6:1–11). These procedures, which perhaps initially had more to do with the cure of souls than with legal regulation, subsequently developed into the *episkopalis audientia.* In this connection we should add that Sohm overlooked the role of tradition in general, even of tradition initiated by charismatic authority. Thus he neglected to observe that the principle of hierarchy obtaining within the original *Ecclesia* possibly served as a formal model for the later, "legalized" Catholic hierarchy.

When we evaluate Sohm's work as a theologian of law and Spirit we must adopt an equally ambiguous judgment. It is understandable and justifiable if in face of an absolute "divine church law" he assumed that the alternative for the Christian church is *aut papa—aut nihil.* But not so much can be said for his view that church law is merely regulative. Here he adopted a laissez faire attitude, as long as charisma could find a place. Sohm's attitude, as well as his lack of concern for New Testament conceptions of law, was conditioned by a nineteenth-century conservative, positivist, formal conception of law—scarcely a Christian interpretation of law. As a consequence, he overstressed the static, abstract character of law and the bondage of law to the past. Indeed, he seems to have been willing to leave regulative law, including church polity, undisturbed if it made no absolute claims. But we must ask, if the Word can be alive, why not also law? Here Karl Barth's view is particularly pertinent and cogent. With considerable persuasiveness (and probably following Bohatec's interpretation of Calvin) Barth rejects Brunner's support of Sohm's antilegalism, by demanding law in the church, *living* law, if the church is to be faithful to its mission in the changing historical situation. Actually, Sohm's interpretation of the Two Kingdom theory led him to an acute dualism. Thus he was able to see no direct connection between law and Spirit, even between law and love. And he was able to see nothing of inwardness in law. Law is external, Spirit is sheer inwardness; love is appropriate only in immediate person-to-person relations. Not that law offers nothing to inwardness: it promotes external freedom for the sake of internal freedom. But law and love, justice and love, in Sohm's view, must be kept in separate spheres.

Accordingly, in an address delivered in 1895 at the twenty-eighth Congress of the Inner Mission, Sohm warned emphatically against any mixing up of the Christian work of love with the social question in any consideration of the theme "Christian-Social." "The social question," he said, "is *only* a question of justice, no question of love." If the Christian is to concern himself with justice, he should leave the Church out of it and proceed to fulfill his worldly vocation or to work as a citizen in a worldly voluntary association. Indeed, Sohm in these ways devoted himself to the extension of suffrage and to the elevation of the working classes against the complacent dominance enjoyed by the bourgeoisie. He had a theory of periodization regarding the history of the social classes—from the medieval aristocracy to the modern bourgeoisie to the contemporary emergence of the worker in his search for dignity and rights. But, in Sohm's view, one should not expect the Christian faith or the Christian church to suggest a direction in the search for justice: "the social classes do not demand or crave for love, they crave for their right."

Considering Sohm's lament over the invasion of law into the church, one would expect him to desiderate the separation of church and state. But so far from being sympathetic with the left wing of the Reformation and with the Nonconformist tradition, he is very critical of any movement that "weakens the power and meaning of church organization." He takes a dim view even of Pietism's formation of *ecclesiolae in ecclesia*. The church as a legal entity within the community requires "as an equal" the support of the state. "The separation of church and state would mean the disappearance of the church from the law!" On the other hand, the church "in the religious sense," as we have seen, stands so high over the earthly reality that it no longer touches the earth. So does Sohm interpret the Two Kingdom theory. It should be added, however, that in his view the church in both the religious and the legal sense must not be subjected to coercion; this view he derives from the Two Kingdom theory of the separation of powers. In this connection he has nothing but praise for liberalism for its resistance to coercion in religion.

If we turn now to consider Sohm's conception of Spirit we find again the dualism we have noted in other aspects of his outlook. Charisma works only spontaneously, from case to case. He sees no connection between charisma and *logos*. Thus he gives no attention to ways in which the charisma relates itself to the analysis of the empirical reality in face of which it will offer love. Nor is there any suggestion that any sort of casuistry is required. In the dimension of Spirit he seems to prefer a purely dispositional ethic, and he gives no indication as to how response to the Spirit involves responsibility for the consequence of action or inaction. Moreover, he fails to consider how Spirit effects consensus among Christians. Some sort of automatic predetermined harmony is relied upon for the church "in the religious sense." This harmony presumably ensues if faith does not allow itself to be yoked to contingent actualities.

It is at this point, however, that Sohm's conception of the invisible church achieves genuine positive significance. The Christian's faith in and loyalty to the invisible church, as we have seen, protects the Christian from idolatry and also from *bondage* to the past. The Christian *Ecclesia* is not to be identified with the worldly ecclesiastical institution, for that is only the Christian "world," not the Christian church. "Visible Christianity," he says, "does not possess the Spirit of God, it is not the people of God, it does not possess the Word of God." Therefore, it is to be properly understood only in its relation to the critical and creative energies of the invisible church. Here Sohm approaches the articulation of what Paul Tillich calls "the Protestant principle." He would readily accept Tillich's statement that "although the Church represents the Kingdom of God in history, it is not the Kingdom of God. It can be perverted into a representation of the demonic Kingdom." But in face of Sohm's dualism of visible-invisible, Tillich, insisting that "there is not a visible and an invisible church as two 'churches'," would deplore Sohm's docetic derogation of the empirical church over against the spiritual church. In this respect Tillich comes nearer than Sohm to Luther's conception of the visible-invisible church. Sohm's dualism, supported by his pathos for inwardness (a kind of *hybris*) led him astray.

For his part, Sohm so much derogates the "worldly," visible church that he says its organization is a matter of indifference. In his view, no polity can guarantee the working of the Spirit that gives birth to love among the brethren; no polity may be accepted as a norm. To absolutize a norm for the organization of the church would constitute the reversion from Spirit to law. The sense of the dualism between the visible and the invisible church, however, prevents Sohm from indicating whether (apart from an absolutistic church) there is any polity that is more or less receptive to the promptings of the Spirit than another. Nor does he show how the invisible church operates in order to make an impact upon the organization of the visible church. There is "no line of connection" from the spiritual church to polity. To find such a line, according to Sohm, is "un-Lutheran."

Sohm's view is that within any polity, except one in which "divine church law" prevails, room can be made for charismatic authority. But if this room is to be found, he insists, we must be able to respond to the Power that is able to exorcise our demonic attachment to the false faiths of ecclesiasticism and of "culture." "One thing is certain," he says. "It is not our culture that will save us, but the gospel alone." In this faith Rudolf Sohm undertook his entire lifework. The question remains, however, as to whether he was able to achieve an adequate understanding of the relationship between the vertical and the horizontal dimensions of Christian faith. It is to figures such as Ernst Troeltsch and Paul Tillich that we must turn for views that are more adequate, because they presuppose a more critical and creative relationship between the Two Kingdoms.

ERNST TROELTSCH was perhaps the European author most influential on teachers of Christian Social Ethics as it developed in America during the twentieth century. James Luther Adams, one of his most persistent interpreters, is still working on the translation and publication of several major Troeltsch essays as this book goes to press. To be sure, Troeltsch has been sharply criticized all during this period by historians, sociologists, theologians, and philosophers. Often they want ethicists to use their methods, ask their questions, and find their answers. But Adams and many others persist in reading Troeltsch precisely because he poses decisive ethical issues by drawing upon historical, sociological, theological, and philosophical materials in a particular way. He thus serves as a model for dealing with necessarily various materials while maintaining a sense of coherence. Adams sets forth aspects of Troeltsch that remain of particular importance in the following chapter.* As so often in his expositions, he also exposes his own concerns.—M.L.S.

CHAPTER 14 · HUMAN RELATIVITY AND
RELIGIOUS VALIDITY: ERNST TROELTSCH

ERNST TROELTSCH was a towering figure in the world of German scholarship during the first quarter of the present century. A professor of theology at Heidelberg from 1894 to 1915, he was closely associated with Max Weber. A professor of philosophy at Berlin from 1915 until the time of his death in 1923, he was the outstanding philosophical theologian of German Protestantism in his period. The scope of his concerns was wide. His writings deal with religious and intellectual history, the philosophy and sociology of religion and culture, historiography and the philosophy of history, metaphysics, theology, and social ethics. Besides his academic pursuits, he was for many years involved in public affairs; indeed, in the Weimar Republic he was at times mentioned as presidential timber.

For Troeltsch the postwar situation as well as the war brought to a focus the confusion and crisis in Western culture that had been the central issue of his previous scholarly and practical effort. A paradoxical situation had become fairly characteristic of the

---

* This essay first appeared in the *Journal for the Scientific Study of Religion*, vol. 1, no. 1 (October 1961), pp. 98–109.

age—on the one hand, endemic forms of dogmatism relying upon false absolutes; on the other, culture relativism, which had emerged as a consequence of the historical consciousness that came to birth in the eighteenth century. Troeltsch's older contemporary Wilhelm Dilthey had spoken of it as "the anarchy of values." Troeltsch's experience of this general state of crisis gave rise to the most persistent tensions of his thought, the tension between the absolute and the relative, and the tension between the claims of a categorical ideal and the demands, the possibilities, and the ambiguities of ongoing history.

In his definition and resolution of these and related issues Troeltsch in certain respects was a harbinger of contemporary existentialism. In face of the absurdity of absolutism (religious, political, and scientistic) on the one hand, and of the emptiness of cultural relativism on the other, he looked for a new statement of the valid ground for meaning. His struggle was a passionate one against meaninglessness. At the beginning of his career he, like his theological teacher Albrecht Ritschl, viewed Christianity as the absolute religion; and he also accepted a Kantian framework as adequate for a philosophy of values. But gradually he came to place more emphasis upon the temporality, the historicity, of religion and ethical norms. This orientation brought to a sharp issue the question of the relation between individuality (with its diversity) and validity (with its claim to transcend the actual). He became increasingly skeptical of rationalism, in its various forms, that claimed to possess a unitary method—whether it be idealist (Hegelian), realist (Marxist), supernaturalist, or naturalist. He held that scientism comes short of being empirical insofar as it screens out unique inwardness and commitment to transcendent meaning. Rationalism had also overlooked the fact that subject and object cannot be understood in separation from each other; a more dynamic and dialectical conception was required. Thus he was prone to stress the tensions, the ambiguities, the relativities of existence. Indeed, personality itself, he argued, exists in a tension between the essential and the existential self. With respect to man's practical relation to the world around him Troeltsch was convinced that interiority can achieve authenticity only through responsible decision and participation in history and community. In his emphasis upon the institutional dimension of the human condition he was quite unlike many of the so-called existentialists.

In this total situation the role of religion he believed, is decisive, for it informs freedom and decision in terms of ultimate demand and support and commitment. His concern with the phenomenon of religion was therefore not merely scientific, in the sense of concern with "objective" description alone. It was for him a living option, an enterprise involving "creation, decision, and fate." New creation and new decision, he believed, are required if the anarchy of values is to be overcome. But in the midst of variety of perspective and in face of the historical, individual character of any culture, where can one find a basis for a standard of values and of religion? What is the ground of validity?

In the ensuing introductory exposition attention will be confined mainly to the writings that reveal his outlook on the philosophy and psychology of religion, the sociology of religion, and the philosophy of history. The periods of development in his thinking accompanied in the main this succession of dominant interests.

THE PHILOSOPHY AND PSYCHOLOGY OF RELIGION

In dealing with questions regarding the nature and the validity of religion, Troeltsch held that everything depends upon the method of approach. Orthodox Christian supernaturalism in vain tries to settle the questions by dogmatic appeal to the fiat of objective revelation. Other groups make equally spurious appeal to an inner miracle of grace, an internalized form of supernaturalism. Naturalism of the scientist variety, on the other hand, dogmatically reduces religion to something other than itself, in terms of either bio-physical or psycho-sociological theory. It denies its independence and integrity by explaining them away. Naturalism as well as supernaturalism appeals to a false absolute. In each instance the false absolute inheres in the method employed.

The essential elements in Troeltsch's critique of the presuppositions of naturalism may be seen in his analysis of positivist psychology of religion. In Troeltsch's time in Germany the debate, pro and con, was largely conditioned by a dualism that may be traced to Kant's distinction between the realm of natural phenomena and the kingdom of ends. Naturalism tries to understand religion, and to estimate its validity, by reference to causal uniformities and necessities attributed to the phenomenal order.

Thus it reduces it to simpler processes and necessities. Under the influence of evolutionary theory, it sometimes seeks for a genetic explanation by assimilating religion to the primitive mentality. And it does these things ostensibly in the name of empiricism. But in all this, naturalism falls short of being empirical, for it dissolves the qualitative differentiae of religion. Moreover, it ignores the fact that no empirical science is competent to deal with the question of validity.

In Troeltsch's judgment, Wilhelm Dilthey proposed a method that, in accord with the Kantian idealism of freedom, makes assumptions more appropriate for the study of human nature and religion. His concept of *Erlebnis*, his definition of the *Geisteswissenschaften*, and his typology of worldviews, are calculated to discern the qualitative aspects of man's inner life and of his cultural creativity. But Dilthey possessed no criterion of validity.

For the sake of further discrimination of the qualitative and individual aspects of experience and for the sake also of approaching a criterion of validity Troeltsch adopted (and further developed) from Windelband and Rickert the distinction between the nomothetic and the ideographic sciences, a distinction determined by the respective characteristic concerns or "interests" of the two types of science. In the former the method is "generalizing," in the latter it is "individualizing." Troeltsch voiced a good many of the criticisms that have been directed against this distinction, viewing the concepts here employed as polar concepts and pointing out also that the distinction may not properly be used to classify the sciences in some simple way. Moreover, he combined and transcended the distinctions in his conception of "individual totalities" and in his concept of types. Nevertheless, it must be noted that he placed too much emphasis on the distinction.

The demand for an ideographic, particularizing method in addition to a nomothetic, generalizing approach transcends the specifically Kantian view regarding the difference between the theoretical and the practical realm. Troeltsch favored a meroscopic instead of a holoscopic approach, to use a terminology made familiar by Richard McKeon of Chicago. The holoscopic outlook, as with Plato, Hegel, and the naturalists, attempts to bring everything under a unitary perspective. The meroscopic outlook, as with Aristotle, Kant, and Troeltsch, presupposes that different spheres of reality should be described by means of quite different types of concept. Referring to both naturalism and Hegelian idealism, Troeltsch says that "monism remains an empty ideal."

But the meroscopic conception as such does not provide a basis for the *validation* of religion and of value perspectives. A third group of sciences, the normative sciences, is required. We must omit exposition here of the refinements of Troeltsch's epistemology and of his psychology of the self. In Kantian (and Neo-Kantian) fashion he distinguishes between the epistemological subject—consciousness in general—and the psychological subject. By reference to the epistemological subject he points to the *necessities* of thought, necessities that function in the nomothetic, the ideographic, and the normative sciences.

Under the aegis of the necessities of thought—a law of consciousness—Troeltsch proposes a means for the validation of religion and of other spheres (logic, ethics, religion) at the normative level. Going beyond Windelband, he asserts that religion "bears within it its own inner necessity and obligatory force in a specifically religious manner." On the basis of this presupposition Troeltsch devises the concept of "the religious a priori," a conception somewhat similar to Rudolf Otto's "idea of the Holy." By this concept he refers to the "law" of the self-apprehension of the unity of consciousness in a transcendent ground. Here he goes beyond Kant to assert a mystical immediacy with the transcendent ground; at the same time he rejects Kantian metaphysical agnosticism. He asserts that in the background of the original Kantian position, and of his own position, is a "metaphysical stance," a modified monadology stemming from Leibniz. "The unconditionality of all that which is a priori," he says, "and the continuity and logical succession of the historical forms of reason seem to point to an active presence of the absolute spirit in finite things, to an activity of the universe, as Schleiermacher says, in individual souls."

But the religious a priori does not function merely within the *Innerlichkeit* of the relation between the individual and the divine. It comes to play in "a world of historical struggle and becoming." Increasingly, Troeltsch became aware of the fact that the individuality of history can impinge upon the normative sciences, and particularly upon the functioning of the religious a priori. In his memorial essay on William James he acknowledged that, within the context of his own transcendentalism, he must give more weight than hitherto to James' lively, concrete awareness of

"multiplicity, irrationality, mere actuality, vital creative power."
Transcendentalism, he saw, cannot explain concrete experience.
The system of a prioris is only a system of *forms* that must be given
content by the world of actualities. The religious a priori cannot
account for the positive religions in their individuality and diversity. Indeed, even the realm of "universal consciousness" is fraught
with contingency.

In his essay of 1910 on "Contingency" (Hastings' *Encyclopaedia
of Religion and Ethics*) Troeltsch clearly breaks through the
Kantian rationalism that informs his doctrine of the religious a
priori. He recognizes that facts as such are irrational and contingent; even the existence of the world itself cannot be derived from
a rational a priori. A variety of "laws" operate simultaneously, and
their conjunction is a contingent matter. Moreover, these laws do
not exhaust reality. Reality in all its richness, both as a whole and
in its components, is an expression of individuality. The consciousness that postulates the laws is itself a part of that individuality. In
short, the world is not generated by consciousness, but rather is
the matrix within which consciousness and freedom emerge. An
elasticity in things is due to a causal nonequivalence. Moral and
religious ideas may be unconditionally necessary, but their content
is dependent upon the actual, historical conditions of human life. In
the light of Troeltsch's recognition of all these conditioning con-
tingencies, it is not surprising that the concept of the religious a
priori does not appear in his later writings.

But this does not mean that the effort to find a standard or to
validate a religious interpretation is a failure or is abandoned.
Troeltsch stands by his view of the unconditional ground, indeed as
a necessity of thought. At the same time, he does not claim to have
"demonstrated" anything. The idea that meaning possesses an
unconditional quality and ground is a matter of faith. Yet, the
orientation to the unconditional serves to ward off the delusion
that "science must dissolve the a priori functions into insubstantial
dependencies and products, of the struggle for existence and of the
most elemental activities, thereby making them into great self-
deceptions of mankind." Ultimately, both science and religion, also
logic and aesthetics, depend upon reference to an ultimate and final
value. "The ontological ought is the key to being."

At this point we should observe that although Troeltsch in this
whole trend claims to transcend Kant by his appeal to the

ontological, he seems not to have considered the possibility of relating the question of standards to an elaborated ontology. He goes beyond Kant in the direction of a mystical philosophy and (as we shall see) of a philosophy of history rather than of a philosophy oriented to the categories of being. In this failure to explicate the categories of being he is to be contrasted with Paul Tillich. Also, his conception of the unconditional, unlike Tillich's, remains within the framework of theism (and of idealism).

The question still remains as to the relation between the ultimate orientation (of religion and of ethical values) and the concrete actualities of historical existence and also the question as to the relation to the positive religions. Before considering these questions further, it will be instructive to examine the major dimensions of Troeltsch's sociology of religion. In this way we shall be able first to observe how he specifically understands the relations between religion as a historical phenomenon and the concrete realities or structures of historical existence.

THE SOCIOLOGY OF RELIGION

According to Troeltsch, sociology as a new way of looking at life and as a special discipline is a product of the historical consciousness. Initially, as presented by its great proponents, it combined descriptive and normative concerns. This combination of concerns was partly due to the fact that it figured in the ideological conflicts emerging after the Enlightenment. Accordingly, the sociology of religion came to birth almost simultaneously with sociology itself. With Marx and Comte, for example, sociology of religion was connected with an attack on traditional religion and its institutions; with Bonald and Stahl it took the form of a conservative defense and counterattack.

This all-embracing kind of sociology Troeltsch believed to be "the source of all errors and confusion." These errors and confusions, whether perpetrated by scientific positivists, supernaturalist theologians, or Marxists, issue from the view that all reality is "accessible to a single method." The attractiveness of this view, "so irresistible to many, depends upon the simplicity of presupposition." Troeltsch shows the paradoxes and inconsistencies to which a monolithic method must resort. Rejecting this approach and rejecting also the kind of sociology that combines descriptive and normative purposes, he views this science as "a separate discipline of general conceptual character which seeks to schematize comparatively the forms and conditions of socialization in general, and thereby it becomes a science ancillary to history and the philosophy of culture, a prerequisite for understanding the always institutionally articulated historical events." He insists that these disciplines should not be confused.

Troeltsch's interest in the sociology of religion and in its possible contribution to his own concerns—history and the philosophy of culture and religion—developed after he came into personal association with Max Weber, beginning in 1897. Writing about Weber at the time of his death, Troeltsch says, "For years I experienced in daily contact with him the infinitely stimulating power of this man, and I am aware of owing him a great part of my knowledge and ability."

Troeltsch was not a professional sociologist, nor did he intend to be. He viewed sociology as a discipline ancillary to his own frankly normative discipline. Yet, his accomplishment in the application of the methods of sociology of religion to the study of the history of Christianity represents a great pioneering effort. As Talcott Parsons says, he is "perhaps the most eminent sociologically oriented historian of Western Christianity." He possessed a fairly thorough knowledge of the work of the major European sociologists of his time and of the nineteenth century. But he did not attempt to set forth a systematic exposition of methods and principles; yet, certain characteristic insights and tools are to be discerned in his historical writings. In this dimension his major interest was in the philosophical presuppositions of sociological method. Moreover, his sociological analyses appear within the context of his study of broad socio-cultural movements; he had no interest in limited studies requiring close analysis of detailed empirical findings. Nor was he in general concerned to discover sociological laws, though he did adapt for his own purposes the Weberian method of "Ideal Types." He wished primarily to discern "from case to case" the uniqueness of milieu within which the mutual interplay between idea and institution, between idea and social forces, takes place. Accordingly, in his *The Social Teaching of the Christian Churches* (1912), he sought to discover the reciprocal influences between ideas, religious groups, and other institutions. In this work, as elsewhere, he stressed the specifically religious character of the

Gospel, the intimate personalism of the Christian ethos, its pathos for communion and community, the close relation between the supramundane God and "asceticism," and Western Christianity's creative adaptability to, and tension with, changing situations. He sought out the ways in which Christianity has functioned as an (indirect) agency of social change. On the other hand, he was so prone to emphasize the obstructions to "heroic religion" at the hands of entrenched power and custom that Max Scheler can say that in this respect he has given us a "sociology of resignation." This phrase of Scheler's should not blind one to Troeltsch's emphasis upon the tremendous innovating power of prophetic Christianity.

In view of the fact that Troeltsch's sociological analyses appear in his writings on the history of Christianity, it is instructive to observe the difference between his method and that which had prevailed among Protestant church historians in the immediately preceding period. The Hegelian and Neo-Hegelian idealists had interpreted Christianity as the unfolding of an idea, according to some uniform developmental principle; they also tended to stress the decisive role of great men. Troeltsch believed it impossible to formulate any such idea or principle. He also rejected the notion that the history of religion can be understood in terms simply of the relations between ideas and persons. As touching the role of great men, he believed the great religious geniuses to be correct in their view that "grace and election are the secret and essence of history." Christianity as a historical religion is and will continue to be inextricably oriented to its founder.

Troeltsch as sociologist of religion is often referred to as a Neo-Kantian. This characterization is scarcely sufficient, and it can be misleading. Despite his many criticisms of Marx, he also learned from him. Indeed, he suggested that some of the orthodox Christians could benefit from a dose of Marxism. Like Weber, he was opposed to either a purely idealist or a purely realist interpretation of the role of ideas in history. As against Marx, he held that ideas may not be viewed in automatic fashion as only the precipitate of economic forces. Even with respect to class stratification, the decisive factor may not be economic. Moreover, the lower classes often represent the most propitious place in society for the emergence of purely religious intuition or organization. On the other hand, class interest may distort a religious idea, slanting it in a tendential fashion. Thus the total socio-economic and cultural situation must be taken into account in the study of the migration and transformation of ideas. In this connection the role of urbanism or of agrarianism and of a natural or a money economy always comes into consideration. In general, then, a religious idea in its impact and in its exfoliation has to be understood by means of a sociological analysis of its influence upon the organizations and institutions emanating from it, and of the influence of these institutions upon it. These ideas and institutions in turn should be seen in mutual relation to other social forces, institutions and their value systems. Moreover, even "in the idea, i.e., the Christian idea, there reside different possibilities of organizational development." In a non-traditionalist society ideas can be detached from their initial social milieu, and can be given new and modified incarnation. In this process, elements latent in the original deposit become evident.

In connection with his view that different possibilities of ethos or of organizational development may be latent within an idea Troeltsch devised his typology of religious associations—the church, the sect, and the mystical type. We do not need to recount here the origin and character of the method of "Ideal Types" (stemming from Dilthey, Jellinek and Weber), or the relation between Troeltsch's delineation of the types of religious association and the characterizations formulated by David Hume, Rudolf Sohm, and Max Weber. Troeltsch never worked out in detail a theory of the dynamics of these types. Nor did he adopt Weber's proposal that differences between sects—in their origin and development—should be studied in terms of their urban or rural setting. In any event, Troeltsch insisted, even more than Weber, that the types again and again interpenetrate in varying ways; and that therefore the actualities should be studied from case to case.

One very important aspect of Troeltsch's use of typology has often been overlooked. In various of his writings he showed that different types of religious association tend to favor social philosophies analogous to the respective types of organization; accordingly, these types of association tend to interpret social-ethical doctrines—for example, the doctrine of natural law—in corresponding fashion.

Less familiar than the typology of associations is Troeltsch's classification of the forms of political organization that have claimed Christian sanction. The types of political organization, he says, may be placed on a spectrum between two poles, according to the relative emphasis upon the spontaneity of the individual or upon the "divinely established" natural orders of society. Thus Christianity from the beginning contained within it both democratic-progressive and aristocratic-conservative tendencies.

But Troeltsch does not view Christianity as possessing a political or economic ideal that it can apply directly. It works by means of mediating elements. In this connection he presupposes a radical distinction between what he calls universal religion and a religion oriented to natural ties. In the undifferentiated society, religion characteristically exercises a direct influence. The great religions of the Orient and the Occident, however, tend to be universal. Here varieties of differentiation obtain, providing tensions between religious and political life or between religious and economic organization. In this situation the forms of religious organization or of nonecclesiastical organization serve as mediating elements through which Christianity exercises indirect and fluctuating influence.

Here we encounter one of the most important conceptions of Troeltsch, the idea of compromise. This concept makes its first appearance in Troeltsch's doctoral dissertation at Göttingen, and it reappears again and again to the very last of his writings. As generally used by Troeltsch, it does not refer to an adjustment that is discreditable. It is rather a concept that points to both the tension and the positive cooperation between Christianity and the world. That is, it points to the dynamic process whereby the universal religion comes to terms creatively with mediating elements in its environment, and even with elements originally alien to it. Sometimes the term "synthesis" is used instead of "compromise," as for example in *Historismus*. Compromise is the means whereby the indirect influence of Christianity has been exercised, the means whereby the ideas latent within the Christian ethos come to fruition, or whereby Christianity has been distorted. Compromise is thus a concept of mediation. It may be effective in the dimension of intellectual, theological construction, in the sphere of the arts, in the political or economic sphere. But not even a highly effective, creative compromise can last. The process must be renewed again and again through thrust and counterthrust. In *The Social Teaching*, for example, Troeltsch observes instances of compromise in the peregrinations of the doctrine of natural law as adopted and adapted by Christian groups, and in the ways in which the church types of religious association, or the mixed types, function. Twice in Western history a major pervasive compromise has been achieved, giving rise to an elaborately articulated social philosophy—first in the Middle Ages and then later in Neo-Calvinism. Like Ranke and Weber, he interpreted developments of this sort to be due in part to the "accident" of the conjunction of major independent forces, social and ideological. Troeltsch points to many compromises that exemplify the working of "accident," for example, the development of early Logos Christology, the cooperation between revealed and natural theology, the initiation and promotion of differentiation through voluntary associations at the hands of Neo-Calvinism and of the free churches precisely during the period of associational expansion in the culture. In his view, Lutheranism through its dualism of the Two Kingdoms eases the tension between Christianity and the world; its compromises therefore have been less transformative than those of Calvinism in the sphere of political and social institutions. Compromise is always a process of give and take, and different compromises exhibit various relative proportions of this give and take.

As is to be observed in a number of examples cited above, a crucial sphere in which compromise occurs is the area of associations. Mindful of the views of Tönnies and Gierke, Troeltsch interprets the history of Christianity in its successive milieus as a sort of dialectical process moving between the poles of community and society (Gierke's formulation of course differs from this). He sees the characteristic dynamic of Christianity, when oriented to the Gospels, to be a leaning towards small associations. In general, his theory of periodization for the history of the West is based upon a typology of associations, ecclesiastical, political, and social. Creative compromise again and again impinges upon or is influenced by these associational structures.

This whole matter of the process of compromise brings us to the heart of Troeltsch's philosophy of history and to his systematic attempt to answer the question of standards that he never permitted to leave his consciousness.

THE PHILOSOPHY OF HISTORY

Just as Troeltsch's untimely death made it impossible for him to work out a systematic philosophy of religion, so also it prevented his completing his elaboration of a philosophy of history. His two last publications were devoted to this subject—*Historismus und seine Probleme* (1922) and *Christian Thought: Its History and Application*, published posthumously. Paul Tillich, in his review of 1923, has given such an embracing analysis of *Historismus* that extensive comment here is unnecessary.

In his philosophy of religion, Troeltsch, in order to establish the integrity and independence of religion, confronted the issues raised by various forms of naturalism. In his philosophy of history he tried to come to terms with historicism, the disposition to consider everything human as historical. Historicism, along with naturalism, he viewed as a major characteristic attitude of the modern mentality. Indeed, in the development of his philosophy of religion he steadily moved away from the placing of emphasis on the a prioris of reason, in the direction of stressing the nonrational, the contingent, the historical; that is, his philosophy of religion veered more and more in the direction of historicism. In accord with this trend he stressed the view that the a prioris of reason are purely formal, that they find their content in the world of historical actualities, and that they thereby become subject to the changes of history. Thus he was brought to confront squarely the issues raised by historicism. Here the question of standards, the question regarding the relation of the relative to the absolute, is faced in its most crucial formulation.

Troeltsch's shift of emphasis is to be observed especially in the fact that he now says in effect: historicism as well as reason has its a priori elements. In his view, it is the task of "the logic of history" to delineate these categories. Here again scientistic naturalism is the counterfoil, for its concepts are drawn from the physical and biological sciences; indeed, they often have been imposed upon the data in terms of a priori conceptions of law and causality. Historicism, aiming to be more empirical in face of its data, tries to construct its categories inductively. Its principal categories have already been mentioned above—individuality, development, contingency, meaning, freedom, novelty. Any surrender of these categories in favor of the conceptual apparatus of naturalism issues in what Troeltsch calls "bad historicism."

Like the other disciplines, historiography seeks for irreducible units. The irreducible unit of historicism is the "individual totality," a complex of data more or less unified by a pervasive meaning and dynamic. This pervasive meaning may transcend the boundaries of national or ethnic scope, as for example in such symbolic conceptions as Renaissance, Reformation, Enlightenment; or it may inform an individual totality that is less than national or ethnic in its purview, such as a style of art or a sectarian religious movement. Every totality, however, must be understood within a larger, more embracing context. If historiography is to grasp more than sheer individuality in history, if it is to classify its data, it requires something more general in character than individual totalities. It will seek to construct typological structures that make comparison and contrast possible. Much of Troeltsch's historical writing may be viewed as an exemplification of his conception of the nature of individual totalities and types. At this point we should observe that Troeltsch's own theory and practice of the task of the historian carries him beyond what he has previously considered to be the historian's peculiar interest, the concern for individuality. Within each individual totality he finds more general features (for example, in his sociological types), and also in comparing totalities he moves to a level of generality (for example, in his typology of faith as productive or non-productive and as universal or naïve). In these ways Troeltsch transcends the simple distinction between nomothetic and ideographic method, though he would insist that any individual totality as a symbolic construction does not exhaust reality. In this sense the concept of individuality continues to function as an irreducible category of the dynamic, contingent historical dimension. Nevertheless, the characteristic work of the historian, and of Troeltsch as a historian, is more of a generalizing enterprise than his explicit delineation of method seems to recognize. At the same time, the ideographic concern is, admittedly, more characteristic for the historian than for the natural scientist.

The actual description of individual totalities carries one beyond the sphere of the logic of history into that of the material philosophy of history where concrete meanings, concrete standards in religion, in the arts, in the areas of economics and politics, appear. Here a distinction very important for Troeltsch comes into play. Already in his *Grund-probleme der Ethik* (1902) he had distinguished between the subjective virtues that concern themselves with the relations between individuals (and between the individual and God) and the objective virtues that require institutional structures and participation. Christianity, for example, with its ethical as well as spiritual orientation, concerns itself with both types of virtue. Moreover, in both spheres it confronts standards of conduct and piety that have their own relatively independent history and content. In its confrontation with these value systems Christianity, when dynamic and productive, has entered (as we have seen) into creative compromise of give and take.

This process of compromise requires what Troeltsch calls synthesis. Here the interpretation of current needs and possibilities, will determine the interpretation of the past and of the latent forces that may be given new expression. Thus the past is not treated as an inert objective mass of data ready to hand; like the present, it lends itself to variety of interpretation in terms of perspectives old and new. Subject and object are therefore involved in a dynamic continuum. History is not *une force qui va*, to use a term employed by Victor Hugo. It possesses to be sure its own limitations and possibilities, and the participant, if wise, will take these seriously into account. In doing so he recognizes the element of fate in history. But the task of achieving new synthesis entails also new decision, new creation, new risk. In this process *history overcomes history*—freedom, fate, obligation, novelty become fused according to personal faith and decision.

The question now arises as to the character and validity of the standards employed in this process of synthesis. Troeltsch's answer to this question is extremely complex. There are three major dimensions in his answer, so far as religion is concerned, and the answer for other spheres is essentially the same. First, insofar as one takes seriously the nature and implications of individuality in history, one must recognize that Christianity or any other religion constitutes a complex or "world" of perspectives in which the believer simply finds himself. Indeed, the ex-believer is fated to be related to this same "world." The human person cannot find a vantage point that transcends this "world," except in the sense that he can be aware of its individuality and his involvement in it. Thus one may not, like Hegel, presume to view the human scene from the perspective of the absolute; history is not yet finished, we do not know its *telos*; moreover, the Hegelian claim to manifest the absolute in the present fulfillment is a form of egregious provincialism. Nor may one, like the supernaturalist, claim to possess a revelation or an historical tradition that is exempt from the processes of history. Nor may one claim to be oriented to the coming unity of humanity; there is as yet no common cultural experience that people of the planet share and that in significant fashion enables them to transcend the individual totalities that constitute their own local, spiritual habitations. Secondly, this involvement of Christianity and of all religions and cultures in their own respective individual totalities should not issue in mere relativism. This outcome Troeltsch views as another form of "bad historicism." Individuality and validity are not incompatible. Here Troeltsch appeals to his Leibnizian perspective; precisely within the dynamic individualities of history one confronts obligation and validity. He appeals also to the Protestant doctrine of justification by faith. In his *Glaubenslehre* (lectures delivered in 1911–1912 and published posthumously in 1925) he rejects every kind of authoritarianism as well as any flattened-out secularist ethos of autonomy; and he speaks for what he calls "autotheonomy," a religious concept that aims to preserve autonomy but in orientation to that which transcends it in the divine promise, demand, and support. The complex of perspectives involved here is presupposed when Troeltsch accepts Ranke's axiom that "every epoch in history stands immediately to God," a view reminiscent of Nicolas of Cusa. Thus he concludes that Christian faith can be valid "for us." "A truth that, in the first instance, is a truth for us does not cease, because of this, to be very Truth and Life. What we learn daily through our love for our fellow-men, viz. that they are independent beings with standards of their own, we ought also to be able to learn through our love for mankind as a whole—that here too there exist autonomous civilizations with standards of their own."

But where is the standard that represents validity in the midst of the "flowing heterogeneity?" This question brings us to the third, and final, perspective to be observed. To put the matter succinctly, we may say that Troeltsch has an ecological, or field theory of standard and validity. Just as Christianity in its history has exhibited an ethos latent with treasures old and new, and just as its effectiveness has issued from the process of creative compromise, so the standard that should obtain today must be discerned in the dynamic unfolding and interplay of perspectives. In Bergsonian fashion he seems to suggest that obligation and validity confront one in the midst of the process of creative evolution. The interplay is not confined to the Protestant heritage. From of old certain fundamental vitalities have been operative: Hebrew prophetism, classical Hellenism, Roman law and government, the occidental Middle Ages. The Christian in face of this complex heritage and in face of the modern mentality with its special qualities may now mainly look toward the development of Europeanism. In the future the interplay of perspectives may be widened. We stand always in the moment of "creation, decision, and fate," in the moment when history must overcome history.

Troeltsch's theory of value has often been compared to that of Whitehead. Of Whitehead it has been said that he Bergsonized Plato. Of Troeltsch it may be said that he Bergsonized Kant and historicized Hegel. The absolute is not available for domestication in history. But from the interplay of perspectives, entered into with faith and with openness, the "platform for new creation" emerges, and with it a recognition of a validity vouchsafed to the relative. "He hath established it upon the floods."

WE CONCLUDE these essays by James Luther Adams with one of his papers on Paul Tillich. His appreciation for Tillich was deep; in fact, his doctoral dissertation was on Tillich, and, besides this one, the only major book by Adams (who edited and contributed to dozens) is *Paul Tillich's Philosophy of Culture, Science and Religion.** The feeling is mutual, and I take the liberty of quoting from Tillich's foreword to the *Festschrift*** written several years ago in Adams' honor:

> It is a great honor and joy for me that I have been asked to write a few introductory words to this book, which is dedicated to the life and work of my dear friend, Jim Adams. Without him I would not be what I am, biographically as well as theologically. He received me graciously when I came to Chicago as a German refugee; he has studied my thought so thoroughly that I have sent to him all those who wanted to know about it, because he knows more about my writings than I do myself; he made the first translations into English of articles I had written in German; he helped me to get a publisher, and I have reasons to suspect that he did many more things for me than I ever have known.
>
> Beyond this personal support, his thought and work have given me a deeper understanding of American Christianity. First and most important is the truth of which he is a living witness, that *agape*, Christian love, is not dependent on trinitarian or anti-trinitarian or other dogmatic traditions (he is a Unitarian), but on the divine Spirit, which grasps men of all creeds through the power which is manifest in Jesus as the Christ. The second thing I have learned from him is the emphasis on the practical, social as well as political, application of the principle of *agape* to the situation of the society in which we live. In this respect he represents the prophetic element in Christianity which much teaching in the churches badly neglects. I even may confess that I feel him as a "thorn in my flesh," when "the flesh" tries to ignore the social implications of the Christian message! He represents in his whole being a warning against a theology that sacrifices the prophetic for the mystical element, though both of them, as he and I agree, are essential for religion generally and Christianity especially.
>
> The third point in which he gave me an example is his extraordinary knowledge of facts and persons and the preciseness and conscientiousness with which he works in all of his theological, sociological, and psychological investigations. There is humility in this attitude which I deeply admire. It is ultimately an expression of *agape*, which cares for the smallest, without becoming small itself.
>
> But there is the other side of him which is equally astonishing: the largeness of interests and involvements in all sides of man's cultural creativity: in the arts as well as in the sciences. Again it is love, the *eros*

* New York: Harper and Row, 1965. Adams has also edited and translated Tillich's *The Protestant Era* (Chicago: University of Chicago Press, 1948), from which the following essay is taken; *What Is Religion?* (New York: Harper and Row, 1969); and *Political Expectations* (New York: Harper and Row, 1971).
** D. B. Robertson, ed., *Voluntary Associations* (Richmond, Va.: John Knox Press, 1966), pp. 5 and 6.

towards the true and the beautiful, which makes it possible for him to unite intensive participation in these functions of the human spirit with his continuous concern for the practical problems of individuals as well as of the society. In theological terminology I could say that James Luther Adams is a living proof of the ultimate unity of *eros* and *agape* and for the possibility that this unity becomes manifest, however fragmentarily, in a human being.

—M.L.S.

CHAPTER 15 · THEOLOGY AND MODERN CULTURE: PAUL TILLICH

THE REFORMATION must continue." With these words Friedrich Schleiermacher, over a century ago, raised a protest against the Protestantism and the prevailing mentality of his time and pointed forward to a new Protestant realization. Protestantism and its culture, he believed, were in need of a Protestant reform.

These words of Schleiermacher could well serve as the epigraph of the writings of Paul Tillich. This does not mean that Tillich recommends, any more than Schleiermacher did, a return to the Reformation. Like Schleiermacher, who was also a theologian of culture schooled in the dialectic of philosophical idealism, Tillich is concerned not only with the religion of the churches but even more with the religious bases and implications of the whole cultural process. In his view, which is based on a realistic philosophy of meaning, religion has to do with humanity's ultimate concern, the concern with the meaning of life and with all the forces that threaten or support that meaning, in personal and social life, in the arts and sciences, in politics, in industry, education, and the church. It is with respect to the total cultural situation, then, that Tillich would say: "The Reformation must continue"; for we are living at the end of an era.

Beginning as a rediscovery of the prophetic message of the majesty of God and emphasizing the doctrines of predestination and of justification through faith, early Protestantism raised a protest against a hierarchical system that had interjected itself between man and God with "a demonic claim to absoluteness." This prophetic message reaffirmed the unconditional character of God. Sin and guilt, the Reformers asserted, cannot be overcome by any mediating human agency. Union with God is received through grace and faith alone. Through this union the sinner paradoxically becomes justified before God. Man's love is the consequence and not the condition of this justification through faith. Analogously, the concept of predestination was the doctrinal statement of the experience of regaining the meaning of life without human activity, an experience that is God's work and that has an explanation hidden from man.

In accord with these Protestant affirmations, the absolute doctrinal authority of the church, the constitutional authority of the hierarchy, and the independent power of the sacraments were all renounced as blasphemies, as attempts by humans to elevate mankind above God and to subject to outer conditions the approach of God to the soul and of the soul to God. Insofar as humanism set up human reason as the final arbiter and adopted an anthropocentric orientation, humanism was also renounced on the basis of corresponding objections. The Reformers cut through all these mediations; they also cut through church history and returned to the source of the message of justification, the Bible.

The positive element taking the place of ecclesiastical authority found its initial expression in the claim of freedom of conscience to interpret the Scriptures, a freedom that was expected to issue in a new unity supported by a providentially inspired harmony. This Protestant freedom of conscience was an "ecstatic" rather than a purely autonomous, humanistic freedom; it was interpreted as the "pneumatic," or, as Tillich would call it, the "theonomous," response of the individual member of the church to the message of the Bible. Obedience to the hierarchical priesthood was therefore supplanted by belief in the priesthood of all believers. Clerical domination yielded, in principle, to radical laicism. The Bible, it was assumed, would interpret itself sufficiently for salvation. Every individual as a monad in the body of Christ would be able to find truth in the Bible. The saving Gospel is there, and the Reformers believed that it would create a unified church wherever it was proclaimed and listened to in faith. Thus, although Protestantism appealed to the individual consciousness and conscience (guided by Scripture and nourished by the religious community), it relied from the beginning upon a hidden automatic harmony. Tillich holds that much of the history of Protestantism and also of modern culture must be understood in terms of this and of corresponding theories of harmony.

But Protestantism could not carry through unaided its resistance to the previously accepted authorities; nor was it able alone to establish new integrations in church and society. It eventually made an alliance with the humanism which it had at first opposed as strongly as it had opposed Roman Catholicism. Philosophical and linguistic exegesis was required for the interpreting of the Bible. Protestantism joined humanism to overcome Catholic exegesis. Here it was assumed that autonomous criticism and Protestant criticism would fundamentally agree. This same pattern was adopted also for other areas of common interest. Gradually the "holy" legend of the Catholic church was dissolved by the modern historical consciousness and by humanistic-Protestant historical criticism; humanistic education was combined with biblical education; scholasticism was supplanted by autonomous science, in which theology claimed a leading role (later to be lost); monastic and feudal conceptions of work were replaced by an inner-worldly asceticism and activism (especially on Calvinistic soil). Belief in harmony between divine and natural law gave rise to a new amalgamation of Stoic and biblical ethics. To be sure, there have been and there still are countertendencies within Protestantism. In Europe, neofeudal types of authority continued to play a role. Moreover, in many quarters rigid forms of ecclesiastical orthodoxy have ignored the original Protestant protest. As a consequence, they have, in principle, maintained the traditional authoritarian outlook. They have merely substituted for the authority of the Roman Catholic church some new absolute, such as the Bible or the confessions of faith, the "priestcraft of the word."

The alliance of Protestantism with humanism gradually developed into an alliance also with a humanist theory of harmony. This development in its outcome must be viewed as simply another dimension of the changes already described; accordingly, it can be best discerned by observing its characteristic negations and affirmations.

The alliance was possible, if not inevitable, because humanism resisted many of the same things that Protestantism resisted.

Tillich, employing a conception familiar in modern myth research, characterizes the pre-Protestant, or Catholic, era in terms of its "myth of origin." In general, this sort of myth expresses man's numinous sense of relatedness to the originating or creative powers of nature and history; it provides a feeling of security and support by relating men to sacred powers of origin rooted in the soil, in the blood, in a social group, or in some other support and sanction of a vital and authoritative tradition. For the Middle Ages the superhuman origin of life was found in a primeval revelation, which was preserved as a holy tradition and guarded as a mystery by the priesthood. This holy tradition found objective manifestation in a sacramental system (which included within it the natural powers of origin). Medieval freedoms, securities, and authorities were supported by this comprehensive myth of origin. Innovation could be introduced only in the name of the "origin." All privileges of "domination," including those attached to the feudal ranks, appealed to the same sanction. Since the system was largely controlled by the priesthood, the latter achieved a certain social independence as the bearer of religion and as the consecrating agent for the sacred powers of origin. Against this medieval myth of origin and the corresponding authorities, both humanism and Protestantism revolted, humanism in the name of an autonomous humanity and Protestantism in the spirit of ancient prophetism and in the name of the doctrines of justification and predestination.

Protestantism, as we have seen, returned to the Bible, where it found not only its own myth of origin but also a sense of mission, a sanction for pushing forward to a new church and society. This does not mean that the medieval myth of origin was wholly eliminated; rather, it was transformed. Just as in ancient Hebrew religion, prophetic and priestly elements were combined, so in Protestantism prophetic elements were grafted onto Catholic sacramental elements. However, in rejecting the claim of the priesthood to be the consecrating agent of the powers of origin, Protestantism initiated a process whereby it would in time weaken its own independence. Partially as a consequence of the principal of radical laicism (implied in the belief in the priesthood of all believers) the modern man has taken a larger share in the shaping of social policy than did his predecessors. Because of these changes, Protestantism has had to depend more and more upon extraecclesiastical social forces for support. It entered more and more, especially after the Enlightenment, into alliance with the developing state bureaucracies or with the bourgeois powers and customs.

Humanism also rejected the old myth of origin and introduced a new conception. According to this new conception, man in his possession of universal humanity was believed to be rooted in the divine *logos*. In its struggle against authoritarianism, humanism can scarcely be said to have developed a myth of origin, but it did create its own "myth of mission" (a term suggested by Michels and not used by Tillich, though it conveys Tillich's idea). This myth of mission drove humanism forward toward the liberation of humanity, which as the bearer of reason and truth was to bring in a new rational order of society. This myth came to its full growth when the enlightened authoritarianism of the early modern period was replaced by liberal and democratic social myths and forms. This full growth took the form of a theory of natural harmony.

In humanism the Judeo-Christian trust in providence was transformed into a reliance upon a pre-established harmony in the cosmos, in the human psyche, and in society. This harmony, it was believed, would progressively engender unity and general well-being if every individual had the freedom to follow his or her own convictions and economic interests; in pursuing self-interests, the interests of the community would be advanced.

This theory of natural harmony may be understood either from the point of view of the human subject—the mind—or from that of the object—nature and the social, productive forces. With respect to the object, the theory of harmony asserted that, in sense perception, nature gives itself to humanity in such a way that a natural knowledge emerges which is adequate for purposes of control; and it asserted that the free sway of all human creative forces—in the cultural area through tolerance, in the economic area through liberal political economy ("laissez faire"), in the political area through the rule of the majority (democracy)—would lead to the rational shaping of society. In other words, it held that the human being may, through a natural harmony, achieve true fulfillment. With respect to the subject, the theory asserted that the categories of the human spirit are the structure-giving elements of nature; hence nature is amenable to rational knowledge and control. Society can be rationally shaped because the human species is undergoing in history an education that will fulfil its rational potentialities. Taken together, then, both the objective and the subjective aspects of the theory of natural harmony presupposed a religious faith in the essential unity and goodness of man and the world and in a spiritual unity between man and nature. It must be noted here that, although certain pessimistic motives of classical Christian thought were ignored, the optimistic worldview that was adopted came primarily from Judeo-Christian, rather than from pagan, sources as did also the activist, world-shaping impulse (which was given marked impetus through Calvinism).

The developments in philosophy during the period of rationalism and enlightenment may be taken as typical of the trends, both practical and theoretical, which gave expression to the theory of natural harmony. From the seventeenth century on, one philosopher after another worked out the implications of the theory of harmony: Spinoza, Descartes, and Leibniz in metaphysics; Shaftesbury and Helvetius in psychology and ethics; Montesquieu, Rousseau, and Adam Smith in political and economic theory; Voltaire and a host of others in the progressivist philosophy of history. Reason, both speculative and technological, both revolutionary and formative, working in the individual and in society, was to usher in the kingdom of universal brotherhood. An original motive power in this drive toward emancipation came, of course, from the recognition of the sacredness of personality, from belief in human rights and human worth. But other ideas also soon appeared, ideas that reflected an increasing tension between the objective and the subjective aspects of the theory.

The enthusiasm for the rational control of nature and society, besides releasing new energies, introduced a new alienation between persons and between humanity and nature, an alienation that would in time disrupt the harmony. Employing a characteristically "existentialist" interpretation of the outlook of modern mentality, Tillich asserts that one of the decisive elements of modern thought is the contrast between "subject" and "object," a contrast that tends to stress the "objectivity" or the "subjectivity" of reality. This dichotomy between subject and object superseded the subject-object unity of the high Middle Ages and became the "prime mover" of Western philosophy and also of modern technological, capitalist society. The sense of the immediacy of the origin, of the creative sources of man's life, was gradually lost. Personality and community became merely objective things, thus losing their intrinsic powerfulness and depth. The attitude toward things followed the same course, partially as a consequence of the developing technology; in the human consciousness "things" lost their intrinsic value and depth. Thus personality, community, and things became the instruments of an autonomous secularism; they became merely objects for control and calculation in the service of man's economic purposes. A spirit of "self-sufficient finitude" invaded the common life. Indeed, religion itself lost its sense of the immediacy of the origin and became one sphere among other spheres; even its God became a "thing" among other things, and the language of religion assumed an "objective," literal character that could only elicit skepticism. In philosophy both realism and idealism exhibited the loss of the sense of immediacy, emphasizing in corresponding ways the dichotomy of subject and object. Romanticism attempted to recapture the lost unity between subject and object (and with it the lost splendor of life) by restoring old myths of origin or by developing new ones, but it achieved only the spurious immediacy of irrationalism, either in the archaism of religious revival or in primitivist organicism and vitalism. Romanticism, however, did not much alter the main trend in capitalist society. Positivism became the characteristic philosophy of a technological society, seeking the domination of the object by the subject. In the spirit of this positivism, the dynamic ethos of capitalist society became increasingly determinative for the Protestant-humanist era.

This characteristic dynamic is epitomized in what Tillich calls "the bourgeois principle." Wherever technology and capital have been at work in the modern world, this principle has been operative. Its success is to be observed in its permeation of almost the entire planet, in a world domination that no one can escape. The definition of this principle can be formulated most succinctly in terms of its goal. The goal of the bourgeois principle is the radical dissolution of the bonds of original, organic community life, the dissolution of the powers of origin into elements to be conquered rationally. Science, religion, politics, art, the relations among the classes—all have been drawn into the crucible of the bourgeois principle. It is true that the bourgeois principle has never been—indeed, it never could be—the sole support of capitalist society. The principle was itself primarily utilitarian and critical; it unconsciously presupposed previously existing creative powers and supports. Just as Protestantism retained and transformed Catholic elements, so modern capitalist society has presupposed and has in varying ways retained contact with the powers of origin. It has not carried through the bourgeois principle in complete consistency. This fact becomes evident whenever the middle classes feel themselves threatened; they then appeal to myths of soil and blood, to nationalism, as a protection of middle-class interests. Yet the characteristic positive preoccupation following from the bourgeois principle has been the creation of means of objective control; and this preoccupation has displaced the intuitive grasping of intrinsic values; both things and persons have been enervated by subordinating them to economic purposes. The spirit of bourgeois society is the spirit that, after having dissolved the primary ties of origin, subjects a "thingified" world entirely to its purposes. This process of "thingification" has been carried through by the motive power of the theory of harmony and progress.

The amalgam of Protestant and humanist faiths in a principle of harmony has produced the modern age with its tremendous creativity; it has produced the modern ideas of tolerance and education and democracy; it has provided the energy and goal of the age of "free enterprise." The practical implications of the theory of natural harmony become especially clear if one observes the contrast between the social and metaphysical presuppositions of the Protestant-humanist era and those of the Catholic era. Catholicism has relied upon a hierarchy that is supposedly based on an ontological hierarchy of being. It has attempted to make the hierarchical system exercise control in all spheres of society. Where Catholicism has been dominant, it has elicited sharp resistance from these spheres, as, for example, in Italy and France. The Protestant-humanist era, on the other hand, has depended upon a hidden harmony. Accordingly, Protestantism has exhibited a greater cooperation and harmony with the evolving autonomous cultural spheres than has Catholicism. (As we shall observe later, this fact must be taken into account in any attempt to understand Protestant secularism.) Moreover, a certain harmony has prevailed within Protestantism itself, despite the lack of authoritative courts of appeal. "A decisive harmony," says Tillich, "has again and again come about automatically. And so the division of Protestantism into numerous mutually antagonistic churches, sects, denominations and movements did not involve any dangers so long as the common fundamental attitude was both positively and negatively unshaken."

Humanism's faith in harmony was for a time no less confirmed by history than was Protestantism's corresponding faith. The residues of earlier social coherence, expanding markets, and relatively free competition, these and other similar factors made it appear at first that the "law" of harmony expressed the nature of reality. The rise in the standard of living for many, the great increase in wealth, and the "success" of Western imperialism made tragedy in history seem (at least to the middle-class mentality) a thing of the past.

But the prevailing forms of Protestantism and humanism are now reaching their limits. The cunning of history pursues elusive, labyrinthine ways, and it makes unexpected turns. Capitalism, with its religion of harmony, has culminated not in harmony but in contradiction and crisis. This turn is no accident.

What earlier seemed to be the natural laws of harmony turned out to be contingent historical circumstances. The theory of the harmony of interests presupposed the eighteenth-century society of small producers and merchants, a society not yet controlled by mammoth corporations. Developments unforeseen by classical liberal economics were to bring about tremendous structural changes—and the breakdown of harmony. Already, within a half century after the promulgation of the theory of the harmony of interests, the liberal utopia began to assume the physiognomy of Lancashire and Manchester. Subsequently, the theory of harmony has more and more become an ideology protecting the interests of the new ruling groups and sanctioning an increasingly destructive application of the bourgeois principle. Instead of producing harmony, the structural changes have in the twentieth century raised the "storms of our times."

These storms have created a darkness so readily visible that it is now almost a work of supererogation to describe it. Whether we think of the far-flung conflicts among imperialisms and of their exploitations in the domestic spheres or in the colonies, of the growth of monopoly and the concentration of wealth and economic power, of the disparity between increasing powers of production and decreasing purchasing power, of the opposition between the classes, of two world wars within our generation, of the inability of capitalism to use the full resources of the economy except in time of war or of radical depression and unemployment (the normal sequel to "normalcy"); whether we consider the "thingification" of man through the rationalization of industry and through his being made into a mere quantity of working power subject to the laws (or chances) of the market, or the "thingification" of nature through its being viewed as something only to be conquered and used, as something only to be shoveled about; whether we think of the prostitution of education to merely utilitarian ends or of the complacently accepted corruption of politics through special interests; whether we think of the irresponsible and commercial vulgarization of the idea industries (radio, movie, and printing), of the increase of agitation, propaganda, and mass-production methods for the influencing of public opinion (with the consequent weakening of individuality and tolerance and responsible discussion), or of the decline of ethically powerful and uniting symbols in the democracies and in the churches—in each and all these tendencies we discern the causes or the consequences of the disruption of "automatic" harmony. This disruption has created a mass society in which reason has lost its depth and dignity (having created a huge impersonal machine that it does not control); in which societal sadism and insensitivity to suffering and injustice are taken for granted; in which the average individual is lost and lonely; in which the fear of insecurity and lack of spiritual roots produce neurosis and cynicism; in which psychiatric hospitals and counseling centers have become major institutions; in which the sense of personal insignificance is compensated by egregious group egotism; in which a flat secularism, the spirit of "self-sufficient finitude," prevails in church and society, exhibiting contemporary man's blunted sense of his relatedness to the creative depths of personality, existence, and meaning; and therefore in which there is a void of meaninglessness, yearning for meaning. This is the world, said Henry Adams in 1892, which is ruled from "a banker's Olympus."

Whether one accepts Henry Adams' dictum in its simplicity or not, one must recognize that Protestantism in its alliance with the evolving middle-class humanism has tended in many respects to become merely the religious aspect of capitalism. Humanist and Protestant harmonisms have together moved from their originally creative phase through a technological stage to become a passionately conservative force. Just as Roman Catholicism first helped to shape the culture of the Middle Ages and then became fettered in the "Babylonish captivity" of the waning Middle Ages and of a petrified Counter Reformation, so Protestantism has helped to form the Protestant era and then, in differing ways in its different forms and countries, has to a large extent become bound in a new Babylonish captivity within capitalist culture. It languishes (all too comfortably) in this prison, or, to change the figure from a Reformation to a biblical one, it is largely a prostituted, a "kept" religion. It has lost its relatedness to an ultimate ground and aim, and thus it has lost much of its original prophetic power. Its God has become domesticated; it is a bourgeois god. In its major effect its ethics are largely indistinguishable from the "ethics" of the bourgeois principle.

As a consequence the Protestantism that offers "religious" embellishment for the bourgeois principle merely aggravates the contradictions of capitalist society. Its appeal to individual consciousness and conscience (detached from the socializing influences of a nourishing spiritual tradition) and its belief that the freedom of the individual by virtue of the centripetal power of harmony moves toward a common center and then issues forth in health and healing for the individual and the society have become a means of evading basic social-ethical issues and of merely protecting the governing powers of the status quo. Philanthropy and social reform emanating from the churches usually assist these governing powers by moving strictly within bourgeois presuppositions. Through its emphasis on economic and spiritual individualism combined with a class-bound moralism, this Protestantism has also helped to dissolve communal symbols and supports. It has been drawn into the general process of dissolution.

It is true that the dissolution described here has not disintegrated spiritual and ethical values in America to the extent visible during recent decades in Europe. As Tillich puts it, "America lives still in a happy state of backwardness." But many of the conditions and attitudes that led to fascism in Europe exist also in America.

The foregoing characterization of the present status of Protestantism is, of course, one-sided and incomplete; indeed, Tillich asserts (as we shall observe presently) that genuinely Protestant motives have persisted in the churches and even in certain aspects of secularism. Yet the tendencies described have been largely responsible for, or have accelerated, the decline of the Protestant-humanist era.

In response to these developments, dynamic movements of revolt have for a century been abandoning the characteristic tenets of bourgeois and Protestant-humanist individualism and automatic harmonism and have been moving in the direction of new (and sometimes of collectivist) forms of faith and society. Some of these movements have opposed the churches and liberalistic humanism as the bulwarks of privilege; other movements have appeared within the churches or in the form of neohumanism. The spectrum of revolt is a wide one. Communism, fascism, and Roman Catholic corporatism assume varying shades of red and black. The Christian socialist movements, neoliberal and neo-orthodox, occupy other positions in the spectrum. In certain areas of the spectrum a desire to "escape from freedom" is evident. The burden upon the individual has become almost too heavy to bear. Consequently, many people relinquish individual religious or political responsibility; they are willing to sacrifice their autonomy in the hope of finding on the path of authority a new meaning in life, new symbols and forms of life. The present attraction of Roman Catholicism and communism must be understood partially in this context. All these movements have been seeking a way out of the Protestant-humanist era.

The whole situation is a paradoxical one for both Protestantism and humanism, the partners of the modern era. Tillich has, in several writings, succinctly described the plight in which Protestantism finds itself. The description applies also to humanism. "That which Protestantism denied at its rise," he says, "is today—*in an altered form*—the demand of the age. That demand is for an authoritative and powerfully symbolic system of mass redintegration: but it was just that—*in a distorted form*—against which Protestantism protested. . . . The Protestant era is finished, after nearly all the historical conditions upon which it rested have been taken away from it." Indeed, the very manner of the rise of Protestantism would seem to have determined its present limitations.

It is clear that if Protestantism is to play a prophetic and creative role in the new situation, it must effect a break and transformation as disruptive and as boldly productive as the changes made at the beginning of the Protestant era; and the transformation must in its effect on the social structure move in a direction opposite to that of the earlier break and transformation.

To inquire, as Tillich does in many writings, as to whether the Protestant era has now come to an end, suggests questions that are importunate for Protestantism and humanism at this epochal moment. It will suffice if we here formulate these questions as they concern Protestantism. Will Protestantism escape its Babylonish captivity and assist reformation again? Will it extricate itself from the disintegration of the mass society of the late-capitalist epoch? Or has it cast its lot irrevocably with the transitory and exhausted forces that now serve as its ideological expression and protection? Will it be able to exhibit again the self-surpassing power of the historic Christian dynamic by disassociating itself from these forces and by giving a sense of meaning, a direction, and a quality of greatness to new forms of thought and life? Or will the coming era take shape in opposition to organized Protestantism? Will it be in any significant sense a Protestant era? Or will it eventually be called a post-Protestant era because of the emergence of some new type of Christianity which will help to determine a new spirit and form of society?

Obviously, no one can today give the answers to these questions (or to corresponding questions that might be posed concerning liberalistic humanism). The questions serve the purpose, however, of giving concrete relevance to a consideration of the problems, the perils, and the opportunities that now confront Protestantism. But they cannot be properly dealt with in the manner of the soothsayer. In considering the problems which they raise, Tillich aims, as he says, "to drive the analysis to a point where the vision of a possible reconstruction" of Protestantism and contemporary society may appear. Hence the title of the volume *The Protestant Era* means to suggest not only that the Protestant era is now approaching its limits but also that the end of the Protestant era would not be the end of Protestantism. Indeed, a new realization might be more in accord with the nature of Protestantism.

A main trend, a characteristic dynamic, of the Protestant era has been expressed, as we have seen, in the bourgeois principle supported by the theory of natural harmony. But the harmony has not come. Instead, men have lost their sense of relatedness to the creative springs of life; community has been frustrated, and neurotic insecurity is the "order" of the day. Insofar as the Protestant spirit has identified itself with the prevailing ethos, it participates in and aggravates the disintegration of our world. The bourgeois principle is insufficient to create community. The questions arise then: by what principle can bourgeois society be criticized and transcended? By what principle can Protestantism regain a prophetic and newly creative power?

Tillich holds that, even if the Protestant era is finished, Protestantism knows a principle that is not finished. Like every other finite reality, Protestantism in any particular historical realization must reckon always with the possibility of its exhaustion. But the principle of Protestantism is not finite and exhaustible. As a witness to this principle, Protestantism is not to be identified with any of its historical realizations. It is not bound to the Protestant era. It can drive forward to qualitatively new creation. It can also, in the name of its principle, protest against the Protestant era and against organized Protestantism itself. The latter are relative and conditioned realities. This does not mean that they are lacking in significance. They are to be understood in the light of the Protestant principle.

Protestantism here confronts the perennial problem of the one and the many, what Emerson called *the* problem of philosophy. This problem, he asserted (quoting Plato), is "to find a ground unconditioned and absolute for all that exists conditionally." The Protestant principle aims to express the true relation between the unconditional and the conditioned. Only by appeal to such a principle can Protestantism transcend its cultural entanglements at any particular time and offer both criticism and creative direction in personal and social life.

This principle is presented in a dual aspect. On the one hand, it is a universally significant principle, pointing to the source and judge of every religious and cultural reality. It points to a moving, restless power, the inner infinity of being, that informs and transforms all conditioned realities and brings new forms to birth. Thus Protestantism can lay no exclusive claim to it. On the other hand, the principle refers to the characteristic possibility, the essential power, of Protestantism as an historical movement. It is the principle by which Protestantism is supported and judged. When Protestantism is not loyal to this principle or when it does not judge itself according to the principle, it is no longer truly Protestant.

Catholicism, in effect, identifies its own historical realizations of the Catholic era with the ground and judge of all religious and cultural realities. Luther called this self-absolutization the "worship of man-made gods." This worship of man-made gods appears in Protestant as well as in Catholic forms, in the sacramentalism of the Word as well as in the sacramentalism of holy institutions and objects. It appears also in the "secular sacramentalism" of capitalism and nationalism. This claim to an absolute authority can conflict with similar claims of other authorities. It can also elicit the resistance of autonomous freedom. At the beginning of the modern era the autonomy that was expressed by humanism and that rebelled against ecclesiastical and political heteronomy, vibrated with a residual religious power. But in both ancient and modern times autonomy has again and again shown itself to be precarious and unstable. It loses its original sense of an unconditional demand for truth and justice; it becomes self-enclosed. As we have observed, this is what has happened in capitalistic society, in which the spirit of self-sufficient finitude now prevails. Increasingly, modern autonomy has degenerated into relativism or into a new heteronomy. Among intellectuals who have been deeply affected by modern historicism, the former tendency is widely evident, but in the culture at large the latter tendency is undoubtedly the stronger. The typical bourgeois man accepts the presuppositions of the capitalist mentality and the societal forms of capitalism with the same rigidity and absoluteness that the Fundamentalist exhibits in his religion. But heteronomy and autonomy do not exhaust the possibilities open to humanity.

The Protestant principle stands in contrast to both these attitudes. The negative implication of the word "Protestant"—a word that arose out of an actual historic protest against ecclesiastical authoritarianism—makes it eminently appropriate to serve as the name and the historical manifestation of the prophetic protest against every conditioned thing that presents an unconditional claim for itself. This negative implication of the Protestant principle has from the very beginning of the Protestant movement included also a protest against any autonomy that forfeits its unconditional source and judge and that rests in its own conditioned self-assertion.

But the Protestant principle is not only negative and critical; it is also creative. Indeed, the critical presupposes the creative element. This positive element is the formative dynamic that sustains the fundamental attitude of seriousness and responsibility that belongs to all creative endeavor. It points to the ground and source of meaning that is present in a singular way in every relative achievement; but it cannot be exhausted or confined in any realization, not even in a definition. This dialectical principle, which combines critical negation and dynamic fulfillment, is the basis for what Tillich calls the "Protestant Gestalt of grace." The ultimate orientation involved here Tillich calls "theonomy." Before defining "theonomy," however, we must give further consideration to the Protestant principle.

This principle has been apprehended again and again in the history of religion and culture. In the West its lineage derives ultimately from Old Testament prophetism with its message of judgment and fulfillment. For the Christian the decisive expression of the essential power and meaning of reality is (in Tillich's formulation) the New Being manifest in Jesus as the Christ. Here the essential power and goodness reveals itself as *agape*, "love," an ontological and ethical dynamic that overcomes the frustrations, the fragmentariness, and the perversions of human existence, bringing together that which is separated. *Agape* is the source of justice and law, supporting, criticizing, and transforming them. It is, on the one hand, a command, and, on the other, it is the power that breaks through all commands. Thus it relates ethical life to the universal and the unconditional, and yet it adapts itself to every phase of the changing world. The Protestant principle presupposes this original critical and dynamic Christian message and its proclamation of the Kingdom of God near at hand. But there is a peculiarly Protestant statement of the principle.

Tillich finds this characteristically Protestant version of the principle in the Reformation assertion of the unconditional character of God and in the idea that the fulfillment of human existence ultimately depends not upon human devices and mediations (of Catholic, Protestant, or secular type) but rather upon justification through faith. He recognizes, however, that the doctrine of justification has become well-nigh unintelligible to the modern man and even to the modern scholar. The situation is partly due to the fact that in some instances the doctrine has come to mean a rule of faith imposed as a "law"—just the opposite of what was originally intended. Tillich has therefore attempted to give the doctrine a restatement in modern terms by devising a Protestant interpretation of a conception that has been used in existential theology and philosophy, the concept of "the human boundary-situation." This restatement presents Tillich's peculiarly Protestant interpretation of the character of human freedom and fulfillment.

Human existence is the rise of being to the realm of freedom. Being is freed from bondage to natural necessity. It becomes spirit and acquires the freedom to question itself and its environment, the freedom to raise the question concerning the true and the good and to make decision with regard to them. But we are in a sense unfree in our freedom, for we are compelled to decide. "This inevitability of freedom, of having to make decisions, creates the deep restlessness of our existence; through it our existence is threatened." It is threatened because we are confronted by an unconditional demand to choose and fulfill the good, a demand that we cannot fulfill. Consequently, each of us as spirit has a cleavage within us, a cleavage that is manifest also in society. There is no place to which we may flee from the demand. And in confronting the demand we can never provide ourselves with absolute security.

The point at which every self-provided security is brought under question, the point at which human possibilities reach and know their limits, Tillich calls "the human boundary-situation." "Right" belief and "right" action, church and sacrament and creed, piety and mystical experience, and also secular substitutes for any of these things, are recognized as false securities. An ultimate and threatening "No" is pronounced upon them all.

But human freedom and existence find support as well as threat at the boundary-situation. This support comes from beyond or beneath the interplay between person and society. What is involved here is the deepest level of human existence. Just where dependence upon the finite creations of spirit is relinquished, a new confidence and a creative impulse arise from the infinite and inexhaustible depths.

This experience of the boundary-situation is not something that takes place in a flight away from the concrete and the temporal. The boundary is, so to speak, at the edge of a particular complex of spiritual and cultural realities. The specific consequences of the experience of ultimate threat and support will therefore be different in the time of Luther or Pascal from what they were in the time of Jeremiah. But always the transcendent significance of, and judgment upon, temporal realities are envisaged anew. One gains at the boundary a paradoxical sense of the immediacy of origin and of threat. Beneath the dichotomy between subject and object a new, a third dimension, the dimension of depth, is discerned. The creative and destructive and recreative powers of being erupt into the consciousness. A new relation to things and people appears. Things are no longer viewed merely as objects for use or as technical means without intrinsic worth. They are seen again in their "powerfulness," which is rooted in the inner infinity of being. In place of "the mutual domination between thing and personality," there appears "a mutual service between personality and things," an "eros-relation." This eros-relation becomes manifest also in a new sense of community and of its depth. In place of the community that breaks the personality and bends it under its yoke, there can now emerge a community of free personalities who know themselves as belonging together through their connection with the ultimate supporting and threatening reality. The personality recognizes something holy and unconditional in the dignity and freedom of other persons; for persons, like things, are seen now to be supported by the inner infinity of being. Here, it would seem, we have Tillich's rendering of Luther's idea of the "love of neighbor" —the consequence of justification.

We do not, however, by our experience of the boundary gain control of the ultimate threat and support. We can *prepare* for receiving the support by exposing ourselves consciously and without reservation to the claims of the unconditional. But awareness of the ultimate meaning and of the possibility of fulfilling that meaning in a particular situation is a matter of "destiny and grace." Neither a church nor any other group can subject the ultimate threat and support to human conditions or techniques. For this reason the radical Protestant attributes only a provisional importance to the church and its forms. Here the radical stands nearer to the secularism that is skeptical of the conventional securities of piety than to any orthodoxy, whether it be "religious" or secular.

In this connection one of the most striking and original aspects of Tillich's rendering of the doctrine of justification should be noted. Luther applied the doctrine of justification only to the religious-moral life. The sinner, though unjust, is "justified" and anticipated. Tillich applies the doctrine also to the religious-intellectual sphere. No act of will accepting "right" belief can be properly demanded by any authority. Devotion to truth is supreme; it is devotion to God. There is a sacred element in the integrity that leads to doubt even about God and religion. Indeed, since God is truth, any loyalty to truth is religious loyalty, even if it leads to a recognition of the lack of truth. Paraphrasing Augustine, the serious doubter may say: "I doubt, therefore I am religious." Even in doubt the divine is present. Absolutely serious atheism can be directed toward the unconditional; it can be a form of faith in truth. There appears here the conquest of meaninglessness by the awareness of the paradoxical presence of "meaning in meaninglessness." Thus the doubter is "justified." The only absolutely irreligious attitude, then, is absolute cynicism, absolute lack of seriousness.

Returning, now, to the consideration with which the concept of the boundary-situation was introduced, we may restate the implications of the Protestant principle as they relate to heteronomy and autonomy. Both these types of "religion" are overcome by what Tillich calls "theonomy" (a concept that had been used previously by Troeltsch and others). In the face of the destruction or weakening of freedom that accompanies heteronomy and autonomy, theonomy goes beyond them both, preserving and transforming an element from each. It emphasizes the commanding element in the unconditional demand for the ultimate good, for truth and justice. This ultimate ground of meaning and existence is not (as in heteronomy) identified with any conditioned reality or social form; yet it calls for obedience. Here an element of heteronomy is retained and transformed. But the unconditional is not arbitrary; it never demands the sacrifice of the intellect; it is not alien to our humanity; it fulfills our inmost nature, our freedom. Theonomy takes over from autonomy this element of intelligibility and self-determination and transforms it. Recognizing that self-sufficient autonomy, as the self-assertion of a conditioned reality, is not able to create a world from within itself and recognizing that every conception of the ultimate good must reflect the cleavage within man and society, theonomy deepens autonomy to a point where the latter is transcended. Theonomy supports autonomy and at the same time breaks through it without shattering it. Thus theonomy brings both heteronomy and autonomy to the boundary-situation, where in differing ways they confront the ultimate threat and support and are transformed. In short, theonomy is the condition in which spiritual and social forms are imbued with the import of the unconditional as their supporting ground and judge.

The critical and creative principle that points to the ultimate threat and support is what makes Protestantism Protestant. It is, therefore, called the "Protestant principle." But it is clear that this principle is no sectarian principle. It cuts through all sectarianisms (both religious and secular) to that which shatters and transforms all self-enclosed forms. Its first word, therefore, "must be the word against religion"; and this means its first word is against every movement that idolizes established forms, whether religious or secular, orthodox or liberal, ecclesiastical or nonecclesiastical. All these idolizations are merely forms of "pharisaism." The Protestant may not attribute a classical status even to the Reformation or to any other period (e.g., the period A.D. 30–33) in a normative sense. "It is of the essence of Protestantism," Tillich says, "that there can be no classical period for it." The principle protests also against any idolization of religious language, whether it be old or new, whether it be in the Bible or in the church confessions.

Thus, Protestantism (or any other religion) always needs the correction that comes from the "secular" protest against any tendency within it to identify itself with the unconditional. In this function, as well as in the challenge of its creative achievement, secularism on Protestant soil may be called "Protestant secularism." The very existence of this sort of secularism shows that grace is not bound up with explicit religion, that is, with those forms whose express purpose it is to serve as a medium of grace. It is "a concealed form of grace," a manifestation of "the latent church." It often serves to remind Protestantism of its own principle and in some cases exhibits a better, even if an unintended, apprehension and application of that principle. Protestantism can appropriate this stimulus only if it stands at the boundary between itself and secularism. When there is a vital relation between church and society, "the church is the perpetual guilty conscience of society and society the perpetual guilty conscience of the church."

These implications of the Protestant principle are given corresponding expression in Tillich's definitions of religion and culture.

Religion is "direction toward the unconditional." Culture is direction toward the conditioned forms of meaning and their unity. Despite this contrast, however, genuine religion and vital culture have ultimately the same roots. "Being religious is being unconditionally concerned, whether this concern expresses itself in secular or (in the narrower sense) religious forms." All sharp divisions between the sacred and the secular must be eliminated in recognition of a transcendent critical and formative power which is present in both religion and culture. "Secular culture is essentially as impossible as atheism because both presuppose the unconditional element and both express ultimate concerns." Implied here is a dialectical view of religion and culture. Religion, in order to achieve realization, must assume form and become culture; in doing so it is religious in both substance and intention. But culture, even when it is not religious by intention, is religious in substance, for every cultural act contains an unconditional meaning, it depends upon the ground of meaning. Yet when religion becomes culture, it may lose its depth and its sense of relatedness to the unconditional; it may degenerate into an absolute devotion to conditioned cultural realities. On the other hand, culture, even in the act of opposing "religion," may rediscover the unconditional threat and support, and it may bring forth new religious creation. Accordingly, the major types of explicit religion appear in implicit form in the history of "secular" culture. With Schelling, Tillich would say that the history of culture is in a broad sense the history of religion. The Protestant principle, in pointing to that universally operative reality that judges and supports all meaningful existence, interprets religion as present wherever there is a uniting of negation and affirmation, of threat and support, of judgment and grace, of crisis and form-creation. Perverted religion and perverted culture appear wherever this dialectic is absent.

The demand is always placed before Protestantism, then, to transcend itself at the boundary-situation and to move toward new realization. It must effect this realization directly in relation to secular realities. This means that its prophetic and creative power must become manifest in a concrete historical situation; it means also that it must combine prophetic and rational criticism (as it has done almost from its beginning). The Protestant principle, therefore, relates "the line upward," the reference to the eternal meaning, to "the line forward," the direction toward the temporal realization of the eternal meaning in accord with the demands of a rational understanding of a particular historical situation. In emphasizing "the line forward" as well as "the line upward" and in demanding a dialectical relation between Protestantism and secularism, Tillich turns away from pietistic indifference to "the world" and history, and stresses the world-affirming and world-shaping dynamic of Calvinism and modern humanism.

In the light of the Protestant principle there can be no *official* philosophy for Protestantism, and there can be no official program for the application of the principle. Yet, if the principle is to achieve relevance in any particular historical situation, it requires both a philosophical elaboration and a program for action. His own philosophical elaboration of the principle Tillich calls "belief-ful" or "self-transcending realism," for it combines realism and a faith that transcends realism. Belief-ful realism "is a turning toward reality, a questioning of reality, a penetrating into existence, a driving to the level where reality points beyond itself to its ground and ultimate meaning." It does not look "above" reality to a transcendentalized spiritual world; it looks down into the "depths" of reality to its inner infinity. "Belief-ful realism" may be characterized as an existential and dialectical philosophy of meaning-fulfillment. . . .

The concept of "meaning" has become almost indispensable in discussions of philosophy of culture and philosophy of history during the past three-quarters of a century, especially since Dilthey gave it a central place in his "critique of historical reason." So great a role has the concept played in recent times that Tillich says the problem of the meaning of history has become the problem of the present period in contrast to the previous period's major interest in the control of nature. This shift of interest is a symptom of the crisis in the culture. Tillich started with the twofold idealistic presupposition that all the spiritual life of man forms an inner unity and that this spiritual life, both as a whole and in its parts, is to be understood only in its religious roots. But in his "self-transcending realism" he goes beyond epistemological idealism and the critical-dialectical method corresponding to it. He is always conscious of the tension between any synthesis and the unconditional quality pointing beyond it. Thus he rejects the idealistic conviction that the antithesis should be thought of only as "sublated" in the achieved synthesis. In this way he replaces the idealistic philosophy of Mind by a realistic philosophy of Meaning.

Perhaps the thinker with whom the most instructive comparison can be made is Karl Barth. Tillich has often been classified with Barth as representative of existential and dialectical theology. But, in his article "What Is Wrong with the 'Dialectic' Theology?" Tillich questions the classification. Tillich asserts that Barth's neo-Reformation theology at its beginning supplied a powerful and radical religious criticism of church and culture; in the face of Nazism it saved the German Protestant church. But he denies that Barth's theology is dialectical; it is, he says, merely paradoxical. Moreover, by interpreting the divine as wholly other and alien to man, it derogates all human culture. It denies significance even to any human questioning concerning the ultimate. By rejecting humanism and autonomy it has created a new heteronomy. Although it opposed the Nazi "Grand Inquisitor" (to use Dostoevsky's term), it has set up its own Grand Inquisitor "with a strong but tight-fitting armor of Barthian supernaturalism" and scholastic confessionalism. Despite its constant reference to crisis, it has come to view everything as being under judgment—except itself. It has "relapsed into the mere reiteration of tradition." It has forgotten the Protestant protest in the name of which it began and is in danger of becoming a merely weakened form of traditional Catholicism. Moreover, in its criticism of culture it has opposed tyranny only for the sake of the church and not for the sake of human rights. And, as a consequence of its supernaturalism and of its Kantian ethical presuppositions, it has for the most part pronounced only an abstract, formal judgment upon the social order—all things are judged and really nothing is decided. This aloofness to the responsibilities of prophetic religion, an aloofness sanctioned by a supernaturalist pessimism, merely assists (by default) the ruling and dominating powers in society. By this aloofness, Barthianism even helped to destroy the religious-socialist movement in pre-Hitler Germany. And it has not yet been able to explicate a positive conception of fulfillment in history. It turns away from a positive decision with regard to the specific situation "here and now." It escapes backward into an otherworldly traditionalism. Despite its avowed existential attitude, which renounces the spectator attitude, it is unable to find a way forward out of the Protestant era.

Tillich's philosophy is one that looks toward meaning-fulfillment in all areas of life. Although many of his formulations of this philosophy reveal the influence of modern intellectual movements, its deepest roots are to be found in the Judeo-Christian apprehension of human existence and fulfillment. This apprehension, implicit in what we have already presented, may be epitomized in three familiar axioms—and affirmation of the essential, if not actual, unity and goodness of existence (mythologically expressed in the doctrine of the Creation) is combined with the recognition of an underivable contradiction in human existence (mythologically expressed in the doctrine of the Fall—which may not be accepted as an historical event or as an explanation of the human condition but as a description of the cleavage in the human spirit and in human society) and with a confidence that the cleavage, the broken unity and goodness, can be restored by the inexhaustible creative power (mythologically expressed in the doctrine of redemption). This Judeo-Christian apprehension, when truly understood, implies a philosophy of history.

In conformity with the historical thinking of ancient prophetism and of the modern historical consciousness, which is in part derived from it, self-transcending realism affirms that the focal expression of these three elements is to be found in history, though the form-bursting and form-creating power arises from beneath the level of freedom and existence. Self-transcending realism is an historical realism. In and through the historical "here and now," in and through the dynamics and structures of history, we experience in widest and deepest dimensions the realization and the contradiction of meaning. Here we encounter in its critical and creative power the ultimate threat and support of human existence. History in all its spheres is the arena of salvation, the realm in which the demands of the unconditional are confronted. Salvation occurs in time and through community, in the overcoming of the demonic powers that pervert both personal and social life. It appears in those forms and structures that give a local habitation to justice and love and beauty. And it is the work of a gracious, affirming, healing power moving toward the fulfillment of being and meaning.

The depth, the tensions, and the possibilities of existence are not really known until one in faith apprehends them through passionate participation in the struggles of history. In other words, the existential attitude implicit in the demand for participation presupposes that the subject comes to know the human situation only by entering into the process of fulfillment, a process in which thought and being are merged and transmuted in the creative life of spirit. The mark of the fullest intercourse with reality is found, then, in the uniting of contemporaneity with self-transcending relatedness to the unconditional; it is found in a "belief-ful," timely awareness and action in terms of the unconditional demands relevant to the present situation. Such an awareness and action, therefore, demands a venturing decision, the taking of a risk.

When people (or churches) do not direct their deepest existential concern to this focus of decision and participation in the "here and now," they miss an unrepeatable opportunity for the expression of meaning in history; in other words, they miss the *kairos*, the "fullness of time." But action or participation is not sufficient. If the action is not accompanied by a decision for the unconditional, then either demonic self-inflation or lack of seriousness ensues. On the other hand, if decision is not accompanied by participation, then knowledge will be abstractly formal or "untimely." Only from an awareness of the inextricable bond and tension between the concrete historical situation and the unconditioned depth of being and meaning can humans avail themselves of truly critical and formative power. The unconditionality of prophetic criticism, combined with the timely resoluteness of formative will under grace, can alone bring the fullness or fulfillment of time, the *kairos*. No aspect or area of life is exempt from the demands of this timely criticism and form-creation; that is, timely in the sense of the *kairos*. Only through timely criticism and action can the significantly new come into being; only in this way can the import and demand of the unconditional impinge upon history. This is the practical implication of the Protestant principle.

In viewing the present social situation at the end of the Protestant era, Tillich sees a negative vindication of the Protestant principle in the consequences of the operation of the bourgeois principle, as well as in the degeneration of self-sufficient autonomy into the current heteronomies of racism, nationalism, and capitalism. These heteronomies have often served to protect the bourgeois principle against radical criticism and thus to negate the Protestant principle. A characteristic consequence of the bourgeois principle (which, it will be recalled, always moves toward the dissolution of the bonds of community life through the rationalization of the powers of origin) is to be seen in the dependence of the working class upon the "free" sale of their physical ability to work, a dependence which, in its turn, relies upon the "laws" (or the chances) of the market. Here the perversion of humanity's essential nature assumes tremendous social dimensions. Even in normal times the fateful threat of insecurity confronts the entrepreneur as well as the worker. This threat, as it has expressed itself in the twentieth century, has more and more torn away the ideological veil that romantic conservative thought and progressivist liberal economics have thrown over the contradictions of capitalist society.

These contradictions, in their most general economic aspects, are three: first, the contradiction between the rapidity of technical advance and the slowness of the development of societal forms that enable adjustment to the technical advance; second, the contradiction between the increasing production power and the decreasing consumption capacity of the masses (bigger and better factories have brought a higher proportion of unemployment); and, third, the contradiction between the assumed liberty of every individual and the actual dependence of the masses on great concentrations of economic power (which determine not only the production and prices of goods but also the manipulation of symbols through the idea industries).

The way out of the present era can be found only if we can be released from the "possession" of the demonic powers that now carry through or protect the bourgeois principle, only if we can be caught up and transformed by newly creative powers emanating from the depths of being and history. Tillich is convinced that we will not even approach this timely moment unless we come to a passionate awareness of the deep void of meaninglessness that the bourgeois principle and its supporting heteronomies have created. The prevailing "neutrality" of the churches to these issues is only a form of ideological concealment of the perversions of the common life. It is true that no Protestant church can properly espouse an official social philosophy or program; to do so would be to violate the Protestant principle. Yet if the Protestant principle is apprehended in a vital and relevant way, it should lead to a turning-away from the void of meaninglessness and to new creation. It should lead to the forging of a principle pertinent to the present historical situation, a principle that in the spirit of radical Protestantism can overcome the bourgeois principle.

This principle might be called the "religious-socialist principle." Tillich has written extensively on this theme; apart from certain collections of his essays, his book, *The Socialist Decision*, deals with this subject. Besides this, he was coeditor of a religious-social-ist magazine for the Kairos Circle in pre-Hitler Germany. Here it must suffice if we give merely a few hints concerning the meaning of the central principle.

Tillich rejects the legalistic or programmatic type of religious socialism that considers socialism to be the precise demand of the Gospels; it attempts to make the Gospels a socialist textbook. He rejects the romantic type of religious socialism that claims that socialism is itself religion; this type of religious socialism rightly asserts that religion does not confine itself to a special religious sphere, yet it stifles the radical criticism inherent in the Protestant principle. He also rejects the practical-political type of religious socialism that simply tries to bring about cooperation between organized socialism and the churches; it tends to emphasize merely practical strategies and fails to scrutinize the basic presuppositions of either socialism or religion in their actual forms, and thus it neglects the need for fundamental transformation of either of them.

In his religious socialism Tillich attempts in a dialectical fashion to dissolve the static opposition of prevailing conceptions of religion and socialism; he aims to understand them in their deepest roots and to transform both of them in the spirit of prophetic religion. Accordingly, he aims to interpret religion and socialism in such a way as to point toward a new concrete Gestalt, capable in the deepest sense of meeting the particular needs of our time. The goal of this religious socialism is the radical application of the Protestant principle to both Protestantism and socialism, to both religion and secularism, in order to free Protestantism from bondage to the religious sphere as a separate sphere and also to make possible a religious understanding of the socialism and the secularism of the Protestant era. This type of religious socialism works primarily on theoretical problems. It is not concerned with the development of blueprints for a socialist system of society; its practical effectiveness, as compared with the theoretical, is in-tended to be small.

Whether or not organized Protestantism will continue its class-bound subservience to the spirit of capitalism is largely a matter of conjecture. There are evidences of change in European Protestantism in the direction of socialism. In the United States there would seem to be a persisting disposition in Protestant circles to rely upon automatic harmony, that is, upon capitalism. In any event, the coming years will bring to birth new forms of collectivism, forms that will vary in different countries. Religious socialism aims to accept the responsibility of delineating the principles that will be in conformity with the theological demands of self-transcending realism, with democratic ideals, and with economic necessities.

The widespread opposition between Protestantism and socialism is to be understood as the consequence of perversions within both of them. Protestantism's opposition is due not only to its Babylonish captivity to capitalism and nationalism but also to a widely held supernaturalist conception of the Kingdom of God as purely transcendent; it is due to the complacency of Protestant liberalism and to the "religious" indifference of Protestant Fundamentalism and Barthian neo-orthodoxy. All these tendencies reveal in varying ways and degrees the absence of a really disturbed consciousness of the magnitude of the struggle that must be made against the demonries of our time. In the face of this situation, religious socialism not only demands that Protestantism should come to a new awareness of the Protestant principle and thus be released from bondage; it also tries to present the special demands of the *kairos* of our time, the demand for a new order of life imbued with new meaning to take the place of an autonomously emptied and heteronomously controlled society.

The opposition of socialism to religion is as false in principle as is the opposition of Protestantism to socialism. The historical roots of socialism are to be found in the prophetic-Protestant-humanist tradition; in the drive forward to the new in history, represented by revolutionary spiritualist movements of the pre-Reformation period and of the left wing of the Reformation; in the autonomous revolt against the powers of origin claimed by an ecclesiastically controlled culture (a revolt moving in the direction of democracy); in the Calvinist and humanist impulse to give a rational, rather than an arbitrary, shaping to society; in the struggle for humanity implicit in all these motifs, as well as in the world-affirming spirit of the Enlightenment. Perhaps the most powerful prophetic ele-

ment in socialism is what has been called its "epochal consciousness," its awareness of the decisive character of the dynamic
structures of a whole period. (The very concept of "the Protestant
era" presupposes this prophetic view that the human situation
must be understood in terms of the integrating and the disintegrating structures of a period.) Tillich believes that socialism is today
more strongly conscious of the *kairos* of our period than is any
other movement, conscious of an impending epochal fate and
opportunity. But it is perverted by the possession of certain
untimely elements that are either residues of the era now in crisis
or new forms of idolatry. Some of these elements were originally
creative ideas, and they are now, therefore, in their untimely form,
all the more dangerous.

Socialism (and especially Marxism) has ignored the transcendent reference of the Protestant principle, and through its false
claim to be a science it has degenerated into a new legalism and a
new heteronomy. By its merely sociologistic interpretation of the
cleavages and corruptions of human existence and by its continued
reliance on an unbroken bourgeois principle (with its naïve belief in
progress) it has transformed originally prophetic expectations for
the future into utopianism. Religious socialism aims to correct the
false anthropology of Marxism and to overcome its heteronomous
and utopian impulses by the achievement of an autonomy deepened by theonomy and by an insistence upon the remoteness of
socialism from the Kingdom of God, however clearly "the decision
for socialism during a definite period may be the decision for the
Kingdom of God."

The religious-socialist principle points the direction out of the
Protestant era by combining elements that have been either
neglected or perverted by both capitalism and socialism. It seeks a
new theonomous society in which the powers of origin supporting
organic community may be broken and yet fulfilled under the
demands of the unconditional; it seeks more than a new economic
system, it seeks a total outlook on existence in which all cultural
areas retain their autonomy. It rejects the metaphysical core of
bourgeois harmonism and socialist progressivism, and it adopts a
prophetic philosophy of history in which anticipation of the new
(as well as the breaking-away from the old) is combined with the
responsibility of planning for freedom. On the basis of these
principles, religious socialism would overcome the fear, the insecu-

rity, the loneliness, the thingification of the masses of men; in such a way it would overcome the contradictions of our disintegrating world. It is clear, then, that if Protestantism or any other group is to meet the demands of our *kairos*, concern for individual salvation will have to be coupled with a concern for "the ultimate meaning and salvation of groups and institutions." But men cannot merely by decision bring about so great a change as this. A power more than human, a power greater than that of the now ruling principalities and powers, greater than that of the present demonries that have men in their possession, must be released. If Protestantism reponds to this *kairos*, the Protestant era will not be at an end. The Reformation will continue. And, surely, in many of these motifs, Tillich may help prepare us for the religious and secular reformation that alone can overcome the crisis of the Protestant era and give new, timely access to what the poet, Gerard Manley Hopkins, has called "the dearest freshness deep down things."

INDEX